SAVE THIS LAND

Nachiketa Das

INDIA • SINGAPORE • MALAYSIA

Notion Press

No. 8, 3rd Cross Street
CIT Colony, Mylapore
Chennai, Tamil Nadu – 600004

First Published by Notion Press 2021
Copyright © Nachiketa Das 2021
All Rights Reserved.

ISBN 978-1-63832-633-5

Cover page
Back: Ranganadi Dam Arunachal Pradesh

DISCLAIMER

All facts stated in the book have been drawn from authoritative sources that are listed in the References section. Every effort has been made to ensure the integrity of the facts, which are accurate at the time of writing. Any inadvertent mistakes, omissions of credit and emerging facts, once brought to the attention of the publisher, will be appropriately rectified and included in subsequent editions.

DEDICATION

I dedicate this book to my wife Shizuka Imamoto. ND.

CONTENTS

Preface *13*

Acknowledgements *17*

1. **Eastern India Must Not Become a Desert** *19*
    Part I: The Fear of Famine **22**
    Political situation during the last decade of the
    British Raj 23
    Serious food shortages in the 1940s 26
    Need for substantial increase in food-grain production. . 29
    Efficiency of food-grain production is still very low 35
    Part II: Destruction of Forests **37**
    Large stretches of forests and scrubland cleared to
    increase the acreage of arable land. 37
    Increase productivity and surrender the appropriated
    land back to Mother Nature. 39
    Social reforms necessary to eliminate the detrimental
    primitive habits 40
    Freedom of the holy cows and unholy goats must be
    restricted 42
    Part III: Rejuvenation of the Mountains **45**
    Revive the mountains – the *mahidharas* – the
    sustainers of the earth. 45
    Saint Achyutananda Das 49
    How do we rejuvenate the *mahidharas*? 51
    Micro-dams in Japan effectively recharge groundwater. . 53
    "Essence of water is plant", Chandogya Upanishad 54
    Pore spaces in rocks of the mountainous region can
    store far more water 55
    Instances of regeneration of forests and hills in India . . . 57

Binjhagiri in Nayagarh district of Odisha 58

Alwar district of Rajasthan 60

Gujarat. 62

Revive the derelict ponds and water bodies. 63

Let us revive the *mahidharas* 66

2. Sea Level Rise and Inundation of Coastal India 69

Rate of sea level rise 70

Sea level rise is not uniform 75

The maximum possible rise of sea level. 78

Sea level rise and coastal inundation 79

Coastal inundation after the last ice age 81

Losses due to sea level rise. 85

Cyclones. 85

Cyclone Fani 88

Cyclone Phailin 88

Lightning strikes in Odisha 95

Catastrophic rise in sea level. 96

Catastrophic submergence of Dwaraka. 97

Threat of tsunami. 98

Odisha tsunami of 318 CE. 99

Harnessing geothermal energy at Barren Island 102

The Indian Ocean Tsunami of 2004. 102

2011 Tohoku Earthquake and Tsunami 105

Nuclear accident and removal of radioactivity 106

Tribute to Prof. Dr. Ken Sasaki. 110

Construction of seawall in Japan 113

Achyutananda's prophecy on sea level rise. 113

Measures to combat the rising seas 116

The Netherlands is up to 6 m below sea level 118

Let the Coastal Works commence. 119

3. Can Global Warming Make the Ganga Run Dry? . . 125

Source of the Ganga. 125

Global warming is not uniform 126

The Gulf Stream 127
Monsoon and its effect on the Himalayan environment . . 129
Global warming and erratic monsoon 131
Heavier rains in Rajasthan 132
Heavier rains at Tehri in Uttarakhand. 133
Cloudbursts in Uttarakhand in the central Himalaya 134
Cloudbursts in Ladakh in the western Himalaya 135
Growth of glaciers in the western most Himalaya. 135
A combination of reasons for the retreat of the Gangotri . 137
The retreating Gangotri and the need for creation of a
series of glacial lakes 140
Need for massive afforestation of the Himalaya now. 143
Conclusion. 144

4. **Management of the Hirakud Dam on the
    Mahanadi** **147**
    Inception of the Hirakud Dam project. 148
    Construction of the dam 150
    Major dam collapses of the world. 151
    Collapse of the Banqiao Dam and the Shimantan
    Reservoir Dam in China. 152
    Collapse of the St. Francis Dam in California. 154
    Collapse of the South Fork Dam in Pennsylvania 155
    Tsunami at the Vajont Dam in Italy 155
    Collapse of Sempor Dam in Indonesia 155
    Dam failure and the Kurenivka Mudslide in Ukraine in
    the Soviet Union 156
    Bombing destruction of the Möhne Reservoir Dam in
    Germany 157
    Notable dam collapses in India. 158
    Deliberate destruction of large dams constitutes crimes
    against humanity 159
    Proposal to protect major dams by Ballistic Missile
    Defence (BMD) Program. 160
    Drafting of a covenant for Protection of World Dams
    and Reservoirs 161

Deliberate destruction of dams during a war be
considered war crimes 161

Salient features of the Hirakud Dam 162

What can trigger a collapse of the Hirakud Dam 163

Reservoir induced earthquake at the Koyna Dam in
Maharashtra in India 163

Possibility of a seismic disturbance at the Hirakud Dam. . 165

Reduction of storage capacity due to siltation. 166

The top priority, flood control, be respected. 167

Policy for disaster management. 168

Important aspects of management of the Hirakud Dam. . 170

Removal of sediments from the reservoir 171

Conclusion. 172

5. **Caring for the Rivers in India.** 173
Growth of Indian civilization along the rivers. 173

Traditional Indian respect for water 176

Inter linking of the rivers 178

History of river linking proposals in India 179

General Sir Arthur Thomas Cotton proposed a national
water grid. 180

Revival of the concept of a national water grid 181

Managing the health of the rivers of India 183

Excavation of sediments from the riverbeds of the
Mahanadi and other major rivers of Odisha for their
revival. 183

Huge global demand for sand. 186

Excavate the moribund Kharasrota 187

Conclusion. 189

6. **Creating Awareness on Water Quality in the City
of Cuttack.** 191
Sources of water for the island City of Cuttack. 191

Toxification of drinking water 192

Obnoxious water hyacinth menace. 195

Sand filled toxic ponds 197
Remedial measures 197
Creation of awareness is paramount 198
Importance of fresh water 200
Contamination of fresh water 200
Cities sinking due to excess drawal of groundwater 201
Excessive drawal of groundwater in coastal habitations
causing saline incursion 203
Public awareness is vital 205
High quality of water in Japan 205

References *207*
Appendix One *231*
Appendix Two *233*
About the Author *237*

PREFACE

Between 2007 and 2013, I wrote a series of popular articles on environment and water that were published on many online newspapers like www.hotnhitnews.com, www.sulekha.com, www.ivarta.com, www.siliconindia.com, and in journals in Odisha such as Geospectrum Interface, Pratishruti Plus, Vistas in Geology, Ravenshawvian etc to create awareness among the masses.

"The doyen of Indian geology" Dr. B.P. Radhakrishna, who was the founder Secretary of the Geological Society of India, was the longest serving Editor of its mouthpiece, the Journal of the Geological Society of India. Dr. Radhakrishna was a profoundly learned geologist and an erudite editor, who read my articles, liked them and advised me to compile them into a book. Dr. Prasanta Kumar Pattanaik, an eminent economist, presently an Emeritus Professor of Economics at the University of California Riverside, read my articles and liked them too. Professor Pattanaik suggested that I get the articles translated into Odia and get them published serialized in some leading vernacular dailies for a wider dissemination in Odisha.

My good friend and colleague Professor Ken Sasaki, a former President of Hiroshima Kokusai Gakuin University (HKGU) of Hiroshima and I had conducted joint research in the general area of water chemistry, water quality, bio-remediation of radioactive pollution, and removal of toxic heavy metals from soil, sediments and water. Dr. Sasaki and I also had collaborated in translating one of his numerous books from original Japanese into English titled, Genbaku Kensui: Dedication of Water Ceremony for the Victims of the Atom Bomb. After the publication of this book on water chemistry and water quality management, Dr. Sasaki urged me to write a book in the general area of environment and water, perhaps by collating my popular articles on the subjects.

Finally, I gathered myself to write this book, Save This Land, which is essentially an expansion and compilation of seven articles, which are: Eastern India must not become a desert, Sea level rise and inundation of coastal India, Can Global Warming make the Ganga run dry? Proper management of Hirakud Dam, Caring for the rivers in India, Awareness of water quality and Creating awareness on water quality in the City of Cuttack. The first five articles were enlarged and updated to become the first five chapters, while the last two articles were merged, expanded and transformed to the sixth chapter of the book.

"An honest tale speeds best, being plainly told", wrote Shakespeare (Richard III, Act IV, Scene IV) and I have tried to story tell the science in these chapters "plainly" so that it 'speeds best'.

Writing this book has been a lonely hike on a long trail in deep woods. In each of these six chapters, I have chosen a topic, analyzed the problem, described the dangers, presented solutions and finally appealed for proaction to save this land. Will anyone listen? This reminds me of Prince Sidhartha Gautama, who after 49 days of meditation under a pipal tree attained enlightenment. The so Awakened One, soon afterwards wished to teach. He was, however, ambivalent, for he believed that humanity is so abysmally ignorant, greedy and hateful that the masses will not grasp the Dharma or the Path, which is far too subtle, profound and onerous. Upon noticing the Buddha's reluctance, the Maha Brahma also known as the Brahma Sahampati or the Heavenly King in Buddhism, himself came down to the Enlightened One to persuade him to teach so that some, however few, will understand the Dharma.

And then the Buddha taught to greatness and millions trod the Path.

In this land, corruption, pollution, adulteration, division, violation, violence, over politicization are rife, yet instead of admission, denialism rules. Admission of problems will open the door for a search for solutions to be implemented. Midway corrections can be made to strengthen the process of elimination of the problems.

People react but never proact, yet, in this book, I appeal for proaction. Will they ever listen? I hope that they do to save this land.

ACKNOWLEDGEMENTS

I have taken liberties in quoting some old Sanskrit and Odia verses, the English translations are mine.

Thankful I am to my friends Barbara Barnes of Riverview in Sydney, Inge Habicht of Bondi in Sydney, Monika Habicht of Redfern in Sydney, Dr. Robert Pallasser of Epping in Sydney, Eciem Leslie of Bronte in Sydney, Marketa Dolezalova of Sydney, Yukiko Takebe of Tokyo and Sydney, Mai Shimizu of Fukuoka and Sydney, Subhadarshini Parhi of Munich, Miwa Satori of Saitama, Sydney and Frankfurt; Asuka Nakano of Fukuoka, Sydney and Budapest; Miho Fujita of Hiroshima, Dr. Kei Sasaki of Kure, Kazumi Kii of Hiroshima, Keisuke Kii of Hiroshima, Maki Ito of Hiroshima, Dr. Miho Nagase of Hiroshima, Masako Ishida of Seno, Mio Hiraoka of Hiroshima, Naoko Nishimura of Matsumoto, Fumiko Takizawa of Matsumoto, Akemi Komoda of Saitama and Sydney, Kumiko Taguchi of Tokyo and Sydney, Miwa Negishi of Saitama and Sydney, Yuko Ishibashi of Tokyo and Sydney, Dr. Aya Sakaguchi of Hiroshima, Dr. Tomoyo Okumura of Kochi, Dr. Aya Katsube of Tsukuba, Yuichi Hosokawa of Hiroshima, Dr. Akasmika Panda of Rourkela, Dr. Gayatri Chaudhari of Aurangabad, Dr. Swayamshree Mishra of Delhi, Amrita Das of Hyderabad and Gunjeet Bhansingh of Bhubaneswar for their support.

I thank my loving wife Shizuka Imamoto for her constant help and support.

Chapter One
Eastern India Must Not Become a Desert

Some three dozen years ago, in December 1985, I had disembarked at Palam Airport of New Delhi from a flight from London to board an Indian Airlines plane to Bhubaneswar, which is the capital of my state of Odisha in eastern India and also my hometown where my parents lived. The three hour long domestic flight then, was scheduled to depart around the midday with a stopover at Raipur in the state of Chhattisgarh in central India. After an early morning fog, the sky over New Delhi was all clear and a bright and beautiful sunny day had unfolded. I had never traversed this aerial route before and I looked forward to the travel, particularly eager to enjoy the panorama of the thick verdant forests and the numerous mountains of the western part of Odisha. After a request at the check-in counter, I had secured a seat by the window to enjoy clear and uninterrupted views.

After takeoff, the plane flew over the semiarid land that adjoined New Delhi and the parched brown earth appeared very different from the green landscape of Scotland, where I had just spent a little over three continuous years conducting research to earn a doctorate degree in geochemistry at The University of Glasgow. I eagerly waited for the plane to fly over the fabled forests of the Vindhya Mountain Range of central India. In those days the governments of various provinces of India claimed to have large proportions of their total land, anywhere between a third and a half or even more, under forest cover. Absence of any readily available satellite imageries like the Google Maps then, made independent verification of the aforesaid claims impossible, which forced the nation accept the exaggerated inaccuracies offered by the governments. In an hour or so into the journey, the plane reached the airspace over the Vindhya and yes, I saw the forests, but they did not appear dense enough. I was disappointed but waited patiently none the less to indulge my visual senses in the sights of the emerald forests, nestled on the mountainous western Odisha.

The dense forests of eastern India, in official government parlance, were termed "reserve forest" that apparently teemed with wildlife. Apparently again, the intense density of the forest canopy in these woods prevented sunrays to reach the ground below. As the plane flew over the mountainous highlands of western Odisha, I did notice the woods, but they lacked the density to be termed thick. The total forest cover, to the naked eye, did not look anywhere near the figures claimed by the governments. I could see plots of cleared land, even homesteads, right at the edge of the "reserve forest". I was shocked at the obvious destruction of forests and quite unconsciously sighed an exclamation in Odia language, '*Deshata maru bhumi hei jibare!*' an English translation of which would read, 'Lo this land will become a desert indeed!' I vividly remember the startled expression my utterance brought upon a high-ranking government officer who sat beside me, and I still visualize the incomprehension writ large on his visage. People did not see the approaching calamity then that we have brought upon ourselves through systematic destruction of forests, which started over half a century ago in the 1960s in India and continues unabated. The percentage of the total area of the various provinces of eastern India under forest cover, in 2009, stood at a little less than twenty.

As I first wrote this article in March 2009, with a heavy heart I had recorded, "By the end of the last month of February, the daytime temperature of Bhubaneswar touched 41°C. In the first week of March this year, several towns in western as well as coastal Odisha recorded their temperatures at or above 40°C. A quarter of a century ago, the maximum temperature for this time of the year, i.e. towards the end of February even early March, practically anywhere in eastern India, never went past 25°C. This time of the year used to be the season of spring, with a touch of chill in the morning air."

Now, in 2021, when I edit the article as a chapter for the book, I lament the complete disappearance of spring from the state of Odisha, where the diurnal maximum even in the month of February routinely goes past 40°C. Where did we banish that spring to and what wrong have we done? Can we do anything at all to invite back that spring or have we lost her forever through the irreversible damages we have caused to our land and climate?

The forests in eastern India, for that matter in the entire country of India, are under a great deal of pressure. Population pressure, a phrase widely used in Indian media, is often blamed as the single most important cause for the retreat of the forests. I disagree with this view and I would like to point out that Japan, where I live these days, in 2009, despite a population density of 339 per square km, which was higher, albeit marginally, than the population density of India at 336 per square km, has over 69% of her total land area under forest cover, as opposed to a mere 20% in India. Once orchards are included in the Japanese definition of forest, in Japan, the total land area under forest cover becomes 79%, say a full 80%. This huge contrast in forest cover becomes even more stark when we note that both India and Japan receive very similar average annual precipitation at 1,200 mm. The average annual rainfall of the state of Odisha at 1,500 mm, incidentally, is very similar to that of Hiroshima prefecture of Japan. I would like my readers to note that the population of Japan is steadily declining and the current population of some 127 million is projected to fall to around 90 million by the year 2050. As the population declines in Japan, the forest cover rises because of the abandoned rural farmsteads getting surrendered to nature. The forests in India, on the other hand, are disappearing essentially due to poor management, brought about by a combination of reasons, which I propose to discuss in the following pages.

Now, at the beginning of the third decade of the twenty-first century, eastern India ranks as the poorest part of the country. The forestlands, as well as the vast stretches of wetlands in this region, are being slowly and steadily taken over by the traditional farmers, who are hell-bent in enhancing the acreage of their landholdings to raise the production of food-grains, essentially to ward off the terrible fears of famine that constantly lurk in the psyche of the inhabitants of eastern India. Prospect of a prolonged starvation that invites death is perhaps a primal fear and the memories of the horrors of the mass starvations of enormous proportions that led to the death of tens of millions, in two hundred years of the British Raj, have remained indelibly etched in the psyche of generations.

Please allow me to start with a description of the political situation in the pre-independent India of the 1940s, to be precise during the Second World War that has a direct bearing on the horrendous famine that was unleashed on eastern India by the British Raj, in the first part of this long chapter discussed in three.

Part I: The Fear of Famine

- ➢ **Political situation during the last decade of the British Raj**
- ➢ **Serious food shortages in the 1940s**
- ➢ **Need for substantial increase in food-grain production**
- ➢ **Efficiency of food-grain production is still very low**

Political situation during the last decade of the British Raj
On the 8th of August 1942, an exasperated Mahatma Gandhi, two months shy of his 73rd birthday, in a most defiant and audacious speech of his life delivered at Gowalia Tank Maidan in central Bombay, served an ultimatum on the British, urging them to quit India immediately. The Mahatma issued a call to the masses to act as an independent nation and his call found huge support among the populace. He threatened the British Raj with mass agitations and his call for civil disobedience would mark the beginning of *Bharat Chodo Andolon* also known as the Quit India Movement. The British Raj responded with unprecedented savagery and arrested almost the entire leadership of the Indian National Congress within 24 hours of Gandhiji's speech to be incarcerated in prisons all over the subcontinent.[1] Within days, well over a 100,000 people that included my idealistic grandfather, were arrested nationwide and mass fines were imposed. Hundreds of thousands of demonstrators that included my 32-year-old grandmother and my 12-year-old father, were flogged mercilessly in the public and thousands of freedom-fighters and innocent bystanders, including women and children, were massacred in army and police firings.

This massive uprising in India happened smack in the middle of the Second World War, which at that point in time was not going very well at all for Britain. Allied forces had suffered a humiliating defeat at the hands of the Japanese, first in the Battle of Malay at the end of January 1942 and then in the Battle of Singapore a few weeks later, on the 15th of February. Lieutenant-General Tomoyuki Yamashita, Commander of the Imperial Twenty-Fifth Army of Japan, having taken 50,000 Allied troops as prisoners in Malay, captured the Allied stronghold of Singapore with only 30,000 Japanese soldiers. British Prime Minister Winston Churchill described the ignominious fall of Singapore, where 80,000 Allied troops had surrendered, as the 'largest capitulation' in

British history. A sizable faction of these Allied troops was Indian, who fought for the British army. Major Fujiwara Iwaichi, Chief of Intelligence of the Japanese Fifteenth Army, saw the Indian soldiers as potential allies, who could help the Japanese fight the British.

Major Fujiwara Iwaichi was in contact with an Indian revolutionary Giani Pritam Singh and they both combined to convince Mohan Singh, an Indian Captain of the British Army, who had just been captured by the Japanese in Jitra town of Malay in December 1941, to form an Army of Liberation for India. Mohan Singh, subsequently, actively recruited among the Indian prisoners of war (PoW) to form the Indian National Army. In a conference held at Bangkok in June 1942 of the Indian Independence League, under the leadership of a Japan based fiercely nationalistic Bengali revolutionary from Chandernagore, Rash Behari Bose, Mohan Singh was appointed Commander-in-Chief of the 'Army of Liberation of India' or the Indian National Army (INA). By the 1st of September 1942, General Mohan Singh of INA would lead 40,000 troops.[2, 3, 4, 5, 6, 7, 8]

While the Japanese Twenty-Fifth Army marched on the Malay Peninsula, the Japanese Fifteenth Army commanded by Lieutenant General Shojiro Ida overcame a weak Thai resistance en route to Burma. Thailand signed a defense pact with Japan and on the 20th of January 1942, General Ida marched into Burma. Despite limited supplies and hostile terrain, 35,000 Japanese troops outmaneuvered the much larger British forces and by the 22nd of February 1942, Japanese troops closed on the capital Rangoon. In a last desperate attempt, General Archibald Wavell, the Commander-in-Chief of the American-British-Dutch-Australian Command (ABDA-COM), ordered holding of Rangoon for as long as possible, only to resign two days later, on the 25th of February 1942, after handing the command to General Harold Rupert Leofric George Alexander. General Alexander soon realized the hopelessness of the British position and ordered the evacuation of Rangoon on the 7th of March 1942. Next day, i.e. on the 8th of March 1942, barely three weeks after the capture of Singapore the Japanese captured Rangoon, the capital of Burma.[9, 10, 11, 12, 13]

One hundred and eighteen yearlong British colonial rule of Malay Peninsula, since the signing of the Anglo-Dutch Treaty in 1824, was overthrown by the Japanese military campaign in a mere sixty days. The Japanese military, moreover, took less than 120 days to liberate Burma that had languished for 120 years under a brutal British colonial rule, since the First Anglo-Burmese War of 1823.[14, 15] Emphasize I must that so intense was the Burmese hatred of the horrendously oppressive century old British regime that after Burma gained her independence from Britain on the 4th of January 1948, the Burmese leadership vowed not to join the British Commonwealth, unlike their compatriots from the newly independent countries of the subcontinent, India, Pakistan and Ceylon.

The ease and the speed with which the Japanese had trounced the Allied forces in Malay, Singapore and Burma, had well and truly terrified the British, in fact, threatened their very hold over India. The British were now convinced of the Japanese military prowess, capable of outmaneuvering the Allied troops to invade and capture eastern India anytime. After the fall of Rangoon, therefore, the Allied forces attempted to regroup in the north of Burma, essentially to thwart the progress of the Japanese military machine. The prospect of a total annihilation at the hands of the Japanese military, presently reinforced by freedom fighters of the Indian National Army and Indian Independence League, the army of Thailand, and a section of the Burmese army, made the British flee Burma by May 1942, before the onset of monsoon downpours. The British and the Chinese sustained some 30,000 casualties in Burma and by July 1942, the retreat of the British forces from Burma was complete, while the Japanese consolidated their position.

Serious food shortages in the 1940s

Between 1920 and 1940, the British colony of Burma was the single largest exporter of rice in the world. Fertile plains of the Irrawaddy and the Arakan region that adjoined the province of East-Bengal of India, produced vast quantities of rice in a British imposed virtual monoculture. The British imported almost 15% of India's total rice requirement from Burma and with the advent of the Second World War, Britain procured even larger quantities of Burmese rice for the British troops. When the Japanese liberated Burma, the British lost access to this vast supply of rice at a time when they needed it most for their troops. The British presently procured that large quantity of rice essentially from eastern India for exporting to their troops stationed in the Middle East and elsewhere, who had been dependent on Burmese rice before.[16]

In a slight diversion, I mention that the principal river of Burma, anglicized as the Irrawaddy, is pronounced very differently in the native Burmese tongue as Ayeyarawati, since the name is derived from the Sanskrit word Airavata, the divine elephant mount of the King of Gods, Indra. The mythical mighty pachyderm Airavata extends his massive trunk into the watery underworld to draw and spray the water into the clouds, which are then converted into life-sustaining rains. In another comparable myth, Vritra Asura or the Vritra Dragon, drank all the waters of the earth draining it dry and then chose to recline in relaxation on the Himalaya, that served as his throne, while humanity suffered a great deal on the parched land. The suffering masses, consequently, prayed and begged God Indra, who moved by their misery mounted Airavata and embarked on a battle to annihilate Vritra Asura to save the world.[17] Airavata tore open Vritra Asura and the waters gushed forth in a mighty river that was named Ayeyarawati. This myth of Vritra Asura is, in fact, an allegory of the last Ice Age, when the fresh waters of the earth were frozen and locked into glaciers that expanded atop the major mountain ranges like the Himalaya. As the climate grew warmer, the glaciers broke up and great rivers gushed forth, resembling great serpents or dragons like the Vritra Dragon, on to the plains. Ayeyarawati channeled the melting glacial waters of the eastern most part of the Himalaya pretty much like Airavata provides water, hence the name. Life-giving River Ayeyarawati sustains the vast plains of Burma.

Let us resume our discussion on the causes of serious shortage of food in eastern India.

In morbid fear of the Japanese advance, the British systematically burnt and destroyed vast tracts of rice paddy fields in the fertile Chittagong region of East-Bengal that adjoined Arakan in Burma. This devilish 'scorched earth policy' of the British and their calamitous move to hoard huge quantities of rice for their troops, drastically reduced the availability of food stock for the people of Bengal.

The British Raj virtually initiated no administrative action, even after the scarcity of food became blatantly obvious. General Archibald Percival Wavell, who had fled Rangoon in February 1942, had been promoted to the position of Field Marshal in January 1943. After Lord Linlithgow retired as the Viceroy of India, in the summer of 1943, the Raj replaced him with Field Marshal Wavell, essentially to rule the colony with an iron hand. Wavell would hold the position till 1947 to be replaced by Mountbatten. When reports of large-scale starvation deaths surfaced, Viceroy Wavell and the Secretary of State for India Leopold Amery wrote to the British Prime Minister Winston Churchill requesting for the release of food stocks for India. Churchill totally disregarded the dire situation and most disgracefully retorted, if the scarcity of food is so severe, 'why Gandhi hadn't died yet', and refused additional supplies. Leopold Charles Maurice Stennett Amery, by the way, was born in India in Gorakhpur to a Jewish Hungarian mother and an English father Charles F. Amery, who worked for the Indian Forest Department. Charles Amery had abandoned his young family and the children were brought up by the mother, who had made great personal sacrifices to educate them. Leo Amery so raised had seen hardship and empathized with the suffering masses in India. Churchill on the other hand hated India, as evident from an entry in Leo Amery's diary where Churchill is recorded to have said in September 1942, 'I hate Indians. They are a beastly people with a beastly religion'. [18, 19, 20, 27]

Churchill's response and disposition were ample demonstrations of the uncaring and contemptuous attitude of the British Raj towards the people of India. The British neglect further intensified the Bengal Famine of 1943-44 that starved at least 3 million men, women and children to death. And as of today, Britain has not arraigned even a single Briton for this horrendous crime against humanity, nor has Britain cared to utter the simple word "sorry" by way of expressing regret for the genocide, let alone making any reparations.

Bengali literature abounds in numerous narratives and firsthand accounts of the famine in 1940s. A particularly heart-wrenching story written in Bengali language, bearing the caption, '*Kaka Ami Bhat Khabo*', narrates the tearful pleadings of a starving little Bengali child begging his famished uncle to fetch him a bowl of rice, which they had no access to. I hope someone translates this story in to English for a wider circulation.

Eastern India endured many famines and starvation deaths during the British Raj. Between September 1865 and December 1866, a most horrendous famine devastated my state of Odisha, which was a part of undivided Bengal then. A full one third, some 1.2 million people out of a total population of 3.7 million, perished in this famine. And the cause of the famine, you have guessed it right, was a total British administrative failure. Sir Stafford Northcote, the Secretary of State for India, in fact, had observed in the British House of Commons, 'This catastrophe must always remain a monument of our failure, a humiliation to the people of this country...'[21, 22] The arrogant British Raj, in the language of a widely respected parliamentarian of India, Dr. Ram Manohar Lohia, had ruled India by, '*bandook ki goli, aur Angrej ki boli*' that in English would read, 'gun shots and the alien language of English'. The Raj chose to learn nothing from their mistakes and maintained an uncaring and contemptuous attitude towards the people of India.

Need for substantial increase in food-grain production
India won her independence on the 15th of August 1947, after being ruthlessly dismembered by Britain into a democratic India, a theocratic Pakistan and a chaotic basket of 564 independent princely states, scattered along the entire length and breadth of the subcontinent. The singular purpose of dismemberment was to ensure that once the most fabulously wealthy and powerful nation on earth, presently reduced to utter impoverishment by the systematic syphoning of wealth over two hundred years of colonial rule, remained indigent and weak forever. I am very aware that many of you are unwilling to accept that Britain systematically destroyed the economy of India and some of you may even go to the length of accusing me of extreme Indian nationalism. To all of you anglophiles, I recommend a book titled, The Case For India, written by a universally admired writer and philosopher, Will Durant.[23] This 228 page book was published in 1930, written by a Pulitzer Prize winning, non-Indian, American writer, who could never be accused of a bias of an Indian nationalistic nature. The book was written most spontaneously, when the author on a visit to India to conduct research for his books on philosophy, saw the systematic ruination of the Indian economy firsthand. Will Durant most eloquently made "a case for India" and most tersely accused Britain of hemorrhaging the colony and the British Raj, in turn, very promptly banned the book.

An Oxford educated eminent economist Dr. Utsa Patnaik, presently an Emeritus Professor of Jawaharlal Nehru University of New Delhi, based on her research conducted on the trade and tax data of nearly 200 years, revealed that the British Raj between 1765 and 1938, in current prices, syphoned USD45 trillion from India.[24, 25] In her book titled, A Theory of Imperialism, published by Columbia University Press in 2016, co-authored with her husband, the equally famous Professor of Economics Dr. Prabhat Patnaik, she thoroughly exposed the enormity of the British theft that utterly impoverished India. Dr. Shashi Tharoor in his 2017 book, Inglorious Empire: What the British did to India[26], also narrates the systematic plunder and the absolute de-industrialization of India by the British, during the two hundred years of the Raj.

After India gained her independence, the British, in particular, and the West, in general, made all manners of derogatory remarks that included predictions of disintegration of India, into a million pieces, by the end of the twentieth century. Say for instance, Winston Churchill in December 1930 in London had most disparagingly vaticinated that after the British departure, 'India will fall back quite rapidly through the centuries into the barbarism and privations of the Middle Ages'. He had also prescribed, 'an army of white janissaries, officered if necessary, from Germany, will be hired to secure the armed ascendancy of the Hindu'[27]. Even 20 years after India's independence, The Times of London, published a number of articles on "India's Disintegrating Democracy", written by the British journalist Neville Maxwell, in February 1967, barely a few weeks before the 4th General Election of India, boldly predicting, "The great experiment of developing India within a democratic framework has failed. Indians will soon vote in the fourth – and surely last – last general election."[27a] The West loved watching the most gorgeous affluent lady, an independent Mother India, presently doing rounds in tattered clothes, clutching a begging bowl, cadging for food-grains. The shortage of food-grains in the newly independent India had been exacerbated, by the disproportionate partitioning of the two fertile food-bowls of Punjab and Bengal of undivided India, with larger areas allocated to Pakistan.

The 1951 census, the first ever of independent India, recorded the population of the country at 361 million.[28] Total production of food-grain in that year was around 51 million tons, which included 20.6 million tons of rice and 6.4 million tons of wheat, which, needless to say, was utterly inadequate for feeding the entire population of the country.[29, 30]

Around this time in 1952, a geneticist and agricultural scientist Dr. Krishnaswami Ramiah (1892 – 1988), who had devoted his life to studying and breeding varieties of cotton and rice, started a program of hybridization which would eventually lead to a significant increase in the production of rice.[31] In the paddy fields of Central Rice Research Institute (CRRI), presently renamed Indian Rice Research Institute (IRRI), located on the outskirts of the City of Cuttack in Odisha, Dr. Ramiah and his team of scientists had carried out extensive hybridization between the Japonica varieties imported from Japan and the Indica strain cultivated in India. The breeding experiments generated rice strains that would eventually provide parent materials for the High Yielding Varieties Programs of 1966. One of these high-yielding rice strains, Taichung Native 1, would make the rice yield of 3 tons per hectare jump to 7 tons in some paddy fields of India.[32]

While the experimentation on rice hybridization progressed, wheat breeding to raise yield, which in those days stagnated at less than one ton per hectare, started too. A geneticist and agricultural scientist by the name Dr. Benjamin Peary Pal (1906 – 1989) started a wheat improvement program at the Indian Agricultural Research Institute (IARI) in New Delhi.[33] This visionary Dr. B.P. Pal was born in a Hindu family in Punjab and was "endowed with a great sense of humor". Dr. Pal passionately loved breeding varieties of roses. In March 1961, his aforementioned program delivered a significant improvement, when a few dwarf wheat strains containing the Norin-10 genes, developed by the famous American geneticist Norman E. Borlaug in Mexico, were grown in IARI.[34] Dr. Borlaug, by the way, would win the Nobel Prize for Peace in 1970. The observed improvements would lead to a National Demonstration Program in 1964, where the yields would exceed 5 tons per hectare. Dr. Pal, as the first Director-General of the Indian Council of Agricultural Research (ICAR), would subsequently oversee the All India Coordinated Wheat Research Project that would truly revolutionize the wheat production in India. With all these rice and wheat breeding experiments in full swing, the total production of food-grains in 1961 reached 82 million tons, which contained 34.6 million tons of rice and 11 million tons of wheat. Although the increase in food production over the decade was impressive, a surge in the total population of India to 439 million by 1961, neutralized all the gains. A poor monsoon would make matters horribly worse in 1966, when the total food production would actually fall significantly to 72 million tons, forcing the government to import a record quantum of 10 million tons of food-grains that year.

In order to address the widespread food-scarcity of the 1950s, the Government of India arranged with the US to import food-grains under the PL 480 program. The Public Law 480 was, in fact, the Agricultural Trade Development Assistance Act of the USA, signed into law, on the 10th of July 1954, by President Dwight D. Eisenhower. The purpose of the legislation was to 'lay the basis for a permanent expansion of our [US] exports of agricultural products with lasting benefits to ourselves and peoples of other lands.' President John F. Kennedy in 1961, renamed PL 480 as 'Food for Peace' program with the statement that 'Food is strength, and food is peace, and food is freedom, and food is a helping to people around the world whose goodwill and friendship we want'.[35]

Between 1955 and 1971, India imported nearly 50 million tons of food-grains from the US under the PL 480 program. I am not interested in getting into a discussion on the pros and cons of PL 480, which flares up every now and then in the Indian media. The wheat imported under PL 480 may well have introduced in India some varieties of noxious weeds, facetiously termed 'The Congress Weed', but let me assure you that the food-grains of this program saved many starving millions. PL 480, moreover, came at a time when other major wheat producing countries like Argentina, Australia and Canada sold their surplus wheat in the international market to countries like the Soviet Union, rather than donate like the US did.

In our modern India of the twenty-first century, politician bashing is by far the most popular pastime, way ahead in popularity of the glitz and glamour filled T20 cricket, the miniaturized version of the gentle languid romance of a sport that takes up to 5 days of competition, often concluding without a winner and much bonhomie between the rivals. I entirely disagree with the most fashionable notion of the Indian intelligentsia that all politicians are bad and corrupt. Let me state my reverence and adulation for an Indian politician Mr. C. Subramanian, who during his tenure as the Minister for Food and Agriculture of India, in 1966, took the bold decision of importing 18,000 tons of seeds of high-yielding varieties of Mexican dwarf wheat. Subsequent hybridization, between the Mexican and the Indian strains, would result in many high-yielding varieties to significantly improve wheat production in India. The initiative of this visionary in collaboration with two other great sons of India, one the agricultural scientist Dr. M.S. Swaminathan and the other, the bureaucrat Mr. B. Sivaraman, who officiated as the Secretary of Agriculture to the Government of India, revolutionized the food-grain production in India. By 1971, the total food-grain production of India stood at 108.4 million tons, which included 42.2 million tons of rice and 23.8 million tons of wheat. In two decades between 1951 and 1971, India's rice production had doubled, and the production of wheat had quadrupled. The total food production was still not enough though for the population that had expanded to 548 million by 1971.

The five aforementioned leaders of the Green Revolution in India, Dr. K. Ramiah, Dr. B.P. Pal, Mr. C. Subramanian, Dr. M.S. Swaminathan and Mr. B. Sivaraman, are not only great Indian heroes, but also heroes of the entire humankind and I salute you gentlemen. India honored Mr. C. Subramanian, quite deservingly so, in 1998, by conferring upon him the highest civilian award of Bharat Ratna.

Despite the commendable scientific advances in the production of food-grains in India and despite the bonhomie of Nehru-Kennedy era of the early 1960s, in 1967, a 286 page book titled, Famine 1975!: America's decision: Who will survive?[38, 39] written by two brothers, William Paddock and Paul Paddock, was published. The book announced imminent worldwide famines by 1975 that would cause millions of deaths. This was no ordinary book, it was a bestseller and the two authors were no ordinary Americans either, they were no Tom, Dick and Harry. William Paddock was an accomplished agronomist and a recognized authority on tropical agriculture and the other Paddock, Paul, was a veteran diplomat, who had spent over twenty years in the US Foreign Service. The central theme of the book was that only the US would be able to provide any help and in the spirit of true humanitarianism, the US must divide the underdeveloped countries of the world into three categories. 'Can-not-be-saved-nations' hence must be ignored, formed the first category, the second category consisted of 'the-walking-wounded' that will survive and the third category comprised 'can-be-saved', so must be helped by the US. India figured as a specific example, with a bold prediction that by 1975, millions of Indians would die of starvation. I invite you my readers to guess the category where India was placed. You have guessed correctly, India figured prominently in their category number one with the recommendation that all these brown little Indians must be allowed to perish, for it is their destiny. Now I invite you to guess where Pakistan was placed. You are wrong, Pakistan was not placed alongside India, but in category three and that meant Pakistan 'can be saved', therefore, must be helped by the US. I always wondered as to what extent this singularly most obnoxious book shaped the prejudiced American foreign policy towards India vis-à-vis Pakistan.

When I first wrote this article in 2009, right in the midst of the global recession brought upon the world by a profligate America, when many iconic American companies and institutions, including General Motors, tumbled like pieces of clothes in a tumble drier, the US appeared incapable of saving itself. And I wondered if that white supremacist arrogance of the 1960s, flaunted so audaciously in the title of the book 'America's decision as to who will survive' came back to haunt them. America's great ally Pakistan is all but a failed state, could collapse as a political entity, while India continues to surge ahead. With the election of the first ever African-American Mr. Barack Hussein Obama as the President of the US, I had hoped that the American foreign policy, based on those white supremacist views of the 1950s and 60s that wreaked so much havoc in the world, is abandoned forever. America escaped the recession by printing the greenback, trillions of dollars' worth. A decade later in 2019, as I rewrote the piece, talk of an American trade war with China appeared to issue a cordial invitation afresh to yet another global recession.

Efficiency of food-grain production is still very low
Towards the end of the first decade of the twenty-first century, India produced around a quarter of a billion tons of food-grain annually. India's total food-grain production in 2008 stood at 227 million tons, which included 96 million tons of rice and 77 million tons of wheat.[40] Ten years later in 2018, food-grain production reached 281 million tons, which included 115 million tons of rice, 99 million tons of wheat and 24 million tons of pulses. In addition, in 2018, oilseeds and

sugarcane production stood at 31 million tons and 380 million tons, respectively.[41] In the process, India has not only become self-sufficient in food, but also has become an exporter of food-grain, a very commendable achievement indeed. Although the total food-grain production has increased very substantially, the average yield per hectare continues to be rather low. With an average yield of 6.5 tons per hectare, China, the largest producer of rice in the world, produces almost 50% more rice than that of India, from a total acreage of 31 million hectares. Because of our average yield of a lowly 3 tons per hectare, in India we dedicate a much larger acreage of some 45 million hectares to rice cultivation. Another major rice producing country, Japan, in an average, boasts a yield of 6.7 tons per hectare.

Some of the lesser rice producing countries such as the US, Egypt and Australia have much higher average rice yields. The US produces around 10 million tons per year at an average yield of 7 tons per hectare, whereas Egypt produces 6 million tons at 9.5 tons per hectare and Australia produces some 2 million tons at an average yield of 10 tons per hectare. Some varieties of rice strains in China are now yielding as much as 18 tons per hectare. Mr. Yuan Longping, one of the most renowned scientists of China who pioneered hybrid rice technology in his country, has boldly predicted a yield of 22 tons per hectare. This 1930 born, 90-year young, dedicated swimmer and volleyball playing scientist was the Director-General of China's National Hybrid Rice Research and Development Centre and received the World Food Prize in 2004. He is very confident that with the adoption of biotechnology, his predictions will come true.[42, 43, 44, 45]

Our average yield of 3 tons of rice per hectare, which incidentally is even lower than the worldwide average yield of 3.8 tons, does not mean that the rice yield is uniformly low throughout India. In the two major rice producing states of Tamil Nadu and Punjab, where rice growing land is irrigated and the use of chemical fertilizers and pesticides is appreciable, rice yield is double the national average at 6 tons per hectare. States of eastern India on the other hand, barring some regions in West-Bengal, have much lower yields, for example, the average yield of rice in Odisha is only a meagre 1.7 tons per hectare. Paddy fields of coastal Odisha yield more than the state average, whereas the yields in the areas that adjoin the Reserve Forests and other stretches of land that were appropriated to increase the acreage for rice cultivation are even less, lower than 1 ton per hectare.

Part II: Destruction of Forests

> **Large stretches of forests and scrubland cleared to increase the acreage of arable land**
> **Increase productivity and surrender the appropriated land back to Mother Nature**
> **Social reforms necessary to eliminate the detrimental primitive habits**
> **Freedom of the holy cows and unholy goats must be restricted**

Large stretches of forests and scrubland cleared to increase the acreage of arable land

Although some regions in the states of West-Bengal and Bihar produce significant quantities of wheat, rice continues to be the staple crop of eastern India. In this section, therefore, instead of discussing the efficiency of wheat production, I restrict myself to rice. Based on the facts on rice yield presented above, we could conclude that the large production of food-grain we have achieved in India is partly because of increased efficiency in yield per hectare, but largely because of an increase in the acreage of arable land through clearing of the forests and appropriation of wetland and stretches of scrubland that fringed every village in the past.

Villagers often cleared large areas of forests to increase the size of their land holdings. In many instances such cleared lands, although rarely suitable for rice cultivation due to unavailability of water, are tortured to produce rice. This phenomenon is best described by the term "agritorture" that I introduce to you, my readers. Every village in eastern India used to be skirted by large stretches of unoccupied barren land and scrubland, where the cattle grazed. Even these poor-quality lands have been appropriated and converted into rice paddy fields. The patches of wetlands and swamps that are so very vital ecologically and for groundwater recharge, disappeared, long taken over by farmers, drained and filled to create more arable land for rice cultivation. The tiny little nondescript ponds that nestled in the scrubs or simply lay scattered around the villages that existed right up to the 1960s and 70s, where frogs frolicked, and innocuous little water snakes wriggled, have disappeared too.

I distinctly remember the croaking of the frogs, the shrill noises and crepitations of the various nocturnal species, announcing their availabilities to the members of their opposite gender, in the evenings of the monsoon months in my grandfather's estate in a village in Odisha in the 1960s. That cacophony, at least the intensity, is well and truly a thing of the past and does not exist in eastern India anymore. Frogs are not alone in dying, we are steadily losing large numbers of both animal and plant species to extinction in India. I contrast the massive extinction of the species of lower life forms in eastern India with the profusion of life around my house in suburban Seno outside Hiroshima, because of the lush environment provided by a forest cover of 80%. The orchestra outside my house, played out in full by the croaking frogs and their myriad creepy crawly companions in the monsoon months, distract me often with their intensity. I see a vast number of playful little frogs everywhere, in the fields and in the parks and even on the roads in Japan, which is an advanced industrialized nation of the world. And the frogs are gone from eastern India, which is essentially rural and agrarian, primarily because we have ruined our environment and we must undo the damage before it becomes irreversible. Frogs, incidentally, symbolize life and their unprecedented disappearance on a massive scale in eastern India, portend the impending tabescence of the land. The disappearance of the frogs should be taken very seriously, as a wakeup call, to prevent the region from becoming a desert.

Increase productivity and surrender the appropriated land back to Mother Nature

In order to prevent the desertification of eastern India, let us improve our crop management practices, which involve proper watering techniques, optimum use of fertilizer and pest control. With improved crop management, even a developing country like the Philippines has demonstrated near doubling of the yield of rice, from 4.5 tons per hectare to 8 tons in certain experimental stations. The second decade of the twenty-first century saw very substantial increases in rice yield in different countries of the world, simply by improvements in crop management. Our priority, therefore, should be a rapid implementation of the improved crop management practices, so that the rice yield in the more fertile stretches of the arable lands of eastern India is doubled, even tripled in a decade. Once we achieve higher productivity, we could transfer all those vast acreages of poor-quality land, so ruthlessly snatched away from Mother Nature, in the last six decades, for agritorture of rice, back to nature. Appropriated wetlands could go back to being wetlands for the frogs to proliferate. The scrublands and the stretches of land, where the forests were cleared, could play host to plantations of native trees or some other varieties of subtropical trees appropriate for the areas. The farmers need not surrender the title to their acreages; they could well tend the plantations and secure handsome returns. Please allow me to cite the specific case of Odisha to show how much land could be safely returned to nature.

The total land area of the state of Odisha is 155,707 square km out of which 61,650 square km make up the total arable land. As of 2009, according to a report published in a respected daily of Odisha, The Dharitri, on the 22nd of April 09, only a total of 28,304 square km of arable land is irrigated. Although the Government of Odisha envisage facilitating irrigation in a big way, only a maximum of 49,900 square km could ever be irrigated, leaving a full 11,750 square km of arable land (61,650 − 49,900 = 11,750) that cannot be irrigated, essentially due to geographical constraints. This 11,750 square km of land, must not be subjected to agritorture to produce rice and must be immediately surrendered to Mother Nature to host a variety of appropriate trees.

Social reforms necessary to eliminate the detrimental primitive habits

Even as the third decade of the twenty-first century or for that matter the third decade of the third millennium commences, and as the Indian Space Research Organisation (ISRO), having successfully commissioned missions to Planet Mars and the Moon, gets organized to launch manned missions to the Moon in the near future, a very large proportion of rural folks from eastern India still continue with their primitive habits that devastate the forests. I start with the age-old habit of collecting firewood from the forests and the scrublands.

We human beings once learnt the art of cooking all those millennia ago, started foraging in the forests not only for food but also for firewood. Nowadays, however, barring a few miniscule numbers of tribes inhabiting the inaccessible forests of India, we have stopped foraging for food in the woods as our agriculture produces enough. Villagers settled on the fringes of the forests in eastern India, however, continue to forage for firewood even today. Collection of firewood is carried out mostly by groups of women, armed with traditional implements to cut and chop small branches and baby trees. These women never cut down the massive trees, unlike the forestry workers and loggers, who are equipped with chainsaws and other more powerful tools and can clear large stretches of forests in a matter of hours. The devastation of the forests by these women, however, is by no means any less severe as they tend to cut down the baby trees which stop the regeneration of the forests. Each bundle of firewood that these women carry home on their heads is equal to at least a few truckloads, in a few years down the track.

This insidious practice of firewood collection that devastates the forests could only be stopped if these women are provided with an alternative fuel to cook their food with, particularly the evening meals. The fuel, moreover, must be very cheap, may even have to be provided free of cost. Such conditions could only be satisfied by the construction of community kitchens, at appropriately convenient locations in the villages. Depending upon the population and the straggle of any village, one or a good few more such kitchens may become necessary. The kitchens would provide the basic facilities of a few stoves, which could be fueled by a supply of commercial cooking-gas or even by biogas, generated from cow dung plants. The women could carry their provisions and utensils to cook the meals, for their respective families, in these community kitchens.

Villages in eastern India, always had community centers in the past, where people met to listen to religious discourses, to hold annual plays and for many other festivities. Establishment of community kitchens may, in fact, revive the important age-old tradition and may bring about closer social interactions. Cooking food in such community kitchens may also help erase the last vestiges of caste prejudices to a significant extent.

Mention I must that by 2019, Hon'ble Mr. Dharmendra Pradhan, the Minister for Petroleum and Natural Gas of the Government of India, had quite significantly expanded the national network of distribution of natural gas across the length and breadth of the country. Natural gas filled cylinders are presently available even in the remotest parts of the country, often subsidized for the poor villagers living in and around the forests. I sincerely hope that people make use of the natural gas for cooking and give up foraging for firewood.

The second primitive habit that I wish to discuss may appear harmless, but is not so. A lot many people in eastern India, perhaps a full 25% of the total population, despite the easy availability of toothbrush and toothpaste, still continue to use *dantakathi* or freshly cut live twigs from branches of a variety of trees for brushing their teeth with, in the morning. A *dantakathi* is typically about 15 cm long and up to 1 cm in diameter. A single *dantakathi* user in a week would easily consume a couple of 1 m long shoots, which could add up to 100 shoots a year. Cutting of all these 100 shoots and the sprigs from a single small tree would essentially prevent it from attaining full growth and adulthood. This primitive manner of toothbrushing by tens of millions in the rural parts of the eastern Indian states of Odisha, Chhattisgarh and Jharkhand are savaging tens of millions of young trees. How do we solve this problem?

The answer is a massive education program to make people aware of the dire need to give up their age-old habit of using *dantakathi* and a program of free distribution of toothbrushes, toothpastes and various herbal and ayurvedic toothpowders or *dantamanjans* in rural areas. Programs of free distribution and education will certainly cost a bit of money, but that would be money well spent for the regeneration of forests.

Freedom of the holy cows and unholy goats must be restricted

When the founding fathers of our modern nation drafted the Constitution of India, they in their infinite wisdom endowed us with the Fundamental Rights that guarantee an individual with the freedom of speech and expression, freedom of association and peaceful assembly and freedom to practise religion. Such rights say for example, Bill of Rights of England and the United States, Declaration of the Rights of Man of France do exist in some liberal democracies. These are indeed a great privilege not enjoyed by the citizens of many countries of the world. Even some wealthy developed democracies do not provide such rights.

In India, our noble founding fathers did not realize that the Rights so meticulously drafted, would also by logical extension apply to the holy mother cow, who after all is our mother. And the cattle population of India have wholly, in full measure, exercised their fundamental rights of speech, peaceful assembly and have vigorously practised their religion of procreation and grazing the greenery to extinction. They have been so successful a species that their number in India in 2012 stood at 191 million, around 13% of the total global cattle count. Add 109 million buffalos and the total bovine count in 2012 stood at a full 300 million. The bovine density per square km of India is 91 and in rural areas of eastern India it is even higher.[46, 47]

Cows are very nice and gentle, give milk, become the subject matter for children right from the age of five up to fifteen or so to write essays on, allow their images to be drawn by children, often under duress, in the primary and junior high school drawing classes. They, moreover, provide free demonstrations of invaluable live sex education, which is not available in the school curricula otherwise, to teenagers. Despite the string of benefits just outlined, the holy cows do cause us significant harm, particularly so in the eastern part of the country, where they are more politically aware. They are, moreover, very conscious of their Fundamental Rights, essentially because of the great grassroots movements brought about by the son of the soil Marxists. Here, moreover, the cattle generally give much less milk, do much less work and cause a lot more damage just like their compatriot Marxist comrades.

The cattle grazing in the forests and the scrubland would eat grass and any foliage within their reach, particularly the new shoots, which not only denudes the forests but also prevents their regeneration. These beasts, moreover, on account of their great weight, pound the earth as they strut and stampede. Their collective pounding marches very effectively drive out the soil moisture, which is the lifeblood of soil. In the absence of soil moisture, the seeds on the ground or the forest floor fail to germinate, which again stops the regeneration of forests.

What could we do to stop the rampaging holy cows that so utterly devastate our forests? The answer is very simple, we must restrict the free movements of the cattle and they have to be confined in pens by their owners. Villages and towns of eastern India have cattle owners, who neither possess enough space to confine their animals, nor have the resources to feed them daily. Every village and town, therefore, must set up community cattle pens for the homeless ones. The era of free movements of the cattle must come to an end and they must be confined to large cow shelters. Fortunately, now in 2021, the Government of India is most actively promoting the construction of cowhouses everywhere in the country. I sincerely hope that the cows get confined to such shelters, where they can be looked after better and, hopefully again, the milk production will rise.

Having discussed the holy cows, let us focus our attention on the unholy goats. According to a report by the Food and Agriculture Organization (FAO) of the United Nations, India's goat tally in 2002 stood at 124 million, which was about 17% of the world goat count of 743 million. India's goat count increased to 149 million in 2018, when the sheep count stood at 74 million.[50] We have around 50 goats per square km of land in India in 2018 and their density is significantly higher in rural areas. Goats are voracious eaters and would often nibble at every blade of grass to completely strip the land of any vegetation. They would even climb small trees to eat the leaves and tender sprigs. Vast expanses of forests and scrublands of eastern India unfortunately receive regular visits from herds of goats to get utterly ravaged and stay denuded without ever getting a chance to regenerate. Just like the cattle, the goats and the sheep must be restrained, if necessary, in community goat sheep pens.

Part III: Rejuvenation of the Mountains

- ➤ Revive the mountains – the *mahidharas* – the sustainers of the earth
- ➤ Saint Achyutananda Das
- ➤ How do we rejuvenate the *mahidharas*?
- ➤ Micro-dams in Japan effectively recharge groundwater
- ➤ "Essence of water is plant", Chandogya Upanishad
- ➤ Pore spaces in rocks of the mountainous region can store far more water
- ➤ Instances of regeneration of forests and hills in India
- ➤ Binjhagiri in Nayagarh district of Odisha
- ➤ Alwar district of Rajasthan
- ➤ Gujarat
- ➤ Revive the derelict ponds and water bodies
- ➤ Let us revive the *mahidharas*

Revive the mountains – the *mahidharas* – the sustainers of the earth
Among the multitude of synonyms for a mountain in Sanskrit and other languages of India, there occurs a word, which is of significance to the present discussion on the prevention of desertification of eastern India. And that word is *mahidhara*, which etymologically means the one who holds the earth or the one who sustains the earth. In our Indian civilization, we respect the mountains, the *mahidharas*, as the sustainers of the earth. So great is our reverence for the Himalaya that in Sanatan Dharma, the Eternal Religion also known as Hinduism, of this glorious country Aryaabarta or the Land of

the Cultured People, presently known as India, it is not just a chain of mountains, He is God. The Himalaya is not only the father of Goddess Parvati who is the consort of Shiva, but also the father of the Goddesses Ganga, Yamuna and Saraswati, the three majestic perennial rivers of India. This deification of the mightiest mountain range is an acknowledgement of the central role He plays in preserving and sustaining our glorious motherland India. Time it is now that we become aware of the singularly most important role the mountains play in sustaining the environment in our Indian subcontinent. And we must also realize the importance of regenerating the mountains, in order to revive the environment and to prevent desertification.

Mountains of the states of Odisha, Chhattisgarh and Jharkhand in eastern India have played important roles too. In the past, say around the independence of India, when these mountains, particularly of western Odisha, were crowned with dense forests, they successfully prevented the onslaught of the hot winds from the arid north-west and semiarid central India. Transpiration from the dense foliage of the thick forests, maintained the relative humidity at much higher levels throughout the year, particularly in pre-monsoon summer months. The combined effect of these two processes, kept eastern India much cooler than the hotter parts of the Indian subcontinent. The cool mountain air, moreover, at higher altitudes always provoked precipitations from the dark monsoon clouds that made eastern India receive much heavier rains than the rest of the country. The dense forests atop the mountains again played a very significant role by arresting the flow of the rainfall that recharged groundwater, at the upper end at higher altitudes, which raised the water table over a much larger geographic area.

As mentioned earlier, the mountains of the states of Odisha, Chhattisgarh and Jharkhand have already undergone extensive denudation. In addition to the recurring damages done by firewood collection and cattle grazing, the rampant unlawful loggings carried out by criminal gangs, often in collaboration with corrupt government officials, are destroying the forests. Another serious menace of the last few years is the vandalism of the pyromaniac criminals, who, just for fun, set the tinder-dry forests ablaze in summer months. These fires annihilate vast swathes of forest that take decades to fully regenerate. Forest fires, in Australian lingo called bushfires, have pretty much become a regular annual event, which cause severe devastations, at times causing enormous casualties. The massive bushfire of February 2009, killed 180 people and injured around 500 in the state of Victoria in Australia.[51] Majority of these bushfires in Australia are deliberately lit.[52]

In Brazil, in August 2019, over 25,000 square km of Amazon rain forest burnt almost entirely up to 99% due to deliberately lit fires, by farmers and loggers, hell bent on clearing the land for growing crops and grazing. The National Institute for Space Research (INPE) of Brazil, confirmed by NASA, stated that some 87,000 forest fires were recorded in Brazil in the first 8 months of 2019. These deliberately lit fires in certain years, clear over 25,000 square km of land in a twelve-month period.[53]

As a result of the serious denudation of the forests on the mountainous terrains of the states of Odisha, Chhattisgarh and Jharkhand, since 2000 or so, the relative humidity in the pre-monsoon summer months comes down to as low as 10%. Heat wave all the way from the deserts of Rajasthan, in the far west of the country, blows unhindered right up to the coastal plains of Odisha at a speed of around 25 km per hour. Consequently, the diurnal maximum, virtually in the entire state of Odisha, surpasses 40°C right from the middle of the month of March. Quite ironically on the 5th of June, which is the World Environment Day (WED), of 2003, the township of Titlagarh of western Odisha experienced one of the highest temperatures ever recorded in Odisha at 50.1°C. If the ambient temperatures of the forests continue to hover above 50°C for a period of time, the dry heat will make spontaneous forest fires a routine occurrence. This extreme dry heat, moreover, repels the moist clouds of the pre-monsoon months, which otherwise would produce rains. Say for example, in 2009, as of the end of the first week of May, there was not a single pre-monsoon shower of any significance in Odisha.

This ambient heat and the hot air blowing all the way from the deserts of Rajasthan, will not only accelerate the extinction of many species of animals and plants, but also seriously affect the rainfall pattern of eastern India. If the rainfall pattern changes significantly, despite the proximity to the sea and despite a long history of very heavy monsoonal rains, eastern India will become an arid land pretty much like littoral Somalia and the adjoining Ethiopia, situated in the north eastern most part of the continent of Africa. I am not indulging in a spot of scare mongering here; I am stating the dire truth. I would like to mention that Ethiopia and Somalia were not always dreary deserts, once upon a time they were lush green too. In order to substantiate my claim, I cite the epic journey, the Queen of Sheba undertook almost three thousand years ago, in the tenth century BCE, to visit the wise King Solomon in Jerusalem. Her entourage from Sheba i.e. Ethiopia carried vast quantities of spices, gold, precious stones and beautiful wood as gifts for the noble king. I want my readers to note the gift of 'beautiful wood', which Ethiopia produced in enormous quantities from her rich emerald forests.[54]

Right up to the beginning of the twentieth century, 30% of the total land area of Ethiopia was under forest cover, which, in the second decade of the twenty-first century, stood at a miserable 4%. One of the oldest human settlements in the world, Ethiopia, has all but become a desert because of systematic destruction of forests.[55]

The inept managers and their corrupt cohorts, blame this extreme hot climate of eastern India of the last two decades on global warming, which has become a convenient excuse to mask all manners of mismanagements and corrupt practices rampant in the states of eastern India. Fashionable it has become to blame global warming for all the ills of the world that include absconsion of Vijay Mallya, the mysterious death of Sridevi, intense urban crime waves and even the worldwide wardrobe malfunction of the supermodels and movie-stars. I admit that global warming is real and upon us, but it is not the root cause of all the evils of the present-day eastern India. The current extreme temperatures here are because of regional warming that we have brought upon ourselves by the denudation of the forests, by the destruction of the bodies of water and by the degradation of the land.

Saint Achyutananda Das

As the third decade of the twenty-first century commences, India is well advanced on her march to achieve the status of a global economic superpower. This great achievement has been possible, to a very great extent, due to a boom in the knowledge-based industries. Quite an irony it is that at a time of a boom in technical knowledge, we are losing the fundamental profound knowledge of living in harmony with nature. This reminds me of the dire prophecy of my forebear, the very great saint and seer of Odisha of the sixteenth century, Achyutananda Das. In one of the verses of his Book of Prophecies he foresees,

> '*Amaa andhakaara, ghotiba mahira;*
> *Agyaana hoiba dharaa, …*', which in English would read,

> 'Blinding darkness will shroud the earth.
> Lost will be the knowledge of the world …' (Translation ND)

I wonder what exactly he meant. Did he foresee blinding dust storms, which are a distinct possibility now in eastern India, in the summer months, on account of the massive deforestation and the consequent soil erosion? Or did he envision something far more sinister, brought about by an extreme weather event or a cataclysm unleashed by a meteorite impact? Or did he foresee a nuclear winter, not so unlikely to envision after seeing the loutish threats of a nuclear devastation, issued by the Prime Minister of Pakistan on the floor of the UN General Assembly in New York, in September 2019. What did you exactly see Oh Saint Achyuta? Regardless of whatever he might have seen, I make a fervent appeal to you my sisters and brothers from eastern India to save this land of our forebear from annihilation. Let us rejuvenate our mountains to at least delay the doom Saint Achyuta prophesied.

Please allow me a spot of indulgence in singing the life and time, in praise of the Odia poet, philosopher and yogi, Achyutananda Das. He was very likely born in the first decade of the sixteenth century in Tilakana village, barely 3 km away from Nemala, where the distributaries of the mighty Mahanadi, the Luna and the Chitrotpala, diverge. After his birth and early childhood in Tilakana, which is some 30 km away from the former capital of Odisha, Cuttack, Achyutananda moved to the famous coastal temple town of Puri by the Sea of Kalinga, presently known as the Bay of Bengal, where his father Dinabandhu Khuntia was in the employ of the Jagannath temple. His grandfather Gopinath Mohanty had also served the holy temple as a scribe. Through his forefathers, Achyuta became a devotee of Jagannath, etymologically the Lord of the Universe, and worshipped Him as the Buddha as well. Austere adherence to yoga, meditation and to the rituals of Buddhist tantra, endowed Achyutananda with great spiritual abilities that made him a prolific author and an incomparable seer. Saint Achyuta, apparently a centenarian, apparently again breathed his last in a state of levitation while seated in a meditative padmaasana posture. My grandfather, Alekh Prasad Das, in his award-winning autobiography, Jibanara Daka, has recorded Achyutananda's spiritual prowess and has stated my family's descent from the seer. The many books of Achyutananda, could loosely be termed as a collection of Books of Prophecies.[56, 57]

How do we rejuvenate the *mahidharas*?

Could we really regenerate our forests on the mountainous terrains of the states of Odisha, Chhattisgarh and Jharkhand; the answer is most definitely yes. In a matter of just two to three decades, these states and much of eastern India could become green again, just like the imageries of the nineteenth century eastern India, so magnificently captured by Bankim Chandra in the most inspirational poem of

> '*Bande Maataram,*
> *Sujalaam suphalaam,*
> *Malayaja sheetalaam,*
> *Sashya shyaamalaam…*', which in English would read,

> 'Bow to You Mother, you are,
> Endowed with an abundance of water,
> Full of bounteous harvests,
> Cool with the vernal breeze,
> Lush green in crops …' (translation ND).

How do we go about regenerating our mountains, the *mahidharas*? In addition to taking the immediate measures of restricting the cattle, goat, sheep and any other herbivores from devouring the forests, the pyromaniac vandals have to be arrested and the firewood collecting folks have to be restrained from ravaging the forests. Clearing of forests, moreover, must be stopped and the illegal logging operation that is going on with the connivance of corrupt officials must come to an absolute end. The biggest step for the revival of the mountains, however, would be a massive program of civil and environmental engineering, which is discussed below.

This program would involve the building of hundreds of thousands, yes you have heard it right, hundreds of thousands of micro-dams that is small dams, weirs and dykes, anywhere from 1 m to 10 m high. Micro-dam building will start right up in the mountains, as well as on the foothills, over the entire sprawl of mountainous terrains, where rainwater cascades down. The construction of micro-dams will also continue across springs, brooks and rivulets that constitute first order streams and on second order streams that emerge from the union of two first order ones, right from their sources up in the mountains, where they originate, to all the way to lowlands where they debauche to the much bigger third order streams. The purpose of these dams is not necessarily to create reservoirs of any great capacities, but simply to arrest the flow of rainwater right at the higher altitudes of the mountains and at the foothills at suitable locations. The arrested rainwater may well form tanks comparable in size to village ponds. Such water tanks, be they tiny or large, simply on account of their location on higher grounds up in the mountains, would have much greater efficiency in recharging groundwater than the village ponds, which are generally located in low lying valleys and in deltaic areas. The Government of Odisha, incidentally, is presently planning to either renovate the existing ponds or to excavate new ones, so that every village has a functional pond. I would also like to mention that any number of such village ponds in low lying areas, which admittedly provide a great many benefits to the villagers, would not help revive the mountains.

Construction of these micro-dams would rarely require any sophisticated high technology, for the structures would be mostly earthen, built with the locally excavated rock, soil and dirt and the central part of these structures, across the streams, could be a simple affair of reinforced concrete. The resultant bodies of water, however shallow they may be, would help recharge the groundwater over a vast area. The consequent increase in soil moisture and the availability of water, high up in the mountains, will significantly help in the regeneration of the forests. Many dead and dying mountain streams would revive and the ephemeral ones will become perennial, which will again ensure a significant regeneration of the forests atop the mountains. The revival of the forests would further enhance the water holding capacity of the soil, which will contribute to a further proliferation of plants and would thus firmly establish a virtuous cycle. As these plants prosper, they would breathe out more moisture which will moisten the mountain air, enhance the relative humidity and cool the environment. The moisture and the cool mountain air would help precipitate rainfalls and avert the dangers of a drastic change to the rainfall patterns.

Micro-dams in Japan effectively recharge groundwater

Please allow me to mention a series of 60 micro-dams constructed across the stream Seno Gawa and her biggest tributary Kumano Gawa, flowing in Hiroshima Prefecture of Japan. The micro-dams were built right from the source, on the top of the mountains, all the way to the lower grounds, on a 25 km long course between Kumano and Kaita towns via Seno town. The purpose of these micro-dams was to recharge groundwater and to manage round the year discharge of water, including the monsoonal rains. I, incidentally, live my life in Japan, on the banks of my elfish little Seno Gawa.

A second order stream Seno Gawa, barely a meter wide at its origin, rises from a mountain Sobagajo Yama of Hachihonmatsu town and flows in a south-west direction for a total length of 22 km, before debauching into the Kaita Bay of the Seto Inland Sea. Seno Gawa, in the process, drains a catchment of 122 square km, 75% of which is mountainous with the highest elevation of 720 m above the mean sea level (MSL) at Oda Yama Mountain. This region, by the way, receives an average annual rainfall of 1,500 mm and hosts a population of around a quarter of a million. A first order stream Kumano Gawa that rises from a mountain west of Kumano town, flows north in a serpentine course for 15 km to tribute Seno Gawa at Seno town. At this confluence, Seno Gawa is 30 m wide and continues to travel south-west to the sea some 10 km away and widens to 100 m or so at its mouth.[58]

The aforesaid 60 micro-dams have been most effective in recharging groundwater that has kept the mountains spectacularly lush and verdant. The mountains are so laden with water that all the tributaries of Seno Gawa that drain the catchment are perennial. I request you my readers to search Kumano and Seno in Hiroshima, either in Google Map or in Google Earth, and see for yourself the lush vegetation on either side of the river and on the adjoining mountains.

And this is what we can do in eastern India, by constructing those hundreds of thousands of micro-dams to revive the mountains and to make the land green again.

"Essence of water is plant", Chandogya Upanishad
Please allow me to quote the second verse of the Chandogya Upanishad that lays emphasis on water for the proliferation of plants and lends credence to my contention of making provision for water first, so that the plants could grow on their own. The Forest Department of the Government of Odisha spends billions of Rupees in plantation drives, without ever making arrangement for water first, and the saplings routinely die due to want of water. The verse, first in original Sanskrit, then in English translation is presented below:

Esaam bhutaanaam prithvi rasah, prithivyaa apo rasah,
Apaam osadhayo rasah,
Osadhinaam puroso rasah,
Purusasya vaagraso,
Vaach Rug rasah,

Rugchah Saama rasah,
Saamno Udgitho rasah. (1:1:2)

Essence of the entire material universe is Planet Earth;
Essence of Earth is water.
Essence of water is plant,
Essence of plant is human being,
Essence of human being is speech,
Essence of speech is Rig Veda,
Essence of Rig-Veda is Sama Veda,
Essence of Sama Veda is Udgita (which is OM). (1:1:2)
(Translation ND).

I draw your attention to the second line that reads, "Essence of water is plant", which means that from water plants grow. Let us, therefore, make provision for water first and plants will grow. Once fresh water fills the pore spaces of the presently barren mountains of eastern India, plants will grow automatically from the seeds, dispersed naturally by the combined action of wind and water and by birds and beasts.

Pore spaces in rocks of the mountainous region can store far more water

However solid the mountains may look, they are remarkably porous, because of the inherent porosity of the rocks and soils they are made up of, and the various joints, cracks, faults and crevasses that pervade the rocks. The porosity of these earth materials of the mountainous Odisha, could be anywhere between 20% and 50%. Consequently, these mountains can hold vast quantities of water in storage that constitute sources for brooks, springs and other first order streams, which merge to generate streams of higher orders. And precisely for this reason, as mentioned earlier, the mountains are revered as the fathers of rivers. In Odisha, the river Mahendra-Tanaya, etymologically daughter of Mahendra, is affectionately named after the source Mahendra mountain, who stands proud as her father.

A full three quarters of the state of Odisha spread over 155,707 square km of land is mountainous, whose mountains boast an average elevation of 900 m above the mean sea level (MSL).[59] This mountainous region, occupying approximately 115,000 square km (rounded down from 116,780 obtained by multiplying 155,707 X 3/4), moreover, contains a series of plateaus that lie at an average elevation between 305 m and 610 m, and numerous intermontane basins and is crisscrossed by rivers of all shapes and sizes. I propose to calculate the total volume of water that could be stored in the pore spaces of the total land mass above the MSL of this mountainous region, in order to demonstrate that this volume is many times more than the total storage capacity of around 10 cubic km of the reservoirs, created by the large dams constructed in the state of Odisha so far. A most conservative estimate of the total volume of water that could be stored in the pore spaces of this entire mountainous region would involve a conservative estimation of the volume of the land, multiplied by a conservative average value for the porosity.

The approximate volume of the total land of this mountainous region is equal to the total area of the land (115,000 square km), multiplied by 300 m (rounded down smallest average elevation of 305 m of the plateaus of the mountainous region), which comes to 34,500 cubic km. The total volume of water that can be stored in the pore spaces of the entire mountainous region, therefore, is 34,500 cubic km multiplied by the lowest average value of porosity at 20%, which comes to 6,900 cubic km. And this volume or the storage capacity for water in the porosity of the mountainous region of Odisha is at least 690 times more than the total reservoir capacity of 10 cubic km (or billion cubic meters – bcm) created so far by the construction of 204 large dams in the state. Out of these 204 large dams, 10 are major project dams like the Hirakud and the Rengali, 50 are medium project dams and the rest 144 are minor irrigation project dams.[60]

Even if we manage to fill up a mere one percent of the water storage capacity available in the pore spaces of the mountainous region of Odisha by water arrested by micro-dams, we will have 69 cubic km of water, which is 7 times the total reservoir capacity of the state created so far. By the way, I would like to mention that the total reservoir capacity of 10 cubic km created by the construction of large dams does not exist anymore, at least a whopping 30% of the reservoir capacity, is well and truly lost due to accumulation of sediments caused by improper management of the reservoirs, rivers, catchment and drainage basins. These issues are discussed further in Chapter Four and Chapter Five. Construction of about 60,000 micro-dams in Odisha will fill up all the available pore spaces of the mountainous land with water, not just down to the depth of the mean sea level (MSL) but beyond. Percolating water will descend deep to great depths to fill up the pore spaces that constitute aquifers, some of which exist hundreds of meters below the MSL.

Micro-dams are much cheaper, safer, faster and easier to construct than the large dams and far more effective in recharging groundwater and regenerating the forests. Micro-dams, moreover, do not displace people.

Instances of regeneration of forests and hills in India
However astounding these simple measures may appear, the claims are not exaggerated. Regeneration of forests and hills and restoration of utterly depleted groundwater, by the construction of micro-dams have already been demonstrated most spectacularly, in a sufficiently large scale, in various parts of India. I discuss briefly three such regions of the country, in this section, in order to convince you my readers that revival of the forests and the mountains and restoration of groundwater are eminently possible.

Binjhagiri in Nayagarh district of Odisha

Please allow me to start this section, with the story of the regeneration of a patch of forest and a 3 km long, 1 km wide, 280 m high nondescript hill, by the name Binjhagiri, in Nayagarh district of Odisha. Binjhagiri, like many other hills of eastern India, suffered serious denudation due to rampant cutting of trees by all and sundry in the 1960s and early 1970s. The residents of the nearby village of Kesharpur and a few other adjacent villages suffered the most, on account of the degradation. Not only did they endure as many as 6 droughts during the space of a mere one decade in the 1960s, but also noticed substantial changes to their climate by the year 1970. By then rainfall had declined noticeably, the air in summer months blew unbearably hot and agricultural production had declined considerably, so much so, that many marginal farmers were forced to abandon their fields and seek employment as daily labourers elsewhere.[61]

A marginal farmer of Kesharpur, by the name Mr. Udaynath Khatei, out of sheer desperation perhaps, resolved to organize the villagers do something to help save the fast deteriorating forest. He was, however, very unsure of a precise plan of action to achieve his goals until the local Divisional Forest Officer (DFO) Mr. Pratap Patnaik provided the initial knowledge and guidance. The villagers, desperate to save their meagre livelihoods, whole-heartedly accepted the leadership of Udaynath and initiated measures to protect the forests. Udaynath was soon joined by two others, an idealistic primary school teacher of Kesharpur Mr. Joginath Sahoo and a compassionate Professor Narayan Hazari, also a resident of Kesharpur. I have the good fortune of knowing Professor Hazari since my childhood, as he was a frequent visitor to our house, because my father Professor Rajendra Prasad Das was his teacher. Professor Hazari taught political science and was always a generous and a noble teacher. The two idealists, Joginath and Professor Hazari, played the vital role of educating the mass movement on protecting the environment. Little did they know that their humble campaign would become a significant mass movement, involving some 22 villages, and the story of their success would receive worldwide publicity.[61] They would, moreover, receive several provincial, national and international awards including the Global 500 Award from the United Nations Environment Program in 1989, 'in recognition of outstanding practical achievements in the protection and improvement of the environment.'

In the very first step, the villagers drastically reduced, by as much as 50%, their own requirements of firewood that they had traditionally obtained from the forest, by cooking once a day, instead of the two meals they normally cooked. A very important second step involved the prohibition of goat and sheep from ravaging the forests. The mass movement then initiated not only its own tree plantation program in the denuded forests, but also provided protection to the plantations carried out by the forestry department of the government. The villagers, moreover, most meticulously guarded the forests day and night, on a volunteer basis, to stop the cutting of trees, by the illegal operators.[61]

This mass movement to protect and regenerate the forests of Binjhagiri, produced remarkable results within two decades and, by 1988, the forests were regenerated to a very significant extent. During this period, the revival of the forests raised the groundwater table of the villages, by as much as 40 ft or 12 m, so that the wells upon reaching a depth of a mere 20 ft could provide drinking water round the year, which in earlier times of 1970, was possible only after digging to a depth of around 60 ft. Soil erosion from the hill, moreover, decreased substantially. And needless to say, agricultural production in those 22 villages around Binjhagiri increased too.

The case of the regeneration of the forest of Binjhagiri is now well publicized in a book titled, Community Forest

Management: A Casebook from India, published by Oxfam.[61]

Alwar district of Rajasthan

The second case of regeneration of forests and hills that I propose to discuss, took place in the arid western part of India, in Alwar district of the state of Rajasthan. This is also the story of an idealist, Dr. Rajendra Singh, who chose to make enormous sacrifices to accomplish his mission against all odds, stacked sky high.

Right up to the 1930s, the district of Alwar that nestles in the vales of the Aravalli hills was green. But then the local prince sold away the forests full of timber up in the hills to logging contractors. In a matter of only ten years, the contractors cut the trees and thoroughly denuded the forests and rains washed away the rich topsoil of the forest floor. Hordes of domestic herbivores of cattle, goats, sheep and camels, grazing grass on the forest lands, nibbled at the new shoots too and that utterly prevented regeneration. Subsequent monsoonal rainfalls on this denuded wasted forest land, raced downhill without ever stopping to recharge groundwater. The absence of soil moisture contributed to further wastage of the land. The denudation of forests on the hills, thus completely reduced the relative humidity and enhanced desertification. Rainfall, consequently, declined too and the entire vicious cycle of desertification, not only intensified, but also continued unabated. By the time a 28-year young Dr. Rajendra Singh arrived in 1985 at the scene, everybody, including the natives of Alwar, had accepted the arid nature of the land as a *fait accompli*. They, moreover, were convinced that the arid land was incapable of regeneration. The young Rajendra Singh and his four friends, who would embark upon the campaign to regenerate the forests, however, visualized the scenario differently.

Rajendra Singh and his Non-Governmental Organization (NGO), *Tarun Bharat Sangh* (TBS) or Young India Guild, took a simple two-pronged approach. The first one was the revival of vegetation on the barren hills, by a prohibition on any further cutting of trees and grazing of the land. The second was the construction of numerous micro-dams to build small water catchments in the hills, valleys and the plains to arrest rainwater. They started their experimentation in a remote village, by the name Bhikampura, in Alwar district.

TBS achieved spectacular success in the regeneration of denuded hills, by placing a total prohibition on grazing by cattle for 3 years, goats for 5 years and camels for 7 years. Vast stretches of wasteland and denuded forests that were given up as hopeless cases, were totally transformed into lush green fields within a decade. However miraculous it may sound, within a time span of only 15 years, quite a few rivers such as Arvari, Ruparel, Jahjajwali and numerous rivulets that were very dead for a very long time, were revived. In fact, river Arvari that had been dead for 40 years started flowing again. Agriculture, which had been reduced at best to a seasonal chore, became round the year activity again. Their simple techniques of rainwater harvesting raised the levels of groundwater considerably and the micro-dams were so effective that the local villagers felt inspired to construct similar weirs wherever necessary. In the process, they would build some 3,500 such water harvesting structures in Rajasthan.

Dr. Rajendra Singh is well known as The Waterman of India. In 2001, he received Ramon Magsaysay Award and the citation read, for community leadership 'to rehabilitate their degraded habitat and bring its dormant rivers back to life'. In 2015, Dr. Rajendra Singh received the Stockholm Water Prize and the citation read, "Today's water problems cannot be solved by science or technology alone. They are human problems of governance, policy, leadership, and social resilience." "Rajendra Singh's life work has been in building social capacity to solve local water problems through participatory action, empowerment of women, linking indigenous know-how with modern scientific and technical approaches and upending traditional patterns of development and resource use."[62] India needs a thousand Rajendra Singh, one for each and every district of the country, to regenerate the denuded forests and the wastelands, to make the country green again.

Gujarat

Please allow me to conclude this section, with a discussion on the restoration of groundwater in the semiarid western state of Gujarat.

The 14th and current Prime Minister of India since 2014, Honourable Mr. Narendra Damodardas Modi, during his tenure as the 14th Chief Minister of Gujarat that continued over 14 years between 7 October 2001 and 22 May 2014, most actively supported Non-Governmental Organizations (NGOs) and communities to develop groundwater recharge projects by constructing micro-dams. Half a million (500,000) such structures that included 113,738 check dams, were built by the end of 2008. These micro-dams very significantly recharged the aquifers, so much so, that by 2014, groundwater tables were fully restored in sixty of the 112 *tehsils,* where groundwater stood utterly depleted in 2004. Gujarat, consequently, became the leading producer of genetically modified cotton in India and the successful use of semiarid land for cultivation made Gujarat's agricultural sector grow at a most commendable average rate of 9.6% between 2001 and 2007.[63] This is truly a splendid display of the process for, and the benefits of, groundwater recharge by the construction of a large number of micro-dams. Modiji you deserve the credit for making the semiarid Gujarat green and now I appeal to you Sir to make eastern India green again.

Revive the derelict ponds and water bodies

The state of Odisha contains 53,845 villages and each village possesses at least a couple of ponds or bodies of water of some kind.[64] The total number of ponds in Odisha, therefore, exceeds 100,000 and the number for the entire eastern India, very likely, exceeds half a million. Such ponds are excellent for recharging groundwater, particularly so, when they are in mountainous areas and plateaus of higher elevations. The mountainous western Odisha, in fact, had an age-old tradition of building micro-dams, locally known as "udaka bandha", where "udaka" means water and "bandha" being dam. "Udaka", incidentally, is a Sanskrit as well as an Odia word, which means water and is the etymological root for the Russian word "vodka". These thousands of udaka bandhas of western Odisha and for that matter, most of the ponds or water bodies in eastern India, particularly so of Odisha, now lay utterly derelict and ruined. The tradition of building udaka bandha must be revived and the derelict ponds must be excavated and renovated, not only for storing surface water, but also for effective recharge of groundwater.

In this context, please allow me to mention that in the second week of May 2017, the summer temperature in Odisha shot up to 46°C and the India Meteorological Department (IMD) issued an orange alert to warn people of severe heat wave conditions. Following the issuance of the alert, the Times of India (TOI) interviewed two experts including me and the statements were reported by Minati Singha in a news item titled, "'Orange alert' across Odisha as temperature crosses 46 degrees Celsius', where she mentioned, "A crippling water shortage and unscheduled power cuts in several parts of the state has made the life miserable for common men. Expressing concern over the rising temperature experts blamed the rise in temperature essentially to the loss of forest cover of western and central Odisha and drying up of rivers and water bodies" (Appendix One).

Please allow me to quote my statement published in the TOI and that read, "Forest cover of Odisha must be raised substantially by proper management of water by the construction of some 60,000 micro-dams in the mountainous parts of the state. All major rivers of the state are dead, and they must be revived by an extensive program of dredging so that they can hold water. Once rivers die civilizations die. Odisha is facing that kind of an unprecedented crisis. The state must revive all derelict and dying ponds, by proper excavation and renovation and the program of afforestation must be intensified. The state government should take a multi-pronged approach and must make it mandatory to install solar panels, rainwater harvesting and rooftop gardening on all buildings across the state, particularly so in the urban areas"[65] (Appendix One), essentially to combat the extreme summer heat and shortage of water.

In August 2018, the Department of Water Resources of the Government of Odisha signed an agreement with the National Bank for Agriculture and Rural Development (NABARD) for "implementation of a project on climate change for massive groundwater recharge… in 15 districts across the state in five years" at a total cost of USD166.30 million. "The South Korea based Green Climate Fund will provide USD34.36 million to the state government as financial assistance through NABARD." "Under the project, 10,000 ponds will be renovated and the recharge structures (shafts) will be constructed to conserve surplus rainwater (in aquifers)."[66] Hopefully all the ponds of the state will be revived soon.

In a slight diversion, please allow me to mention that the capital of the state of Odisha, Bhubaneswar, is a good few thousand years old city of temples and contained many celebrated ponds, all of whom now stand utterly silted up and most of them are derelict and dying. All these ponds need systematic excavation, then renovation, for a proper revival. The city of Bhubaneswar, moreover, is built on a vast undulating terrain that was drained by a series of 24 first and second order streams that originated from the hills in the west. The largest of these streams, since time immemorial, bore a most dignified name, "Gangabati Nadi" or the Gangabati River. This second order stream in her twenty-first century version is utterly defiled, clogged and barely flows as the derogated Gangua Nala or the Gangua Drain. This drain is now choked full of industrial and medical effluent, untreated raw sewage and "night soil", a euphemism for pure and unadulterated human excreta. Oh my darling Gangabati, you are a maimed ravaged river of a testimony to the callousness of the population of the capital city of Odisha, who so very boastfully espouse the richness of their culture of cleanliness. Shame, shame, what a shame!

My clever brethren of Bhubaneswar, including the high and the mighty in the government, you have completely filled flattened all the smaller streams and encroached upon the wetlands and the floodplains with the construction of an entire range of dwellings, right from the shanty to the high-rise, which most severely obstruct drainage and, in fact, demonstrate your total disdain for the very concept of drainage. And the net result is a drastic fall in water table, due to a lack of groundwater recharge, horrendous contamination of the aquifers and routine outbreak of hepatitis of epidemic proportions, extensive urban water logging even after a moderate rainfall. The rainfalls, in fact, convert asphalt roads into raging rivers that regularly inundate houses even to the level of upper floors. The floods, moreover, instantly metamorphose most passenger cars into submarines, while the rest are transformed into powerboats that take off at great speed, in all directions, to entertain the stranded denizens.

However smart you corrupt land-grabbing criminals may consider yourselves, your chicanery does not go unnoticed, in fact, the whole world sees it and I hope that someday you face the heavy hand of the law. All those dwellings, built on the floodplains, by you, urban vandals, must be bulldozed to liberate the 24 streams of Bhubaneswar from your clutches and they must be excavated and fully rejuvenated.

Let us revive the *mahidharas*

In the summer of 2008, the government of the state of Odisha announced a plan for the planting of trees over an area of 100,000 hectare (1,000 square km) every year. This is a well-intended policy that I welcome. This policy can be fruitful, only if proper attention is paid to the selection of the right species of plants, depending upon the topography, type of soil, rainfall patterns and micro-climate of the various parts of the state. Plantations of trees are required everywhere, but afforestation necessary for the regeneration of the denuded forests, atop the mountains, is crucial. Let these plantations of trees proceed, hand in hand, with the construction of those numerous, hundreds of thousands of micro-dams.

If we do not act now and continue to procrastinate in rejuvenating the mountains, a time will come that is not too far away, when the damages will be considered irreversible. Let us act now before it is too late and let us launch the Program of Revival of the *Mahidharas*.

Soon after the publication of this article in 2009, I, as usual, sent copies by email to many of my friends that included fellow academics, scientists and environmentalists. One such gentleman, has access to and is in the habit of forwarding interesting articles to, the scholarly Chief Minister of Odisha Honourable Mr. Naveen Patnaik, who is an accomplished writer and is keen on the preservation of the environment. I have, therefore, reasons to believe that the studious Chief Minister (CM) did see this article. Sometime later in early 2010, the CM took a meeting of some of the senior most officers of his government and resolved to undertake a program of large-scale construction of micro-dams in Odisha.

The then Principal Secretary to the Government of Odisha for the Department of Water Resources, had participated in the meeting and was given the responsibility to implement the said program. I have known this Principal Secretary for a long time, as a most brilliant student. I, in fact, had the privilege of teaching geology to this bright lad, by the name Suresh Chandra Mahapatra, nearly four decades ago in B.Sc. Geology Honours class at Ravenshaw College, between 1980 and 1982. Suresh studied geology well, stood first in B.Sc. and after completion of M.Sc. (Tech.) in Applied Geology from the venerable Indian School of Mines, joined the Oil & Natural Gas Commission (ONGC) of India as a geologist, before qualifying for the Indian Administrative Service (IAS). He went on to establish himself as a fine officer and in due course became the Principal Secretary of Water Resources and in 2021, rose to the topmost position of the Chief Secretary to the Government of Odisha. You have made me immensely proud Suresh. This dynamic IAS officer, Mr. Mahapatra, took up the responsibility of constructing micro-dams most diligently.

A few years ago, when I visited Suresh in his office, he projected numerous photographs of patches of lush green vegetation that had grown, on their own, around the micro-dams, in hundreds of locations in western Odisha. The little streams that ran dry, immediately after the monsoonal downpours, presently boasted surface water even in pre-monsoon summer months, because of the newly constructed micro-dams. Availability of water on the stream beds, not only facilitated the spontaneous growth of native plants, seeds of which were dispersed by birds and beasts, but also regenerated forest cover and raised groundwater table. Availability of surface and groundwater, moreover, solved the problem of drinking water, not only for the villagers, but also for their domestic animals and the wild beasts. Micro-dams, consequently, have become immensely popular among the rural populations of western Odisha, who are now clamoring for the construction of many more.

In March 2020, the Minister for Water Resources of the Government of Odisha stated that a total of 14,588 micro-dams were constructed in Odisha, in a 10-year period between 2010 and 2019, irrigating some 1,47,000 hectares of land[67]. This is indeed a piece of excellent news. I was also encouraged to hear Mr. Suresh Chandra Mahapatra IAS, mention a policy decision of the Government of Odisha to construct 4,000 micro-dams per year for the foreseeable future. And I fervently request the Government of Odisha to raise the number to 10,000 per year, so that Odisha can get the 60,000 or so micro-dams it desperately needs, constructed in the next 5 years, which will make Odisha green again. I sincerely hope that the required number of micro-dams get constructed in Odisha, during the present 5-year tenure of the CM Mr. Naveen Patnaik.

Ten years ago, when I wrote this article, I had appealed and called upon the Chief Ministers of all the states of eastern India, for that matter of all the states of India, to lead by example of planting trees and had waxed lyrical,

Let the leaders show the way,
By planting one tree every day.

Now a decade later, too late it is, to revive the barren mountains and forest floors of eastern India by merely planting trees and the only way out is construction of hundreds of thousands of micro-dams to provide water for plants to grow.

I, therefore, appeal to you all to construct those 60,000 micro-dams necessary in Odisha alone and some 500,000 in the entire eastern India, to make this part of the world green again to save this land.

Chapter Two
Sea Level Rise and Inundation of Coastal India

"Global warming is making sea level rise", I wrote in 2008 and proceeded to state that sea level, however, will not rise appreciably overnight, not in months, not even in years. The rise will assume dangerous proportions only over a substantial length of time, perhaps over decades. The assertions, I warned, are not designed to make you complacent my readers and comforted them by saying that you need not panic either. I criticized the sensationalist movies and documentaries that show the sea invading deep into eastern India, inundating the capital of West-Bengal Kolkata, which as Calcutta was once the capital of British India. In these documentaries, moreover, the ancient capital city of the state of Odisha, Cuttack, situated at the apex of the delta of the Mahanadi, some 70 km inland, within a matter of seconds, submerges under the invading sea. These movies very successfully scared millions of viewers, without ever telling much on how to combat the rising sea.

As I rewrite in 2021, well over a decade after the original article was written, I would like to mention that we have not only lost a precious dozen years, but also have become aware of a much faster melting of the Greenland ice sheet, which once completely melted will raise the sea level by a massive seven meters, over a period of a mere decade or two.[1]

I, therefore, propose to impart a sense of urgency to the issue of sea level rise and draw your attention to a news item published in the Times of India of the 30th of October 2019, written by Denise Lu and Christopher Flavelle of NYT News Service with a caption that screamed "Rising seas will erase more cities by 2050, new research shows". The running caption of the same article was titled "Mumbai at risk of being wiped out by 2050". This piece of news is based on research carried out by Scott A. Kulp and Benjamin Strauss of Climate Central and published in the most respected journal, Nature Communications.[2,3] These two researchers used Artificial Intelligence (AI) to accurately interpret the extent of inundation and state that some 300 million people of the world, living on coastal tracts, will lose their land to the rising seas by 2050.

Sea and nature in general have been more kind to us human beings than we would care to admit. Nature always gives us plenty of warning before doing anything drastic and, by the same token, the sea gives us a good many years to protect our landmass from her transgressions. As sea level rise accelerates due to global warming, coastal India faces inundation. Although sea level rise is inevitable, the inundation of coastal India is not, and certainly not a *fait accompli*. If we decide to initiate collective action, in a scale comparable to the mass movement led by Mahatma Gandhi, we could successfully combat the rising seas, at least for a good few centuries. In this article, I propose to discuss the various aspects of sea level rise and emphasize the preventive measures that could be undertaken to save coastal India, from the ravages of the rising seas.

Rate of sea level rise

Earth scientists equipped with geological, geochemical and palaeontological (from the study of fossils) evidence have proved the existence of ice ages in the earth's history.[4] During an ice age, the temperature of the earth's surface and the atmosphere decline significantly that cause substantial accumulation of glacial ice. The most recent ice age, in the earth's history, commenced around 110,000 years ago, peaked around 20,000 years ago and ended around 10,000 years ago. While stating these ages, I have deliberately provided round numbers in consideration of the fact that at different parts of the globe, the last ice age peaked and ended at somewhat different times. If I may further elaborate on the regional variations, I could even state that the last ice age ended anywhere between 10,000 and 15,000 years ago.

Soon after the ice age peaked, glaciers started melting and released vast quantities of water into the sea. Sea level, consequently, started rising and has risen about 130 m in the last 18,000 years. The rate of sea level rise in the past, however, has not been uniform, initially very fast it was and then it slowed down. Most of the sea level rise, therefore, took place between 18,000 and 6,000 years before present. Let me clarify the commonly used term 'before present', which is precisely what it says and means 'ago' in common parlance.

Since 3,000 years before present till the end of the nineteenth century, sea level was practically constant and did not rise much.[5] The rate of sea level rise during this period was a mere 0.1 to 0.2 mm per year. Since 1900 CE, however, sea level has been rising more rapidly at the rate of 1 to 2 mm per year. These numbers in millimeter do not appear large and daunting, but when accumulated, say over a period of a century, they do assume menacing proportions. In 100 years since 1900 CE, sea level rose by 20 cm, which is not insignificant.

In the early 1990s, satellite altimetry was employed to very precisely record sea level rise. Please allow me to explain briefly satellite altimetry, which is an advanced piece of space technology for accurate measurement of height. Satellite altimetry very precisely measures the time taken by a radar pulse to travel from the satellite antenna to an exact point on the surface of earth and back to the satellite receiver. These data eventually provide the exact height. TOPEX/Poseidon joint satellite mission between NASA of the US and CNES of France launched in 1992, has measured sea level with unprecedented accuracy. Results of TOPEX/Poseidon satellite altimetry observations show that since 1993, sea level is rising at the rate of 3.1 mm per year.[6, 7]

A logical question that arises is precisely how high will sea level rise to, say by the end of the twenty-first century? This is a difficult question and many groups, scattered all over the world, are actively engaged in providing an answer, but let us try none the less. If the current rate of sea level rise, as ascertained from satellite altimetry, remains constant at 3.1 mm per year, then by 2100 CE the rise would be 310 mm or 31 cm. Such a rate, if remains unchanged indefinitely, is not much of a cause for concern for the near future. This rate, however, is extremely unlikely to remain constant, which renders the calculated projection of sea level rise by 31 cm, by the year 2100 CE, extremely naïve. We, moreover, know that the intensifying anthropogenic global warming, would considerably accelerate the rise of sea level through two main processes and they are, increased pace of widespread melting of glacial ice and thermal expansion of sea water.

Rise in sea level due to melting of glacial ice is easy to understand, but the phenomenon of sea level rise due to thermal expansion, although quite simple, may be somewhat unknown. Let me, therefore, start with an explanation of thermal expansion, which is essentially a property of any matter, solid or gas or liquid, to expand when heated. Sea water, which has a huge capacity to absorb heat is no different and expands in volume upon heating, thus raising sea level. If sea water temperature were to rise by say 1°C by 2100 CE, the resultant rise in sea level could reach 40 cm. A near complete melting of all the mountain glaciers of the world would make sea level rise by about 35 cm, which could well happen by 2100 CE if global warming continues unabated. A combination of these two factors alone, therefore, could raise sea level by 75 cm by 2100 CE.

Let us now analyze the contributions from Greenland and Antarctica, which are still somewhat uncertain at this stage. In my 2008 version of this article, I quoted an authoritative study of September 2008 that claimed that Greenland Ice Cap that experienced losses of 257 cubic km of ice per year due to melting, would lose 465 cubic km of ice annually, by the year 2080 CE.[8, 9] Meltwater from this body of ice raises sea level by 0.6 mm per year now, which would rise to 1.0 mm annually by 2080 CE. On the basis of this study, if we arbitrarily accept contributions from Greenland Ice Cap to raise sea level by 0.6 mm per year till 2050, which then rises to 0.8 mm per year till 2080 and finally to 1.0 mm per year till 2100 CE, we get a sea level rise of 7.5 cm by 2100 CE [(0.6 mm X 50 years) + (0.8 mm X 30 years) + (1.0 mm X 20 years) = 74 mm = say 7.5 cm in 100 years].

The southern continent of Antarctica that holds the single largest volume of ice, fortunately, is also the slowest to melt. The current and future rates of glacial melt or the volume of ice breaking off as icebergs to enter the oceans, however, are very uncertain. In 2008, a well-respected study reported that 85% of the entire coastline of the continent was observed, between 1992 and 2006, to assess the total glacial contribution towards the oceans. The observations were made by highly sophisticated satellite interferometric synthetic aperture radar. The results of this study revealed that the total contribution from Antarctica that included East and West Antarctica and Antarctic Peninsula was about 200 cubic km per year, which is comparable to the contribution from Greenland Ice Caps and could raise sea level by 0.5 mm per year.[10] Although this rate of contribution from Antarctica may rise very rapidly in the future, given the uncertainty, let us accept it to be similar to that of Greenland Ice Caps of 7.5 cm by 2100 CE. This statement will raise howls of protests from my colleagues, but let us accept it for the time being. The total contribution from Antarctica and Greenland to sea level rise by 2100 CE is, thus 15 cm.

These simple calculations of the total contributions from all the sources that I had shown in the 2008 article, projected a sea level rise of 90 cm by the year 2100 CE.

The uncertainty in calculating the contributions from Antarctica, is essentially due to an interesting possibility of global warming causing higher precipitations, in the central part of the icy continent. These much heavier snowfalls may result in greater accumulation of glacial ice, than losses due to a combination of melting or breaking off into the oceans. The net contribution of Antarctica may thus even become negative. I would like to briefly touch upon the state of mass balance in the cryosphere, a term that embodies all the deposits of ice and snow in the world. Each year a significant volume of sea water, capable of lowering sea level, evaporates to precipitate in Antarctica and Greenland as snowfall. If no ice or ice meltwater were to return to the oceans, sea level would fall. This, however, did not happen in the last few centuries as large volumes of ice entered the oceans and a mass balance was maintained. Global warming is now all set to disturb this mass balance.

The Intergovernmental Panel on Climate Change (IPCC) chaired by a scientist from India, Dr. Rajendra Kumar Pachauri, in its Third Assessment Report (TAR) of 2001 predicted that by 2100 CE, global warming would raise sea level anywhere between 9 cm and 88 cm.[11]

I would like to state that in 2007, the IPCC shared the Nobel Prize for Peace with Al Gore of the US. Dr. Pachauri made his country proud when on the 10th of December 2007, he accepted the prize on behalf of the IPCC.[12]

The IPCC-TAR considered all the relevant factors of thermal expansion, mountain glaciers, glacial ice of Greenland and Antarctica, groundwater, soil moisture and permafrost to arrive at their result. I hope that my readers will bear in mind that this study was published in 2001, after which a lot more information on the melting of glacial ice emerged. In view of the new information, the lower limit of 9 cm rise by 2100 CE appears a gross underestimation. There are many, who claimed that even the upper limit of 88 cm was an underestimate and sea level could rise much higher.

Given my obsession with roundness and quite rightly so, for the earth is round, the sun is round, the moon is round and most importantly the cricket ball is round, let us accept again a round figure of 100 cm or 1 m rise of sea level by 2100 CE for our ensuing discussions, instead of 90 cm that I have demonstrated earlier.

Now in 2021, we have reasons to believe that sea level rise may actually accelerate, and it could rise by 2 meters or more by 2100 CE.[3]

Sea level rise is not uniform
We all know that water maintains the same level. We have seen this fundamental property of water well exhibited everywhere, say in a cup of tea, in a bucketful of water and for that matter, in a bigger container like a swimming pool. How come then I claim that the level of sea water or for that matter sea level rise over the entire globe is not uniform? In order to explain this apparent intrigue, I must remind you my readers that the earth is a fast-spinning sphere, hurtling around the sun at a great speed. Let me expand a little on the speeds of this vast spinning top, which is also a spaceship.

Any place on the equatorial surface of the earth, if viewed from a distance in the space, is travelling at a speed of 1,670 km per hour, which is twice as fast as a jumbo jet in full flight! I will show a simple calculation to convince you of this great speed. The equatorial radius of the earth is 6,378 km that makes the equatorial circumference 40,076 km (2 X Pi X 6,378 km = 40,076 km). Any point on the equator covers this distance during the course of one full day, which is about 24 hours, at a speed of 1,670 km per hour (40,076 ÷ 24 = 1670 km). The speed of revolution of the earth, around the sun, is even faster and let me present the calculation to convince you.

Earth's orbit is elliptical, which requires calculating an average value for the radius for calculating the circumference. The average radius of 149.5 million km [(152 million km + 147 million km) ÷ 2] when multiplied by 2 Pi gives a circumference of 939, 336, 203.4 km, say 940 million km. Our spaceship Earth covers this distance in 365 days and 6 hours travelling at a speed of 107,000 km per hour [940 million km ÷ (365.25 X 24 hours) = 107, 232 km per hour]. Earth races round the sun, at a speed that is at least a hundred times faster than that of a commercial airplane, whose cruising speed is no more than a 1,000 km per hour.

Having demonstrated these calculations on the speeds of rotation and revolution of Planet Earth, I would like to veer off the main theme, in order to lavish praises on the Father of Astronomy Aryabhata[13] (476 – 550 CE), who in the fifth century CE that is over fifteen centuries ago, very accurately calculated many aspects of the spinning earth. Aryabhata was very likely born in the erstwhile state of Kalinga, which adjoined Magadha and stretched from the Ganga in the north to the Godavari in the south and embodied the present-day states of Odisha, Andhra Pradesh, Jharkhand and parts of Bihar in eastern India. Equally possible it is that he was born further south, in the southern-most state of Kerala. In any case, after his education, he adorned the court of the king of Magadha at his capital city of Pataliputra, which now bears the name Patna that forms the present-day capital city of the state of Bihar. All those Indians who enjoy slandering and disparaging the poverty-stricken inhabitants of today's Bihar, must realize that this is the state, which was once Magadha that for centuries remained the heart and soul of the most prosperous and fabulously wealthy India. Let no one deride the poor of Bihar, for their desperate poverty is due to a wrong set of policies and complete incompetence in implementation of various developmental programs of the state. Let us remember that every part of India was affluent, at some point or the other, in the past. Let us, therefore, not deride each other on account of our relative wealth or poverty of the present-day. And let us all unite, for India is one, regardless of our regionalism, in order to eradicate this desperate poverty.

Aryabhata's seminal work Aryabhatiyam was translated in to Arabic in the ninth century CE and subsequently, it journeyed further west. Four hundred years later, in the thirteenth century CE, this treatise on astronomy was translated into Latin. The Latin version of Aryabhatiyam, provided the foundation for the growth of astronomy in Europe. I want my readers to appreciate that the Hindu astronomers of India, built the foundation for European astronomy to stand and flourish. Aryabhata, in a chapter of his treatise entitled *Gola*, which means circle or sphere, very categorically demonstrates the sphericity of the earth, way before any European astronomer even had the vaguest inkling as to the size and shape of our planet. Aryabhata's calculation of the equatorial circumference of the earth at 39,968 km, is only marginally less (by 62 km) of 40,076 km that we accept today. His calculated duration of one complete rotation of the earth around its axis, which in common parlance is stated as 1 day, is absolutely correct at 23 hours 56 minutes and 4.1 seconds. Aryabhata also calculated the value of Pi with remarkable accuracy and laid the foundation of many disciplines of mathematics that included trigonometry and mensuration. My reverential bow to you master, Aryabhata.

Coming back to the issue of nonuniformity of sea level rise, I hope that I have convinced you my readers that sea water is perched atop the vast spaceship called Earth that travels at a tremendous speed and is held tightly by the earth's gravitational force. Earth's gravity, incidentally, shows subtle variations across the globe depending on the composition and structure of the crust, which is the uppermost layer, say, the skin of Planet

Earth. The crustal structure and composition vary, from place to place, based on their rock and mineral assemblages and their disposition. Sea water, thus experiences subtle variations in gravitational pulls at different locations, which affect sea level. Earth's rotation, moreover, and the consequent Coriolis force and trade winds, whip the sea water to different levels at different places. For example, sea level is currently 50 cm higher than the mean sea level at various Indonesian islands located between 0° and 10° S latitudes. Nonuniform changes in temperature and salinity of sea water and ocean circulations also contribute to the spatial variability in sea level.[14, 15, 16, 17]

Having convinced you of the spatial nonuniformity of sea level at any given point in time, let me assure you that at some places of the globe, sea level could rise higher than the mean sea level rise.

The maximum possible rise of sea level

In order to determine the maximum height sea level could rise to, we need to discuss the total volume of ice present on our Planet Earth that could completely melt. The Antarctic landmass of 13.6 million square km holds 30.1 million cubic km of ice, which constitutes about 91.5% of the total ice on earth. Greenland and the Arctic contain 2.6 million cubic km of ice, which constitutes 8% of the total. Himalayan, alpine and other ice caps, ice fields and valley glaciers combined, carry 0.2 million cubic km of ice, which makes up the rest 0.55%. The total volume of glacial ice of the world is thus 32.9 million cubic km. If all these glacial ice melt, the world oceans spread over a total area of 362 million square km will rise by a maximum of 80.4 m.

The obvious question that arises now is how long the sea would take to rise to the maximum possible level of another 80 m. We are aware that after the last glacial maximum, since 18,000 years before present, sea level rose by 80 m in about 8,000 years. The rise was thus an even one meter in a hundred years, a rate of rise identical to our projection for the twenty-first century. Based on this rate, we can as well say that another 8,000 years will elapse before sea level rises to the maximum. This logic may not be correct though, for the simple reason that anthropogenic global warming has utterly disturbed the global climate, which in turn has provided the momentum for an accelerated pace of melting of glacial ice. If the rate of melting of glacial ice doubles, which is a real possibility, and then remains steady, which is unlikely, 80 m rise could happen in the next 4,000 years. If the rate of melting of glacial ice continues to increase after doubling, sea level may rise to its maximum potential even sooner, but very likely not before a couple of millennia.

Sea level rise and coastal inundation

Sea level rise will devastate the low-lying coastal areas of the entire world. Mainland India, endowed with a long coastline of 5,700 km, will not escape the wrath of the seas. The total length of the Indian coastline is much longer at 7,500 km, when all the island territories of Andaman and Nicobar, and Lakshadweep are taken into account. A 1 m rise in sea level, say by 2100 CE, will practically submerge the entire Lakshadweep group of islands and absolutely nothing can be done to save them. Let me, therefore, concentrate on the threats to the mainland of India. In my 2008 article, I had presented an estimate of the total area of the vulnerable coastal land of India facing inundation, upon a 1 m rise in sea level. The 2008 estimate, however, was based on a simple premise that the gradient of the 480 km long coastal tract of Odisha is such that a 1 m rise in sea level will make the sea transgress by 1 km. This simple model, based on land topography, gave an estimate of the total coastal land in Odisha likely to be inundated by a 1 m rise in sea level at 480 square km. The northern and central parts of the coast of Odisha are alluvial and flat, whereas the southern coast is rocky and steep. The coastline of Odisha, therefore, was considered a good representative for the entire country. The 2008 estimate of the total land of India vulnerable to marine transgression at 5,763 square km, for the total length of the 5,700 km long coastline of the mainland is, therefore, not entirely wrong, but not absolutely correct either. A much more accurate estimate could be obtained by using Artificial Intelligence (AI), which makes vast improvements in digital elevation models (DEM) as demonstrated by Scott A. Kulp and Benjamin Strauss of Climate Central, published in Nature Communications in October 2019.[3, 18] The simplistic estimate of 2008 could well prove to be an underestimation and the total area threatened by inundation would be much larger.

The northern most part of the east coast of India, where the many distributaries of the Ganga and the Brahmaputra have created the largest delta of the world, is barely above sea level and is most vulnerable to sea level rise. Bulk of this Ganga-Brahmaputra deltaic system is situated in Bangladesh and the rest in the Indian state of West-Bengal, which thus is the most vulnerable state in India. The riverine Odisha that lies immediately to the south of West-Bengal is also very vulnerable, for the hexa-deltaic plains it hosts, created by the Subarnarekha, the Budhabalanga, the Baitarani, the Brahmani, the Mahanadi and her distributaries, and the Rusikulya, in a traverse from the north to the south. Further south along the east coast, occur the huge deltaic plains laid by the Godavari, the Krishna and the Penna in the state of Andhra Pradesh, followed by the Kaveri delta of the southernmost state of Tamil Nadu. All these deltas being low-lying are vulnerable to inundation when sea level rises. Although the west coast of India does not host large deltas, it is not immune from the threats of sea level rise. Kutch region of Gujarat, greater Mumbai and southern parts of Kerala will be utterly devastated by the rising seas.

In the 2008 article, I quoted that a 1 m rise of sea level will inundate 1,810 square km of land in Gujarat, 1,220 square km in West-Bengal, 670 square km in Tamil Nadu, 550 square km in Andhra Pradesh, 480 square km in Odisha, 410 square km in Maharashtra, 290 square km in Karnataka, 160 square km in Goa and 120 square km in Kerala. In view of the improvements in the digital elevation models (DEM) mentioned earlier, these numbers will most definitely get a substantial upward revision. I hope that the enormity of the problem India faces due to sea level rise dawns on you, my readers.

Coastal inundation after the last ice age

Many people in India and, for that matter, in the advanced industrialized countries of the world are still not convinced of the problem of sea level rise. In order to convince you, I mention that sea level rise by 130 m, since the last glacial maximum 18,000 years ago, has inundated over 250,000 square km of land in the west coast of India. On this submerged land, which was once coastal Gujarat, flourished the grand city of Dwaraka that Sri Krishna built all those millennia ago. Thanks to the many underwater surveys and excavations most diligently carried out by the archaeologists of the venerable Archaeological Survey of India (ASI) and by the marine scientists of the National Institute of Oceanography (NIO), we have now discovered two extensive submerged ruins, one off the present-day city of Dwaraka, at depths between 15 m and 20 m below sea level. The other one, ruins of a vast metropolis that stretches for 9 km on the seabed of the Gulf of Khambhat (formerly known as the Gulf of Cambay), lies at a depth between 25 m and 40 m. These second ruins, now termed the Gulf of Khambhat Cultural Complex (GKCC), lying 40 km off the coast of Surat in Gujarat were a monumental discovery in December 2000.[19, 20, 21] Either of these ruins could be Sri Krishna's Dwaraka.

Although this submerged land of the continental shelf off the coast of Gujarat has experienced episodes of uplift as well as subsidence, only reasonable it is to attribute the depths of the two underwater ruins, essentially to sea level rise. Please allow me to make an attempt to ascertain the age of submergence of Dwaraka, based on information from the global sea level rise. A 15 m rise of sea level took place over a period of 8,000 years and 25 m to 40 m rise took place over a period of 10,000 years.[22, 23, 24] On the basis of these ages, I feel confident to state that Sri Krishna's Dwaraka was inundated at least 8,000 years ago. This information also implies that the fratricidal war between the Kauravas and the Pandavas, description of which constitutes the subject matter of the greatest epic Mahabharata, took place at least 8,000 years ago.

This set of ages of 8,000 and 10,000 years contradicts, quite rightly so, the speculative age for the Mahabharata at 1,000 BCE, which was proposed by the nineteenth century Europeans, essentially British, whose prime interest was to distort the history of India to perpetuate English supremacy.

And to their utter shame and disgrace, countless historians of India, even in this twenty-first century, seven decades after the independence of India, keep parroting the English version of Indian history. I appeal to you the historians of India, to take cognizance of the vast amounts of archaeological and geological evidence pouring in, in the last two decades or so, and to rectify the horrendous distortions of Indian history to restore the dignity, it so richly deserves. Instead of remaining armchair bound, it is time for you lot to don SCUBA (Self-Contained-Under-Water-Breathing-Apparatus)   gear   to explore and excavate the Indian continental shelf off the coast of Gujarat, Odisha, Andhra Pradesh and Tamil Nadu to gather more evidence to reconstruct the rich past of India. As a student of geology, earth and environmental sciences, I have climbed mountains and dived in the seas and earned my right to advise you, the armchair historians of India, to wake up from your slumber. And most importantly, let the ages you determine of the various historical events like the Mahabharata, inundation of Sri Krishna's Dwaraka, antiquity of Ramayana, the Vedas and the Jagannath Puri, not get stunted by the writings of

British historians. Do not get carried away by the British invention of Aryan invasion of India hypothesis at 1,200 BC. This figment of British imagination was designed to place a very low ceiling on the much older Indian civilization. I would also like to state that the Mahabharata was never a myth, it is history, albeit richly embellished and most eloquently narrated by the greatest writer in human history, Vyaasadev.

Age of the pieces of pottery, recovered from the Gulf of Khambhat Cultural Complex (GKCC) during underwater explorations in 2003 and 2004 by the scientists of National Institute of Oceanography (NIO), determined in the laboratories in Oxford in Britain and in Hanover in Germany, is 31,000 years.[21] This discovery has most comprehensively discarded the utterly incorrect premise that the Indian civilization started because of Aryan invasion around 1,200 BC. India was the cradle of urban civilization, which started much earlier, at least 31,000 years ago, when vast cities flourished in the deltaic plains of the Saraswati River, so eloquently praised and admired in the Vedic literature. The last ice age reigned then, and sea level was at least 130 m below the present level and much of the Indian landmass was covered by glacial ice. As the ice age came to an end, sea level rose and many of those vast cities like the GKCC on the west coast of India as well as cities on the east, were submerged. Glaciers also retreated, creating space for the construction of new urban centers at higher altitudes and latitudes of the landmass of India. In all probability, it is the urbanized Indians who moved beyond the geographic confines of the subcontinent to create urban settlements elsewhere in the Middle East and The Mediterranean.

Having provided an example of a massive submergence from the west coast, I present here another small but interesting observation from the east coast of India. All through the history of Odisha, the site of the famous Jagannath temple at the coastal township of Puri has been referred to as a mountain, often described as Neelakandara or Neelachala or even Mahameru. Since neela is blue and the words kandara, achala and meru mean mountain, etymologically Neelakandara and Neelachala mean the Blue Mountain and Mahameru means the Great Mountain. In this twenty-first century, the site of the Jagannath temple is barely 10 m to 15 m above the mean sea level (MSL), which hardly qualifies as a mountain. I want my readers to appreciate that these very words Neelachala, Neelakandara and Mahameru connote history and when I take you back in time to 18,000 years before present, when seas were 130 m below the present level, the site of the Jagannath temple suddenly assumes an impressive height of say 150 m (130 m + 10 m or 15 m). The present Jagannath temple, which is not even a thousand years old, did not exist then, but the precursor or the previous incarnation of Jagannath, Neela Madhava or the Blue Vishnu, who is much older than Sri Krishna, adorned that Blue Mountain. By rising 130 m, the sea has submerged much of that imposing Blue Mountain that presently appears as a mere mound.

During the last ice age, I might as well state that the snow line was much lower.[25, 26] The Himalaya was of course all covered with glaciers, but mountains in the deep south of Tamil Nadu and Kerala also had ice caps. The snow line in locations at 10° latitude existed at a mere 1,000 m above sea level, which means that the Nilgiri Hills, that have an altitude of around 2,500 m today, hosted glaciers then. At 20° latitude, snowline was down to 600 m, which means that practically all the higher mountains of the Aravalli, the Vindhya, the Western Ghat and the Eastern Ghat ranges cradled glaciers. The Mahendra Giri of Odisha at 1,200 m and the adjoining hills of the Eastern Ghat in Andhra Pradesh, hosted a massive complex of glaciers. Should my fellow earth scientists start careful research for glacial geomorphological features and glacial debris in these mountains, they may find some. Sediment cores from suitable lake beds in these mountainous areas would produce pollens of temperate flora that flourished during the last ice age. I would also like to add that practically all the rivers of peninsular India were snow fed and drained glacial meltwater in the past.

Losses due to sea level rise

The rising seas now threaten to inundate the deltaic plains of the east coast of India, which are well and truly the bread baskets of the country, for they provide prime agricultural land. Agricultural productivity of these fertile tracts is often double the average productivity of the country. On the west coast, the rising seas threaten the vast commercial and industrial complexes. As sea level rises, coastal erosion will increase very substantially along the entire shoreline, groundwater quality will be compromised. Storm surges will become much more frequent as well as intense and will destroy the infrastructure.

Because of global warming, the surface water temperature of the Arabian Sea, the Bay of Bengal and the Indian Ocean that generate the South West as well as the North East Monsoon, will increase, which in turn will make monsoons more intense. I offer a simple analogy of a kettle full of water on a stove, to explain the rise in intensity of the monsoon system. When the kettle is heated gently, the water boils slowly and does not produce much steam. On the other hand, when the kettle is heated strongly, it absorbs a lot more heat, which makes the water boil vigorously, which generates copious amounts of vapor. Likewise, a hotter sea surface will generate much more vapor and an intense monsoon than that of a cooler sea.

Cyclones

A more intense monsoon system will not only raise the peak wind speeds of the storms, but also increase their frequency. In the last quarter of a century, we have already seen some very severe storms and downpours in India, Bangladesh and Myanmar. I will give an example from each of the three above mentioned countries. The super cyclone of 29, 30 and 31 October 1999 that devastated the state of Odisha, had wind speeds over 260 km per hour, perhaps reaching as high as 300 km.[27, 28] Widespread torrential rains that accompanied this category 5 cyclone, poured between 60 and 80 cm of rain over the vast Mahanadi basin, spread over an area of some 141,600 square km, in the three-day period.[29] The maximum rainfall during the storm was even higher at 95 cm, recorded in Bhadrak district of Odisha. I want my readers to appreciate the scale of this almost one-meter rainfall in three days, which is higher than average annual rainfall of many parts, even many countries, of the world.

The super cyclone caused a 6 m high storm surge, above the astronomical tide, recorded at Paradip port on the 29th of October 1999. This surge was probably 8 m high, at some other coastal locations and travelled 20 km inland. The lethal combination of the cyclone, flood and the storm surge killed over 10,000 people, 400,000 heads of cattle, 2 million domestic animals and uprooted or broke 90 million trees. A vast majority of these trees had stood tall for generations and some for centuries! Destroyed were crops over a land area of 17,110 square km and 275,000 homes, which made 1.67 million homeless. The damages by this super cyclone, also known as the Paradip cyclone, were simply unprecedented in the history of Odisha that made at least 5 million farmers lose their livelihood. This cyclone affected Myanmar too.[30]

Bangladesh has seen many devastating cyclones and the last very severe cyclonic storm that wreaked utter devastation, appeared on the 15th of November 2007. This category 5 Cyclone Sidr attained peak wind speeds of 260 km per hour and caused a storm surge of over 5 m that inundated the low-lying coastal regions. Despite massive evacuations of the order of 2 million people, the cyclone, the heavy rains and the storm surge united to cause 10,000 fatalities. Cyclone Sidr of 2007 is generally considered to be the strongest to have stormed Bangladesh since 1991 that had caused over 143,000 fatalities.[31] Cyclone Sidr utterly destroyed the mangrove forests of an entire one quarter of the vast Sunderban, which is a world heritage site on the Ganga-Brahmaputra delta. So total was the devastation that the forest will take at least 40 years to regenerate. This cyclone affected the Indian states of West-Bengal and Odisha too.

On the 2nd of May 2008, a category 4 tropical cyclone Nargis that ravaged Myanmar reached peak wind speeds of 215 km per hour and seriously damaged the capital city of Yangon. Vast areas of the low-lying Irrawaddy delta were inundated by a combination of torrential downpours and a 3.5 m high storm surge that caused at least 146,000 fatalities.[32]

Because of global warming, extreme weather events will not only intensify but also will become far more frequent. Once in a century super cyclone, will become once in a decade events and once in a decade extremely severe cyclones will become annual events. More ominously, the cyclone season, instead of remaining restricted to four months in a year, like it is now, will expand to become a perennial all season phenomenon. We got a glimpse of the future in 2019, when the cyclone season in the east coast of India started in April with the devastating Cyclone Fani[33], which utterly ravaged coastal Odisha, particularly the City of Puri. The cyclone season continued right up to the month of November, when very severe cyclonic storm Bulbul[34] made landfall on the 9th of November and devastated West-Bengal and Bangladesh. In November 2019, the sea surface temperature in the Bay of Bengal off the coast of Odisha was 28 even 29°C, which is very high and unprecedented. In the year 2020, very severe cyclonic storm Nivar made a landfall in the southern-most state of Tamil Nadu on the east coast, almost at the end of November on the 26th. Exactly a week later, cyclonic storm Burevi, the fifth named storm of the 2020 North Indian Ocean cyclonic season, made landfall in north Sri Lanka on the 2nd of December 2020. In a decade or two, I assure you, my readers, that with the intensification of global warming, the cyclone season will start right in the month of February and end in January, to make sure that cyclones become a round the year event for the east coast of India.

Cyclone Fani

Because Cyclone Fani came so early in the year, in the month of April, does not mean that it was any weaker than the cyclones that visit later, in their usual monsoon season. Fani was just as strong and during rapid intensification before landfall, attained a 1-minute sustained winds of 250 km per hour and packed quite a mean punch to kill 89 people in India and Bangladesh. Fani was an extremely severe cyclonic storm, according to cyclone classification of the India Meteorological Department (IMD) and was classified as a Category 4 tropical cyclone on the Saffir–Simpson hurricane wind scale (SSHWS). Fani, in fact, is now recorded as the strongest tropical cyclone to strike Odisha since the 1999 super cyclone described earlier. With a sustained wind speed of 185 km per hour, Fani made landfall at Satpada, near the City of Puri, on the 3rd of May 2019 to utterly ravage the temple town.

Cyclone Fani originated from a tropical depression at 2° N latitude, west of Sumatra in Indonesia in the Indian Ocean, on the 26th of April and travelled around 2,500 km to reach Bangladesh at 22° N latitude on the 4th of May. Sea surface temperature, incidentally, of the Odisha coast on the 25th of April was 31°C. Please note these high sea surface temperatures in April and in November, mentioned above, are all due to global warming.

Cyclone Phailin

Please allow me to discuss Cyclone Phailin[35], essentially to showcase the excellent disaster management expertise Government of Odisha has developed, in the second decade of the new millennium. This extremely severe cyclonic storm Phailin, originated as a tropical depression on the 4th of October 2013, in the Gulf of Thailand to the west of Phnom Penh in Cambodia and some 400 km west of Ho Chi Minh

City in Vietnam. In the next few days, the system moved westward, went over the Malay Peninsula and on the 6th of October, moved out of the Western Pacific Basin to reemerge in the Andaman Sea, the next day, on the 7th of October. Then early on the 8th of October, India Meteorological Department (IMD) started monitoring the system as Depression Bay of Bengal 04 (BOB 04).

The system moved west-northwest and sailed over the Andaman and Nicobar Islands. Then it developed into a cyclonic storm and moved into the Bay of Bengal on the 9th of October, when IMD named it Phailin. Next day, on the 10th of October, Phailin intensified into a very severe cyclonic storm and on the 11th of October, Phailin further intensified into an extremely severe cyclonic storm. Around 10.30 pm Indian Standard Time (IST) of the 12th of October 2013, Phailin made landfall at Gopalpur on Sea of Ganjam district of Odisha. After landfall, Phailin persisted in causing heavy rainfall over many districts of Odisha, say for example, in a 24-hour period on the 13th of October, the township of Banki that is some 100 km inland received 361 mm of rain. The copious rains engendered serious floods. Phailin continued to weaken and by the 14th of October, the cyclone reduced to a mere low pressure before a total dissipation.

Once the India Meteorological Department (IMD) and other foreign agencies confirmed that Phailin was headed straight for Odisha, the immensely popular Chief Minister of the state, Mr. Naveen Patnaik, driven by his duty of care and concern for the welfare of the people of his province, announced a policy of zero casualty during the management of the imminent disaster. In order to implement this ambitious yet arduous policy, the Government of Odisha mobilized all relevant agencies such as the Odisha State Disaster Management Authority (OSDMA), field level officers of various services of the Government of Odisha, Cyclone Shelter Management and Maintenance Committees (CSMMCs), the Odisha Disaster

Rapid Action Force (ODRAF), Odisha State Armed Police (OSAP) in collaboration with national agencies like the National Disaster Management Authority (NDMA), National Disaster Response Force (NDRF), Central Reserve Police Force (CRPF) and the Indian Air Force (IAF) to evacuate around a million people, from the coastline to cyclone shelters, flood shelters and safe buildings on higher grounds. Some 30 Non-Governmental Organizations (NGOs) helped the government agencies too.

The Government of Odisha took a proactive approach, quite rightly so, and prepared well to deal with the imminent disaster. At the Odisha State Disaster Management Authority (OSDMA), the path, intensity and magnitude of the cyclone and updates from the India Meteorological Department (IMD) were continuously monitored. The OSDMA carried out extensive mock drills at all the cyclone shelters and ensured that all installed equipment was fully functional. The Cyclone Shelter Management and Maintenance Committees (CSMMCs) were mobilized to facilitate mass evacuation.

Just as roared in, the very severe cyclonic storm Phailin, the Government of Odisha through the above-mentioned agencies did a sterling job, in creating awareness among the people on likely devastations and the need for evacuation to higher grounds. The evacuation of all people, living within 0 and 10 km from the coastline, started at around 9 am on the 11th of October, some 36 hours before the expected landfall, and proceeded smoothly, because the masses were convinced of the good intentions and sincerity of the governmental efforts. Cattle and other livestock were moved to safe higher grounds too. The government opened 4,197 free kitchens to cater to over two million people, consisting of the evacuees and the vulnerable, affected by the cyclone. The government also opened 338 medical relief centers and dispatched 185 medical teams. The cyclone, heavy rains and consequent floods, just as expected, caused extensive devastation to rail and road infrastructure, transportation, power lines, public buildings, houses and uprooted a large number of trees.

This Phailin led natural disaster, despite the precautions caused 44 fatalities, destroyed 256,633 houses and affected 13 million people. The combination of cyclone and flood, inflicted a 50% loss on the standing crops on 1,292,967 hectares of land and adversely affected 44,806 fishing and 1,564 artisan households.

Within 24 hours of the landfall, the Government of Odisha cleared all major highways and roads and made elaborate arrangements for providing safe drinking water and electricity. The Indian Air Force (IAF), moreover, airdropped some 5.7 tons of dry food in inaccessible areas.[36]

Despite the losses, management of the Phailin disaster, when contrasted with the poorly managed super cyclone of 1999, was generally acknowledged in Odisha and beyond, quite correctly so, as a spectacular success. The people of Odisha much appreciated the excellent management of the disaster and developed an even stronger admiration for their much popular Chief Minister Mr. Naveen Patnaik, who went on to achieve a massive electoral win again in the April 2014 General Election, held barely six months after Phailin struck.

Following the landfall of Phailin, Margareta Wahlstrom, the UN Special Representative of the Secretary General for Disaster Risk Reduction, in a telephone call to the Chief Minister, commended the Government of Odisha, by saying that "The Odisha government managed to reduce human deaths during Phailin by evacuating around one million people from the seaside areas. The authorities also made people aware of the areas which were vulnerable and saved many lives."[37, 38] The UN Special Representative praised Odisha with the words, "Today, Odisha is a global leader in disaster management and risk reduction," and concluded by saying, "Timely dissemination of information about the severity of the cyclone was the main reason behind minimal human loss."[37, 38]

Mr. Pradipta Kumar Mohapatra IAS, then a Principal Secretary and the Special Relief Commissioner of Odisha was given the overall responsibility to provide the leadership to manage Phailin, making him, in other words, the command-and-control head of the Government of Odisha and he did a sterling job. I request you my readers to allow me to lavish praises on this gentleman, whom I had the pleasure of teaching geology in the early 1980s at Ravenshaw College, where he did his undergraduate Geology Honours studies. Pradipta was an outstanding student and after completion of his B.Sc. Geology Honours, he enrolled for M.Sc. (Tech.) in Applied Geology at the venerable Indian School of Mines. After completion of his M.Sc. he successfully wrote the Civil Services Examination, conducted by the Union Public Service Commission of India, and qualified for the much-coveted Indian Administrative Service or the IAS. Pradipta secured a very commendable high rank of 3 among a 1,000 or so successful candidates, selected for the Civil Services in 1988. During his career as an IAS, he held many responsible positions and earned a substantial reputation as a very capable, honest, upright administrator of impeccable integrity. This 1988 Batch IAS went to Southern Cross University in Australia for his mid-career training in the year 2001 to do an MBA, where I renewed contacts with him after a gap of some two decades. During the Phailin crisis, he worked round the clock, directed all District Magistrates of the coastal districts and conducted a most successful evacuation of a million people, from the coastline into safe houses on higher grounds. I am proud of you and I salute you Pradipta, you are a great son of this country. A day after the Phailin landfall, I sent him a message saying, "Go and sleep well now". Mr. Pradipta Kumar Mohapatra IAS is now the Additional Chief Secretary to the Government of Odisha.

Ever since IMD named the storm on the 9th of October, it accurately tracked and predicted the course of Phailin. During the course of the day, on the 12th of October, the Director-General of IMD, Dr. Laxman Singh Rathore, kept announcing a wind speed of 220 km per hour plus minus 15 km for Phailin at landfall, in contradiction of the much higher wind speed forecasts made by various foreign agencies.

After Phailin made the landfall around 9 pm of the 12th of October, with wind speeds between 200 and 210 km per hour, gusting up to 220 km per hour that whipped the storm surge to a height not exceeding 3.5 m above the astronomical tide, all predictions made by India Meteorological Department (IMD) and boldly announced by the Director-General Dr. Rathore, proved absolutely correct. The following day, the 13th of October, IMD received a worldwide recognition for the accuracy of the predictions, while the inaccurate forecasts of the American and British agencies became obvious. In a press meet on the 13th, in a calm and composed matter of fact tone, without the slightest hint of arrogance, Dr. Rathore stated, "Being a national meteorological department we cannot predict the way other agencies do, as this will lead to a panic like situation. We stuck to our stand and told the media what we have been saying since the start. Our predictions proved to be more or less accurate." A picture of confidence and dignity Dr. Rathore also mentioned, "They have been issuing over-warnings, we have been contradicting them." And "they" were the foreign agencies such as "the American Joint Typhoon Warning Centre (JTWC) of the US Navy and the US Air Force, Britain's Met Office and many private forecasters like London based Tropical Storm Risk" who had "assessed Phailin as a "super cyclone". The JTWC had predicted "wind gusts could reach as high as 315 km per hour", which did not happen. "They" also had predicted that the storm surge could reach heights of 6 m, which did not happen, either.[39, 40, 41] IMD made India very proud indeed.

Just as Phailin, roared in, Dr. Rathore remembered the Hirakud Dam, which is one of the largest multi-purpose river valley infrastructure projects of India. The reservoir created by this hydroelectric dam built on the Mahanadi, holds some 6 billion cubic meter (bcm) or 6 cubic km (km^3) of water.[42, 43, 44, 45, 46, 47, 48] I had written an article titled, "Proper Management of Hirakud Dam" that was first published in 2008 and with some necessary updation and modification, presently constitutes the Chapter Four of this book. Soon after the publication, I had sent a copy of the said article to Rathoreji, who happens to be a voracious reader, and he had read my article. He realized that the unexpected heavy rainfall the upper catchment of the Mahanadi was about to receive, with Phailin moving further inland in the next 24 hours or so, Hirakud would receive vast quantities of water that could overwhelm the huge dam. Right then, in the middle of the night, Rathoreji rang up the Home Secretary of the Government of India and apprised him of the imminent danger of Hirakud getting swamped. Rathoreji then rang up the Chief Secretary of the Government of Odisha and advised him to instruct the Chief Engineer of the Hirakud Dam, to open a large number of sluice gates of the dam, to release water to create room in the reservoir, for accommodating inflowing runoff from the upper catchment. The sluice gates were flung open immediately to release water, from the reservoir that stood at a level of 629 ft, barely 1 foot short of the absolute upper limit of 630 ft, to lower it to the level of 623 ft. Discharge of such a vast quantum of water created a medium level flood in the deltaic regions of the coastal districts, just as Phailin roared in, but the Hirakud Dam was saved. By the time Phailin dissipated and rains stopped after a few days of the landfall, the inflowing water from the upper catchment raised the water level of Hirakud to 629 ft again. Subsequently, in a disaster management seminar organized by the IMD and the government in the capital city of Odisha, where Rathoreji and I were in attendance, I at one stage narrated the efforts of Rathoreji that he himself had told me, in averting a disaster at Hirakud. I had also summed up by saying, "This gentleman Dr. Rathore, a valiant Rajput of honor and integrity, has saved Odisha" to a most appreciative and grateful audience. I always called him a valiant Rajput since our days in the Department of Science and Technology of the Government of India in the late 1980s. Dr. L.S. Rathore[49] is currently the permanent representative of India with World Meteorological Organization of the United Nations and the Chair of Intergovernmental Board of Climate Services of the United Nations. He is a member of the advisory committee of National Disaster Management Authority (NDMA) of India. My deepest bow to you Rathoreji.

Lightning strikes in Odisha

Of late, because of the rising summer temperatures that have reached new highs and availability of vast quantities of moisture, because of much higher sea surface temperatures, lightning strikes have become far more frequent and numerous in Odisha. In 2019, Odisha accounted for 9,37,462, around 16% of the total, cloud to ground lightning strikes of India that cause thousands of deaths and much destruction.[50] Lightning strikes in the second decade of the new millennium have become a major natural disaster in Odisha, causing over 400 deaths annually. In the year 2017, some 465 people died because of lightning strikes. Around 85% of these lightning strikes occur between the months of May and September.

Following the Cyclone Phailin of 2013, four Doppler radars, indigenously built by Indian Space Research Organization (ISRO) and Bharat Heavy Electricals Ltd (BHEL), were installed in Odisha by the India Meteorological Department (IMD) to monitor and predict severe weather events like thunder storms, hailstorms, cyclones and tornadoes within a radius of 300 km of each installation.[51, 53] With these advanced observational tools, the IMD could accurately forecast and issue advisories on lightning strikes. An eminent meteorologist Prof. Uma Charan Mohanty[52], internationally known for his pioneering research on Indian summer monsoon and tropical cyclones, played a key role in getting the Doppler radars installed in Odisha. I have known this most affable erudite scientist and academician, Dr. U.C. Mohanty, who is now a Professor Emeritus at IIT Bhubaneswar, since the beginning of my tenure with the Department of Science and Technology of the Government of India in 1989. Installation of the Doppler radars was sanctioned by the Director-General of IMD Dr. L.S. Rathore.[49]

Thanks to the adoption of the early warning systems that included installation of 4 Doppler radars, 6 lightning detection sensors and an agreement with Earth Network of the United States, the deaths have now fallen by some 30%.

Catastrophic rise in sea level

Coral reefs, built by marine coral polyps, are found in warm tropical and subtropical oceans across the world. These sub-sea structures, made up of calcium carbonate, rise with the rising sea and also maintain a faithful record of the sea level. In the last decade or so, a very large number of deep core samples from the coral reefs all over the world were collected to be analyzed, to provide solid evidence on variations in the rate of sea level rise in the postglacial period.[54] Based on the geological evidence, we now know that there were three major periods of rapid sea level rise, presently termed "*meltwater pulses*". The oldest rapid rise, or the *meltwater pulse 1A0,* occurred between 19,000 and 19,500 years ago. The next rapid rise, *meltwater pulse 1A,* occurred between 14,600 and 14,300 years ago, when sea level rose by 13.5 m within a span of 290 years, centered at 14,200 years ago. The last rapid rise, *meltwater pulse 1B,* occurred between 11,400 and 11,100 years ago, when the sea level rose by 7.5 m over a period of 160 years, centered at 11,000 years ago.[55]

Extensive geological evidence "derived from analyses of ice cores, glaciers, lake and marine sediment cores, and terrestrial sequences" show that Planet Earth experienced a massive meteorite impact, during the Younger Dryas cold-climate period of earth's history, say between 12,900 and 11,700 years ago, pretty much during the meltwater pulses discussed above.[56, 57, 58] The Younger Dryas, incidentally, is named after the alpine tundra wildflower Dryas octopetala, whose leaves are abundant in lake glacial sediments, like the ones found in the present day lake sediments of Scandinavia. The Younger Dryas impact theory, received considerable support from research work published in 2018 and 2019, and posits that Planet Earth collided with one or more fragments from a huge 100 km diameter comet, remnants of which continue to exist within the inner solar system to the present day. The comet or asteroid fragments, some measuring more than 4 km in diameter, impacted the huge ice sheets of Greenland, North America, South America, Europe and western Asia some 12,900 years ago, causing a massive deluge that raised the sea level instantly by at least 3 or 4 m. This catastrophe led to the collapse of vast ice banks that led to further instant rises of sea level.

The inundation of the entire littoral city of Dwaraka on the Gujarat coast, in a matter of hours as described in the Mahabharata, could well have been caused by this catastrophic rise in sea level.

Such a catastrophic rise in sea level, occurred in the past and could well happen again, in the future.

Catastrophic submergence of Dwaraka

A most eminent academic of Harvard University, Prof. Diana L. Eck, in her 382 pages long book titled, "India: A Sacred Geography" has transcribed the catastrophic submergence of the City of Dwaraka, 36 years after the end of the Mahabharata war. The description is in the Mausala Parva or the Book of Clubs, the sixteenth of the eighteen books of the Mahabharata, as witnessed by Prince Arjuna. Please allow me to quote verbatim the description of the submergence as follows:

> "The sea, which had been beating against the shores, suddenly broke the boundary that was imposed on it by nature. The sea rushed into the city. It coursed through the streets of the beautiful city. The sea covered up everything in the city. I saw the beautiful buildings becoming submerged one by one. In a matter of a few moments it was all over. The sea had now become as placid as a lake. There was no trace of the city. Dvaraka was just a name, just a memory."[59, 60, 61]

A painting of Sri Krishna's City of Dwaraka, based on its descriptions in the Indian epics of Mahabharata and Harivamsa, was executed during the reign of the Mughal Emperor Akbar.[62] The painting, presently lodged in the Smithsonian Institute of the USA, shows the sprawling city bound by ramparts punctuated by an archway and containing mostly two-story and some three-story buildings. Going by the narrative of the inundation of the city quoted earlier, a rapid rise of sea level by at least 10 m is necessary for total submergence of the city. Such a rapid rise, in a matter of days, probably did occur following the catastrophic asteroid impact during the Younger Dryas, some 12,900 years ago. The submergence of Dwaraka, as argued earlier in the text, happened at least 8,000 years ago. In view of the confirmation of the Younger Dryas catastrophe, I would like to say that Dwaraka submerged 12,900 years ago. As the Mausala Parva states that Dwaraka submerged 36 years after the Mahabharata war, only logical it is to say that this great war Mahabharata, took place at least 13,000 (12,900 + 36 = 12,936) years ago.

Threat of tsunami

A tsunami[63] is a series of waves generated by earthquakes, volcanic eruptions, meteorite impacts, landslides and underwater explosions, in a large body of water like a sea or a large lake. Large tsunamis have tens of meters high waves and possess enormous destructive power that can utterly devastate coastal areas of entire ocean basins. Virtually all littoral countries have experienced tsunamis. Tsunami is a Japanese word that means 'harbor waves', because in Japan they were observed to pound the harbors following earthquakes. The oldest recorded tsunami[64] of 479 BCE, devastated a Persian army that was poised to attack a seaside town named Potidaea in Greece. Based on geological evidence we now know that 1.4 million years ago, an entire one third of the East Molokai Volcano of Hawaii, standing some 900 m above the sea, collapsed in to the Pacific Ocean, generating a massive landslide that produced a megatsunami of an estimated local height of 2,000 feet (610 m) that utterly destroyed the surrounding Hawaiian Islands, before racing to the shores of Mexico and California some 3,800 km away.[65]

The present-day population of India were not aware of the devastating effects of a large tsunami, until the 2004 Indian Ocean Tsunami struck the east coast of their country on the 26th of December 2004. This Indian Ocean Tsunami was not the first and will not be the last to visit India. Tsunamis can inundate vast tracts of land in India, particularly so on the east coast.

Please allow me to discuss the inundation of coastal India due to a tsunami that struck Odisha in the year 318 CE. I will also discuss the 2004 Indian Ocean Tsunami and the megatsunami of 11 March 2011 that followed the Great East Japan Earthquake.

Odisha tsunami of 318 CE
During the four-year reign of King Subhan Deo that started in 318 CE, 'A Yavana, or foreigner, named Rakta Bahu (the Red-Armed)' mounted a maritime invasion of Odisha (p.239-241, p.445)[66]. This Greek General embarked his vast army containing troops, horses and elephants on vessels and

anchored at a distant offshore, to spring a surprise seize on the Jagannath temple of Puri. The straw feed of the animals and their voluminous excreta, however, drifted ashore and alerted the townsfolk, to the presence of a substantial enemy lying hidden offshore, to attack them at the next available opportunity. King Subhan Deo fled Puri with the statues of the deities, to the dense forests of western Odisha, some 250 km away, to escape the impending attack. The Yavana army, in due course, launched a murderous attack on Puri, only to find the king and the deities missing. Upon enquiry, the invaders learnt that their presence was discovered by the straw and dung brought ashore by the sea. Now, please allow me to quote, "Enraged with the ocean for disclosing his secret, Rakta-Bahu drew out his armies to chastise its waters. The sea, on observing such formidable preparations, retreated for nearly a cos – the infatuated Yavanas rushed on – when the tide suddenly returning with tremendous noise and fury, swallowed up a great portion of the army and inundated the whole country to a frightful extent. The flood reached inland as far as the Baronai Pahar of Khurda, taking with it immense quantities of sand. It was at this time that the Chilika lake was formed by the irruption of the waters of the ocean."[66]

A little further down in the text of his article titled, An Account, Geographical, Statistical and Historical of Orissa Proper, or Cuttack published in 1822 in The Asiatic Researches, Vol. 15, Andrew Stirling wrote, "A real irruption of the ocean may have occurred in the same age, and this natural calamity", he speculated, was ascribed to "bloody wars, revolutions and other moral evils, which afflicted the country at the time" by the "ever active invention of the chroniclers".[66]

You are right Mr. Stirling; this chronicled description is indeed that of a natural calamity, very likely that of a massive tsunami. Sea water retreating for a cos, which is a unit of length that stretches about 3km and then roaring back "with tremendous noise and fury" is indeed the signature of a massive tsunami that reached the present day Barunei Hill, which lies some 40 km inland, as the crow flies from the coast at Puri. The foothills of Barunei, at present, lie at an elevation of 40 m above the mean sea level. This tsunami of 318 CE that devastated the coastal Odisha, therefore, was very likely 40 m high.

Do tsunamis attain such large amplitude? Yes. Many such massive tsunamis have registered their signatures in geological history that is deciphered from the rock records. Could a tsunami of such large amplitude ever hit coastal Odisha again? The answer is again yes. Occurrence of a massive earthquake, of a magnitude between 8 and 9 in the Richter scale, in the Andaman and Nicobar Islands, could easily generate a 40 m high tsunami that could lash the east coast of India in a couple of hours. A catastrophic volcanic eruption in Barren Island, located some 140 km east of the Andaman and Nicobar Islands, could generate a massive tsunami too.

These tsunamis have wavelengths anywhere between 10 km and 500 km and they can race around at astonishing speeds of 700 km per hour, just as fast as a jumbo jet. The speed of a tsunami depends on the depth of the water and is given by the equation, speed = square root of acceleration due to gravity, g, multiplied by the depth of water, H. The value of acceleration due to gravity, g, is 9.8 m per second square.[67] The average depth of oceans is 3,688 m, so the speed of a tsunami could be 190 m per second or 684 km, say, 700 km per hour. The average depth of the Bay of Bengal or the Sea of Kalinga at 2,600 m is a little less than the average depth of oceans.[68, 69] In the Bay of Bengal, therefore, a tsunami will travel at a speed of 160 m per second or about 575 km per hour.

The capital of the Union Territory of the Andaman and Nicobar Islands is Port Blair, which is more or less equidistant from Kolkata that lies at a distance of 1,300 km in the northern most part of the east coast of India, and Chennai that lies at a distance of 1,350 km in the south. A massive tsunami travelling at a speed of 575 km per hour in the Bay of Bengal, generated by an equally massive earthquake in the quake prone Andaman and Nicobar Islands, could reach Kolkata and Chennai in a mere two and a half hours, to utterly devastate the entire east coast.

Harnessing geothermal energy at Barren Island

Barren Island[70], incidentally, is India's eastern most territory and this 8 square km uninhabited island has an active volcano that has erupted more than ten times, since the first recorded eruption of modern times in 1787. The last eruption was in 2017. I propose that geothermal energy be harnessed on this island to generate electricity, which could be used for electrolytic dissociation of desalinated seawater to produce hydrogen and oxygen gases. Hydrogen gas could be compressed into cylinders, which will become the fuel for cars and buses to ply on the roads of Port Blair and elsewhere, to make Andaman and Nicobar Islands free of air pollution. By the way, while the hydrogen generation market was valued globally at USD115.25 billion in 2017, in 2019, world H_2 production was a huge 70 million tons.[71] In 2019, the global green hydrogen market alone was valued at USD 786.9 million and between 2020 and 2027, is poised to grow at a compound annual growth rate (CAGR) of 14.24%.[72] My proposal to harness geothermal energy at Barren Island to generate hydrogen is certainly not farfetched, in fact, is a very feasible idea.

The Indian Ocean Tsunami of 2004

The Indian Ocean Tsunami of 26 December 2004 that killed an estimated 227,898 people in 14 countries that rim the Indian Ocean and the Bay of Bengal, originated from a massive undersea megathrust earthquake that occurred off the west coast of northern Sumatra in Indonesia.[73] A rupture along the fault between the Burma Plate and the Indian Plate, of the south Asian part of the earth's crust, caused this Indian Ocean earthquake that registered a magnitude of 9.1 to 9.3 in the Richter scale and reached a Mercalli intensity up to IX in certain places. A series of large tsunami waves this earthquake produced grew 30 m tall, a full 100 ft high, as they travelled inland.

This Indian Ocean Tsunami, utterly devastated Indonesia's northern province of Aceh of the island of Sumatra. According to the Ministry of Health of Indonesia, 131,026 people died and some 37,000 went missing. Nearly a million and a half Sri Lankan's were displaced from their dwellings, because of the tsunami that engendered 31,229 deaths and 4,093 never returned home. The famous Sri Lankan tourist train, the Queen of the Sea, packed with holiday makers was totally destroyed causing some 2,000 deaths. The Government of Thailand reported 5,395 deaths, 8,457 injuries and 2,817 missing in addition to the extensive damages endured in the six southern provinces facing the Andaman Sea. Independent media reports emanating from Myanmar announced 90 deaths, while the claim by the eye-witness estimates was 600. The Maldives reported 82 deaths and 26 missing, presumed dead. Malaysia despite its proximity to the epicenter, escaped the tsunami lightly with only 68 deaths and 5 missing, essentially because the island of Sumatra protected its western coast.

India endured some 10,749 deaths mostly in Tamil Nadu, the southern-most state of the east coast facing the Bay of Bengal, and an estimated 5,640 people went missing mostly from the Andaman and Nicobar Islands. The above two numbers, of late, have been revised downward by 1,458 and 2,927, respectively.

In this connection, please allow me a detour to mention that in 2017, on the sidelines of a meeting of a DST (Department of Science & Technology) committee on FIST (Fund for Infra-structure in Science & Technology), a fellow member of mine, Prof. Kuppuswamy Porsezian, then a Professor of Physics of Pondicherry University, mentioned that the 2004 Indian

Ocean Tsunami dumped huge slabs of ice on the beaches of Chennai in Tamil Nadu that left the locals absolutely baffled. They were clueless on the source and apparently there were conjectures in the vernacular press, on the provenance being at the far-off Antarctica, separated by the vast tropical seas. Upon further enquiries I learnt that those slabs of ice had evaporated leaving smaller volumes of water than what would have been expected from a comparable block of ice made up of pure water. I realized that these were, of course, large chunks of methane clathrate or methane hydrate or hydromethane, dug up from the recent marine sediments by the gouging actions of retreating seawater and then thrown up on the beach by the tsunami.

Methane clathrate $(CH_4 \cdot 5.75H_2O)$ or $(4CH_4 \cdot 23H_2O)$ forms in cold subzero conditions in oceanic sediments, when methane gas gets trapped within a crystal structure of water, forming a solid that looks like normal ice.[74] This methane clathrate contains 1 mole of methane gas (CH_4) for every 5.75 moles of water that corresponds to 13.4% methane by mass.[75] Methane clathrate can be harvested to produce methane gas and the oceanic methane clathrate deposits are simply enormous.

Incidentally, during my tenure at the DST as a Senior Scientific Officer – Grade One, I had revived a national coordinated project titled The Deep Sea Fans of Bay of Bengal in 1989. These deep sea fans are in fact the seaward extension of the vast Ganga-Brahmaputra delta. This enormous blanket of marine sediments is some 3,000 km long, 1,000 km wide and between 8 and 16 km deep and is loaded with huge quantities of hydrated methane.[76, 77] Japan has already developed technologies for extracting hydrated methane from the marine sediments of the Sea of Japan. India, hopefully, will harness this vast resource of hydrocarbon from the sediments of the Bay of Bengal.

Now, on resumption of my discussion on the 2004 Indian Ocean Tsunami, I would like to emphasize the enormity of this catastrophe that lashed the villages and coastal communities of Somalia on the east coast of the African continent, some 4,500 km away from the epicenter of the earthquake that triggered the tsunami. In Somalia, 50,000 people were displaced from their homes, the death toll was 176 and 136 went missing. Further south on the east coast of Africa, one person drowned in Socotra island of Yemen and 3 people died and 6 went missing in Seychelles.

The enormous devastating power of the 2004 Indian Ocean Tsunami was again noticed when a 1.5 m surge was observed at Struisbaai in the Western Cape of South Africa, some 8,500 km from the epicenter. Two people died in South Africa too.[78]

2011 Tohoku Earthquake and Tsunami

At 14.46 hours, in the afternoon of a spring Friday on the 11th of March 2011, the Pacific coast of Japan was struck by a massive undersea megathrust earthquake of magnitude 9.1 in the Richter scale. The epicenter of this most powerful earthquake ever recorded in Japan, was some 70 km east of the Oshika Peninsula of Tohoku. This 2011 earthquake is mentioned in Japan as the Great East Japan Earthquake and is the fourth most powerful earthquake in the world since 1900, when modern record-keeping began. This Great Earthquake, physically moved the entire main island of Japan, Honshu, to the east by 2.4 m (8 ft) and shifted Planet Earth on its axis, anywhere between 10 cm and 25 cm.[79]

This earthquake generated powerful tsunami waves that reached a height of some 40.5 m (133 ft) in Miyako in Tohoku's Iwate Prefecture. Further south in Sendai, this tsunami racing at 700 km per hour travelled 10 km inland, after giving the residents of this most beautiful city only a ten-minute warning. The enormous height of the tsunami that was beyond anticipation, washed away over a hundred evacuation sites. The invading tsunami killed people mostly by drowning and caused 15,899 fatalities, 6,157 injuries and 2,529 persons went missing. The tsunami, moreover, caused colossal damage to infrastructure and 121,778 buildings 'totally collapsed', 280,926 buildings 'half collapsed' and 699,180 buildings were 'partially damaged'.[79]

The tsunami propagated through the entire Pacific Ocean region, striking the shores of faraway Chile in South America, some 17,000 km away, with waves 2 m high.

Nuclear accident and removal of radioactivity

The tsunami utterly overwhelmed the Fukushima Daiichi Nuclear Power Plant complex, causing a stoppage to electric power generation. Within a few days, the onsite electrical generators installed to provide emergency power supply to the cooling systems, ran out of fuel. This caused a total shutdown of the cooling system leading to a buildup of heat, which in turn generated hydrogen gas. In the absence of any ventilation, crippled by the unavailability of power, hydrogen gas kept building up in the containment structures of the reactor and eventually exploded. The three nuclear reactors, of the Fukushima Daiichi Nuclear Power Plant, experienced the level 7 meltdowns. The nuclear accidents and the partial meltdowns led to the evacuation of all residents within a 20 km radius of the power plant.[79] I must mention that the Japanese scientists and engineers through their sheer determination and ingenuity, averted a total meltdown of the nuclear reactors, thus preventing a horrendous nuclear catastrophe.

The World Bank estimated the total economic cost of the Great East Japan Earthquake and tsunami at USD235 billion, making it the costliest natural disaster.[79]

This tsunami induced aforesaid nuclear accident, released large amounts of radioactive materials, mostly consisting of three radio-nuclides namely, cesium-137, strontium-90 and iodine-131 that spread throughout the local and regional environments, because of their relative volatility, to contaminate soil, water and sediment of the entire area. These three radio-nuclides Cs-137, Sr-90 and I-131, in fact, had accounted for most of the harmful effects following the Chernobyl nuclear accident in 1986. Consequently, purification of the soil, sediment and water, and expeditious treatment of contaminated materials became necessary to make a full recovery from the nuclear disaster in the Tohoku area of Japan. Within a few months of the accident, most of the I-131 disappeared because of its short half-life of 8 days and despite a much longer half-life of 28 years, Sr-90's amount of diffusion from the power plant was quite low. The main culprit of the radioactive pollution in Fukushima, therefore, was Cs-137, with a half-life of 30 years, which needed to be removed from the contaminated water, soil and sediment.[80, 81]

Removal of radioactive Cs-137 from water and soil is conducted mainly by physical and chemical processes using zeolite and clay, and by chemical treatment. Carbon magnetite materials that effectively adsorb Cs-137 are recovered with a magnet. These techniques, however, even after a successful accomplishment of adsorption of Cs-137, require vast storage facilities for the contaminated soil, sediment and water wastes. This limitation, therefore, required the developments of technologies that reduce the volume of wastes generated after treatment. In addition, more efficient, convenient and low-cost technologies needed to be developed, in view of the long-term needs for practical removal of radioactivity from the contaminated area.[80, 81]

Biological treatments by growing plants such as sunflower on contaminated soils have been tried, but their effectiveness in removal of radioactivity was rather low, which, therefore, could not be employed to purify the radioactively polluted soil. Microbiological removal of Cs-137 using a fungus Paxillus involutus and cyanobacteria, Synecchocystis and

Rhodococcus erythripolis and Rhodococcus sp. were reported. Large scale removal of Cs-137 using those means to decontaminate soil, water and sediment, however, was not reported. Removal of Cs-137, moreover, from the contaminated soil of Fukushima by physical and chemical processes, was not conducted. Removal of radioactivity in Fukushima, initially involved the physical removal and transfer of vast quantities of the contaminated surface soil to a storage facility in another location.[80, 81]

This is when, in the summer of 2011, only a few months after the nuclear accident, I had a good chat with my collaborator senior colleague and good friend Prof. Dr. Ken Sasaki of Hiroshima Kokusai Gakuin University (HKGU) of Hiroshima, regarding designing a bioremediation research project to remove radioactive Cs-137 from the contaminated soil, water and sediment of Fukushima. Dr. Ken Sasaki had conducted an enormous amount of research in Hiroshima to remove toxic heavy metals like arsenic (As), selenium (Se), cadmium (Cd), mercury (Hg), copper (Cu), lead (Pb), zinc (Zn), cobalt (Co), nickel (Ni), chromium (Cr) and elements like uranium (U), thorium (Th) and non-radioactive cesium (Cs) from contaminated soil and water using a strain of photosynthetic anaerobic rod-shaped gram negative purple bacteria, Rhodobacter sphaeroides, which he had engineered in his laboratory. Prof. Ken Sasaki, then the Professor of Bioengineering and the Director of Mei-Sui Bio Research Institute of HKGU, had conducted some 15 years of excellent bioremediation research using Rhodobacter sphaeroides for improving water and soil quality. Prof. Sasaki, who in a couple of years would become the President of Hiroshima Kokusai Gakuin University, readily accepted my suggestion. Prof. Sasaki, in fact, by then had reported successful simultaneous removal of uranium (U), strontium (Sr), cobalt (Co), and cesium (Cs) by photosynthetic bacteria Rhodobacter sphaeroides, confined in porous ceramic beads. Prof. Sasaki, moreover, had demonstrated an almost 100% successful removal of non-radioactive cesium (Cs), from a sample of artificially contaminated water containing a concentration of 5 mg/L of the said metal, by treatment with an immobilized strain of Rhodobacter sphaeroides, within 2 to 3 days.

Prof. Ken Sasaki, his most capable son Dr. Kei Sasaki, who is presently a Lecturer of Hiroshima Kokusai Gakuin University and a Director of Mei-Sui Bio Research Institute, and I, designed experiments to remove and recover radioactive Cs-137 from contaminated soil and sediment in Fukushima, by using arginate beads, containing immobilized photosynthetic bacteria Rhodobacter sphaeroides.[80, 81] A simple aerobic treatment system led to removal and recovery of between 73.2% and 81.9% radioactive Cs-137 from contaminated sediment and removal of between 59.5% and 73.3% from contaminated soil. After treatment, radioactive Cs-137 incorporated into the immobilized beads were recovered, which upon incineration were reduced by more than 97%, without ever scattering any radioactive Cs-137 to the immediate surroundings.[80, 81]

In further experimentations, immobilized photosynthetic bacteria, Rhodobacter sphaeroides, cultured on porous ceramic beads of 2 cm diameter, effectively removed and recovered more than 90% of radioactive Cs-137 from contaminated sediments, after 3 to 14 days of aerobic treatment in an outdoor 60 L vessel. The removal and recovery from soil was a little lower, between 42% and 73%. The weight and mass of the harvested beads, moreover, could be reduced by more than 97% after desiccation. This technology of removal and recovery of radioactive Cs-137 had, therefore, considerable advantages over other technologies that demanded very large storage facilities in Fukushima. After removal of radioactivity, vegetables like Komatsuna or Japanese mustard spinach (Turnip leaves) and Chingensai (Green pak choi) were cultivated on remediated soil. The above vegetables, grown on these treated soils showed a radioactivity content lower than the recommended limit for edible foods in Japan, i.e. less than

100 Bq per kg.[80, 81] Incidentally, the becquerel (Bq) is a unit of radioactivity. Remediation treatment using Rhodobacter sphaeroides containing ceramic beads, therefore, appeared to be a compact and suitable technology that made significant contributions towards agricultural recovery in radioactively polluted areas of Fukushima.

Tribute to Prof. Dr. Ken Sasaki

My dear readers, please allow me a diversion to pay tributes to my friend Prof. Dr. Ken Sasaki, who was seven years my older and succumbed to lung cancer at a relatively young age of 69, in the early summer month of May of 2018. Prof. Sasaki was an outstanding bioengineer and synthesized his strain of Rhodobacter sphaeroides that he used very successfully for bioremediation of soils and wastewater, contaminated by a whole range of industrial pollutants including toxic heavy metals. Ever since the nuclear accident at the Daiichi nuclear power plant of Fukushima in 2011, Prof. Sasaki then a hexagenarian, worked tirelessly with the zeal of a young samurai to bioremediate the radiologically contaminated agricultural fields of Fukushima area. Dr. Sasaki would regularly drive over a thousand kilometers from Hiroshima to Fukushima, carrying his instruments and agricultural implements for his experimentations there. He would then return to his office and laboratories to resume teaching at Hiroshima Kokusai Gakuin University that he served so very sincerely since the late 1970s, when he took up employment there as an Assistant Professor. Prof. Sasaki was an institution builder and he did a great deal for the welfare of the students and the university. He played a key leadership role in the university, to ensure the impartation of highest quality education and training to the students.

Prof. Sasaki was a much-admired educator, not only within the university, but also in Hiroshima and beyond. He was a darling of both the print and electronic media that he used well, to educate both the public and the policymakers on the importance of maintaining water bodies sparklingly clean, to ensure sustenance of water quality of the highest order. The disciplined people of Hiroshima have paid heed to his advice and in their gratitude, affectionately named him the Mizuno Sensei or the Water Guru.

A prolific writer on water chemistry, water quality management, wastewater treatment, bio-recycling, bioengineering etc. Prof. Sasaki, dedicated his early years to a systematic recording of the water chemistry of all the important water bodies of Hiroshima area that contained many famous hot springs, ponds, wells, streams and rivers, at least twice a year, before and after the monsoonal rains, year after year, every year. This most impressive data base of water chemistry that he built over a period of forty years, without any interruptions whatsoever, is absolutely unique and incomparable in the world. After his demise, his son Dr. Kei Sasaki is continuing the work of recording the water chemistry of all the water bodies of Hiroshima.

A compassionate visionary Prof. Sasaki was, and he had a great deal of love for humanity. He firmly believed that water, to be more precise, a body of fresh good quality drinking water was the greatest heritage of humanity. And I agree with his views entirely and I propose that the bodies of good drinking water be recognized as the greatest heritage of humanity, all over the world.

Barely a fortnight before the occurrence of the Great East Japan Earthquake of the 11th of March 2011, Prof. Sasaki was in India with me to sign a Memorandum of Understanding (MoU). We signed the MoU between my two universities, Ravenshaw in Odisha, where I was a Professor of Geology, the Dean of Administration and the Dean of the School of Earth Sciences and Hiroshima Kokusai Gakuin, where I was a Visiting Professor. The MoU facilitated exchange of students and members of the faculty and collaborative research. As a part of the student exchange program, Miss Amrita Das, an M.Sc. Computer Science student of Ravenshaw, visited Hiroshima Kokusai Gakuin University for a period of six weeks. In so doing, Amrita became the first ever exchange student of Ravenshaw University to visit a university in a foreign land. Upon returning home, she successfully completed her M.Sc. and secured a good position with an IT major. Amrita is now well placed in the IT industry.

As a part of collaborative research, we analyzed the waters of two famous hot springs of Odisha, Atri and Tarabalo, for their chemistry and radon (Rn) content and we were pleasantly surprised with a discovery of a significant presence of radon. Atri possess Rn in concentrations of 0.03×10^{-10} curie (Ci) per liter of water and the concentration for Tarabalo is 19.16×10^{-10} Ci per liter.[82] Incidentally, the curie (Ci) is a unit of radioactivity and named in honor of Pierre Curie, but some consider it to be in honor of his wife Marie Curie.

While the Rn content of Atri hot spring is low, the Rn content of Tarabalo is significant and comparable to that of the famous hot springs of Hiroshima in Japan that average around 80×10^{-10} Ci of Rn per liter of water.[82] Uranium bearing sandstones, mudstones and shales of the underlying Athgarh sandstones of Gondwana age appear to be the source of Rn. Waters of Atri and Tarabalo contain small amounts of organic matter and Tarabalo also contains minor counts of bacteria, which could be easily eliminated with proper maintenance and these two hot springs can be developed into major health and tourist resorts.

During the five-year tenure of the said collaboration, I joined Prof. Sasaki to translate his book on water chemistry and water quality management, from the original Japanese to English that was published in Japan in 2013 bearing the title, Genbaku Kensui: Dedication of Water Ceremony for the Victims of the A-Bomb.[83]

After seeing firsthand, the poor state of water quality in Odisha, a most generous Prof. Sasaki gave me unfettered access to his proprietary technologies and permission to use his strain of Rhodobacter sphaeroides for bioremediation, to improve water and soil quality anywhere I wished, particularly so in India. May your noble soul, Prof. Sasaki, rest in peace.

Construction of seawall in Japan

In the aftermath of this most devastating tsunami, the Government of Japan decided to construct a 14 m high and 400 km long seawall, along the entire north east coast of the main island of Honshu, to protect the most vulnerable stretch of land from the Pacific Ocean tsunamis. On a 25 m deep foundation stand the 14 m high concrete seawall, buttressed by a 40 m wide bank of earth covered with concrete. The seawall is interspersed with floodgates that are kept open to allow the rivers to discharge into the sea. The gates are designed to close during tsunamis. The deepest seawall, some 63 m deep, is in the steel city of Kama Ishi. As I write this book in January 2021, construction of this great seawall is proceeding smoothly.[84]

The economic aspect of global warming and sea level rise will probably emerge as a new interdisciplinary subject in the near future. Instead of attempting any calculations to put a price on future damages, caused by coastal inundation in India due to a combined effect of sea level rise, storm surges and tsunamis, I would merely make a generalized statement that the economic losses will run in to thousands of trillions of rupees.

Achyutananda's prophecy on sea level rise

Achyutananda's Books of Prophecies contain bold predictions of the sea inundating coastal Odisha. His prophecies describe in detail a week of incessant rains and the events leading up to the marine transgression and subsequent inundation of the sprawling stone staircase, comprising twenty-two steps, known in Odia as the *Baaisi Paahaacha* of the Jagannath temple of Puri. On the 3rd of September 2008, a respected Odia daily the Dharitri in its editorial cited Achyutananda's prophecies of fish swimming on the *Baaisi Paahaacha*. Achyutananda further elaborates the marine transgression with graphic details of sea water submerging the pedestal in the sanctum sanctorum of the temple, presently adorned by the deities.

My grandfather used to describe me these prophecies, when I was only a child studying under his tutelage in a primary school in his village. I failed to comprehend the concept of marine transgression and did not quite fathom the deluge then. Consequently, I never really understood the prophecies. And as luck would have it, I moved to Puri for my high school education and saw the Jagannath temple and the sea. I distinctly remember a classmate of mine, who hailed from the township of Puri, telling me of the prophecies again, which, by the way, are a part of the established folklore of the holy temple town, since their issuance in the early part of the sixteenth century. My friend had quoted that the 65 m tall Jagannath temple will be submerged completely. I had dismissed his words out of hand and I never paid much attention to what he had said. Whenever I frolicked on the vast sandy beaches of Puri and on the premises of the Jagannath temple, I was most reluctant to accept that this revered temple could ever be so overwhelmed. I dismissed the prophecies as figments of imagination or superstition, at best.

Only after I embarked upon my studies in geology, which took me to many parts of this magnificent planet we call home and lodged me in quite a few venerable universities and institutions of the world, I learnt that marine transgression and regression are geological facts. They, moreover, have occurred regularly in the earth's history, I learnt. I realized that the sea level could indeed rise to inundate the Twenty-two Steps of the Jagannath temple, which are barely 10 m to 15 m above the mean sea level. The deluge, in fact, could entirely submerge the Jagannath temple, the top of which stands just about 80 m above the mean sea level, as prophesied. As explained earlier, 80 m is the upper limit of sea level rise, should all the glacial ice of the world were to melt away. Call it a coincidence or a remarkably accurate prophecy by a remarkably accurate seer, the choice is yours. It is about time that the world learns of this very great seer and his prophecies.

On the 15th of September 2008, a mere 100 km per hour storm, whipped off a 6 m storm surge that inundated 20,000 hectares of agricultural land, tens of villages and severely affected thousands of families of coastal Odisha. In April 2019, a severe cyclone Fani, with a wind speed of 180 km with gusting speed of 200 km, made landfall 20 km south of the township of Puri. A 2 m high storm surge it whipped, inundated Puri and caused massive damages to the numerous hotels on the beach. A strong cyclone, with wind speeds of 300 km per hour, could create a storm surge of 10 m height. Should a surge of this magnitude hit the coastal township of Puri on a full moon day at high tide during the monsoon, sea water will indeed inundate Puri and the Twenty-two Steps of the Jagannath temple. This could happen any time now, say by the middle of this twenty-first century, even before a substantial rise in sea level.

So confident was Achyutananda of his prophecies that in one of his writings in Odia he says:

'Parbata sikhare phutiba kain,
Achyutara katha taliba nahin';

which when translated into English would read:

Water lilies will bloom atop the mountains blue,
Mark Achyuta's words, for they will come true.
(Translation ND).

However astounding this prediction may appear, it is not all that far-fetched. Let me explain very briefly how this could eventuate. The very site of the Jagannath temple, Neelachala, which as explained earlier was once an impressive mountain, is barely above sea level thanks to the rising sea. As the sea rises even higher, places along the coast which were once hill tops during the last ice age, will be waterlogged ponds where lilies will bloom.

Achyutananda's confident prophecies scare me and give me the feeling that the people of the east coast of India, perhaps will do nothing to combat the rising sea, which will transgress and inundate this rich and fertile stretch of land. I feel deeply hurt, when I visualize the inundation of Puri, where I completed my high school education and spent some very happy teenage years frolicking on those beautiful sandy beaches. Some of my dearest friends whom I have loved and admired, hail from this holy and enchanting township. Visualization of the inundation of their lovely houses, which have stood as indelible landmarks in my life's journey, pains me immensely. Let us unite and initiate preventive action to combat the rising sea, for inaction would make Achyutananda's prophecies come true much sooner than we wish.

Measures to combat the rising seas
Now the big question arises, is there anything at all that could be done to combat the rising seas, particularly at a time when global warming continues unabated, making sea level rise inevitable. Let me respond that although sea level rise is inevitable, coastal inundation at least for the next few centuries is avoidable, provided we take preventive action. Let us discuss the preventive action we could take.

Bengal has devised its own unique set of techniques to deal with problems of any magnitude. Considering the current state of affairs in West-Bengal, I would assume that the threat of sea level rise would be confronted by the battalions of comrades led by their formidable leaders, who would assemble on the beaches and raise their voices in unison to shout:

Sea level rise, *nahin chalega nahin chalega*.
Bay of Bengal! *Wapas jao wapas jao*.

Although this kind of slogan shouting has been very successful in driving away industrialization, employment, growth, prosperity and the Tatas from West-Bengal, I do not foresee this technique succeeding in forcing the Bay of Bengal to retreat. For the benefit of my non-Indian friends, I provide a glossary of the revolutionary terminology just used: *nahin chalega* – will not do, *wapas jao* – go back.

I am at pains to record that West-Bengal in the third decade of the twenty-first century, is a mere shadow of the Bengal of a century earlier. In those heydays, Bengal produced a great many luminaries, who led social reforms, educational reforms and industrialization in India. The leaders, intellectuals and nationalists of Bengal led the Indian freedom movement through their phenomenal organizational skills, inspirational speeches, salutation of '*Jai Hind*' (introduced by a Germany based Thiruvananthapuram born Tamil Indian nationalist revolutionary Dr. Chempaka Raman Pillai[85, 86] and immortalized by Netaji Subhas Chandra Bose as the battle-cry of Indian National Army) and the passionate songs of '*Vande Mataram*' (written by Bankim Chandra Chattopadhyay), '*Amar Sonar Bangla*' (written by Rabindranath Tagore), '*Qadam Qadam Badhaye Ja*' (marching song of Indian National Army, written by Pandit Vanshidhar Shukla and composed by Ram Singh Thakuri) that reverberated across the length and the breadth of India to unite a nation. So vociferous were the Bengalis in their protests against the colonial rule that the panic-stricken Viceroy Curzon, cowered to apply the time-tested nefarious British tactic of 'divide and rule' and partitioned their state on the 16th of October 1905 along religious lines, in order to subjugate them.[87] The division of the state into East and West-Bengal was designed to pit the Hindus against the Muslims, who spoke the same language of independence of

India then. I would like my readers to remember that it is the British Raj that had sown the seeds of the partition of India, with the division of Bengal.

Having praised you so much my Bengali friends, I would like to mention that time it is now for West-Bengal, the state which will suffer most in the east due to sea level rise, to provide leadership on the east coast to combat the rising sea. I appeal to you my sisters and brothers of Bengal to unite, let us put aside the divisive politics and embark upon a collective mass action, to combat the menace of the rising sea.

And let Gujarat, the state that is going to suffer the most in the west, take up the leadership of the west coast. My sisters and brothers from Gujarat, you produced the greatest leader of the twentieth century world, Mahatma Gandhi, and now in the twenty-first century you have produced a world leader in the Hon'ble Prime Minister of India Narendra Damodardas Modi, and you certainly can provide the leadership now.

The very first step in the preventive action, to combat the rising seas to save our coasts, is the creation of awareness among the masses, through a comprehensive education program to ensure their active participation. In the second stage, we must embark upon a truly epic program of coastal-engineering works, on a scale unprecedented and perhaps at least ten times bigger than the endeavors of the Dutch in Holland, in the last 65 years.

The Netherlands is up to 6 m below sea level
The Netherlands, informally known as Holland, along with Belgium, when ruled by Spain and Austria, before 1581 CE, were known as the Low Countries. The very word 'nether', means lower or under. Consequently, the Netherlands means the country of low-lying lands. The total geographic area of Holland is about 41,526 square km, half of which lies below sea level and was covered by the sea, lagoons and swamps. In

the last eight hundred years, the native Dutch people have reclaimed bulk of this land by pumping sea water back into the sea. The Dutch are so proud of their land reclamation efforts that they have a saying, which in English would read, 'God created the world, but the Dutch created Holland'. The reclaimed areas of the country are called polders, which now constitute the heart of the Netherlands. Amsterdam, the capital and the largest city of the country, is built on a polder and lies almost 6 m below sea level.

The Netherlands is located on the low-lying deltaic plains of the Rhine system and in 1953 experienced a massive flooding disaster that killed nearly 2,000 people and destroyed 47,000 buildings.[88] Following the inundation, a vast construction effort known as the Delta Works was undertaken in 1958, which continued right up to 2002, 'to end the threat from the sea'. The project involved the construction of 3,000 km of outer sea-dykes or ramparts and 10,000 km of inner canal-and river-dykes. The outer sea-dykes are 50 m thick at the base and 15 m high with a flattop. This Delta Works remains one of the largest construction projects in human history and has very successfully protected the Netherlands from inundation by sea.[89]

Let the Coastal Works commence

Let us draft a master plan to combat the rising sea. And please allow me to propose a name for this master plan, the Coastal Works, which would include all the coordinated projects of coastal-engineering, delta-works, river-engineering of both east and west coasts of India. The rising seas, presently, do not threaten the entire coastline of 5,700 km of the mainland of India, therefore, let the very first stage of our endeavors be focused on the most vulnerable parts, which are the numerous low-lying river deltas. Protection of these deltas from the ravages of the rising seas would require a well-coordinated construction of an extensive network of dykes, embankments, dams and revetments. Building materials for the earthen structures could be sourced primarily by the excavation of sediments from riverbeds and from the shallow continental shelf of the seas.

The first line of defense against the rising sea would be a massive flat-topped outer-dyke of comparable cross section to that of the outer-dykes of Holland, at 15 m high and 50 m wide at the base. The flattop of the outer-dykes could be as broad as 8 m to host a two-lane highway. The outer-dyke would be accompanied by a substantial inner-dyke running essentially parallel to the first, and a very large number of equally substantial cross-dykes to link the inner- and the outer-dykes. The building of the network of dykes will create a large number of freshwater lakes of different shapes and sizes depending upon the topography, which must be managed carefully. In certain localities, substantial strips of land of the continental shelf, currently under sea, could even be reclaimed.

The combined length of the network of dykes of the Coastal Works, would easily be ten times longer than that of their Dutch counterpart. The cost of the Coastal Works will be in thousands of billions of rupees, which is expensive, but if we do not take up this project, the losses will be in thousands of trillions of rupees. The Coastal Works will take decades to complete, but let us not delay the start.

At the moment in India, on certain coastal areas of the east as well as the west, coastal-engineering projects are ongoing. Although these projects were not designed for combating sea level rise, their scopes could be expanded to lay the foundations for the Coastal Works. Say for example, dredging on coastal waters is going on at Dhamra of Odisha for setting up a new seaport and at Chilika lake for keeping a channel open from the sea to the lagoon. These kinds of dredging could be expanded and modified to build the outer-dykes. The Ministry of Environment of the Government of India, moreover, has initiated an Integrated Coastal Zone Management Project (ICZMP) for the Odisha coast.[90]

This plan was initially drafted for implementation along two stretches, first, on a 40 km long one from Gopalpur to Chilika lake and second, an 80 km tract between Paradip and Dhamra.[90] ICZMP is a commendable program designed to prevent coastal erosion and the scope of this program could be substantially expanded. Coastal towns and villages under immediate threat from the sea and storm surges are getting protective dykes constructed by the government. These are good and welcome moves, but this piecemeal approach is not enough. The time now it is, to draft a master plan for the entire country and initiate appropriate projects.

Please allow me to remind you that India now has a massive, hugely ambitious and successful space program that had a most humble beginning, only five decades ago in 1962. Indian Space Research Organization (ISRO) launched India's first interplanetary mission on 5 November 2013, when the Mars Orbiter Mission probe Mangalyaan successfully lifted off from the First Launch Pad at Satish Dhawan Space Centre of Sriharikota in Andhra Pradesh. Mangalyaan successfully reached the Martian orbit and, in the process, made India the very first nation in the world to do so in its maiden attempt. Mangalyaan is orbiting Mars since 24 September 2014.[91, 92, 93] Six years earlier, on 22 October 2008, India's first lunar probe Chandrayaan-1[94] had been successfully launched from the same Sriharikota and the two components of the probe, a lunar orbiter and an impactor, had successfully accomplished their objectives.

The far more ambitious Chandrayaan-2[95], successfully launched from Sriharikota on 22 July 2019, consisted of the indigenously built lunar orbiter, the *Vikram* lander and the *Pragyan* lunar rover. The scientific objectives of the Chandrayaan-2 mission were to map and study lunar topography, to study mineralogy and elemental abundance of lunar surface, to study the composition of the lunar exosphere and to locate and assess the abundance of water. The main objectives of Chandrayaan-2 lander were to prove the ability to soft-land and to operate a robotic rover on the lunar surface. Chandrayaan-2 reached the Moon's orbit on 20 August 2019 and made orbital positioning maneuvers for the landing of the *Vikram* lander. The *Vikram*, however, crashed on the lunar surface instead of making a soft-landing, apparently caused by a software error. Even though the Chandrayaan-2 failed in fulfilling all its main objectives, the mission was reasonably successful and these Chandrayaan and Mangalyaan space missions are huge achievements indeed.

Our space program, in general, has helped immensely in raising the quality of life of the entire nation. If our space program could achieve so much in a mere fifty years, we surely can do a lot in the foreseeable future to protect our country from the rising seas. Our nation, therefore, must pay some attention to protect the landmass by taking up the Coastal Works. If we manage properly, India will continue to prosper very substantially even in this era of global warming. I must, however, record that quite difficult a task it is, to motivate a people who are so utterly obsessed with the present that they can hardly visualize even tomorrow, let alone a few hundred years from now.

Our Indian empires of the past were the most prosperous and successful seafaring nations. The Kalinga empire of the east coast was immensely prosperous, due to maritime trade and commerce with far-off lands of Java, Sumatra, Sinhala, Malaya, Siam, The Philippines and many other countries of the world. All those thousands of years ago, perhaps tens of thousands of years ago, Kalingan merchants and scholars settled in those far off lands to set up urban centers, so much so that till this day the natives of Malaysia are called Keling[96] or Kling and our epic Ramayana as Ramakatha is celebrated in

Java and Sumatra even today. The present-day Bay of Bengal, right up to the middle of the nineteenth century, by the way, was known as the Kalinga Sea or The Sea of Kalinga.

I would also like my readers to recall that Emperor Ashoka's sons Prince Kunala and Prince Mahendra and daughter Princess Sanghamitra carried the sacred Bodhi plant to Sinhala from a sea port of Kalinga, to spread the message of peace and love, following the Kalinga war in 261 BCE i.e. 2,280 years ago.[97] The Pandya and Chola Empires of Tamil Nadu were major maritime powers, way before the advent of the Christian Era. I would also like to state that these empires of the past were adept in river-engineering and very likely on coastal-engineering as well. The oldest surviving dam of the world, the Grand Anicut on the Kaveri of Tamil Nadu attests to my assertion. This 330 m long, 4.5 m high and 20 m wide dam was built across the Kaveri by King Karikala of Chola Dynasty, more than two thousand years ago, in the first century BCE to irrigate around 280 square km of land in the fertile delta, and the dam is still functional.[99]

The Government of India is most vigorously implementing the Sagarmala, etymologically the marine garland, a program for a comprehensive world-class modernization of existing ports and port-led development of India's 7,500 km long coastline and 14,500 km long potentially navigable waterways. In a meeting held on the 25th of March 2015, the Union Cabinet of the Government of India approved the concept of Sagarmala, which envisions to "integrate the development of the ports, the Industrial clusters and hinterland and efficient evacuation systems through road, rail, inland and coastal waterways, resulting in ports becoming the drivers of economic activity in coastal areas".[100, 101] The various existing and planned coastal highways of the various coastal states and the Sagarmala program, could well become a major component of the Coastal Works to create barriers to combat the rising seas.

We have a rich history in building dams, managing water and dealings with the sea. And we did all this even before Holland was conceived as a nation. So, if the Dutch could construct their Delta Works to protect their land that lies 6 m below sea level, we could do better and safeguard Mother India from the threats of the rising sea. And in years to come we could export our expertise of the Coastal Works to other countries in distress.

Construction of protective seawalls and 20 m high dykes, strategic retreat to involve gradual planned relocation of low-lying coastal settlements to higher grounds, further inland of at least an elevation of 10 m above the astronomical high tide, will protect this land perhaps for a few more centuries. And this we must do for future generations.

Let the Coastal Works commence to save this land.

Chapter Three
Can Global Warming Make the Ganga Run Dry?

Global warming is real and upon us. How will global warming affect the rivers in India, will they all dry up? Can the holy Ganga, the river that has shaped and sustained the Indian civilization through the ages and who, we Indians, revere as the life-giving mother, run dry! Many climate experts and environmentalists, in the first two decades of the twenty-first century, made dire predictions of the Ganga becoming seasonal. Some doomsayers even went to the extent of boldly predicting the river to become ephemeral by the year 2035, which is barely half a generation away! Is it possible that the Ganga will run dry by 2035! Is this calamity an inevitability that should be accepted as *fait accompli* or is there anything we, the people of India, collectively can do to save the holy Mother Ganga from extinction? This profound issue demands examination and I propose to engage you my readers in a serious debate.[1]

Source of the Ganga
The Ganga originates from the Gangotri glacier, which is one of the largest valley glaciers of the Himalaya, located in the western part, in the state of Uttarakhand. The Gangotri, some 30.2 km long and between 0.5 and 2.5 km wide, reclines at altitudes between 4,120 and 7,000 m above the mean sea level (MSL). This recumbent glacier originates in a cirque, which is a natural amphitheater like structure at the base of a mountain, immediately below the locally highest Chaukhamba peak. The Gangotri glacier is fed by three main large tributary valley glaciers namely, the 15.90 km long Raktvarn, the 22.45 km

long Chaturangi and the 11.05 km long Kirti. Eighteen smaller tributary valley glaciers feed the Gangotri too. The total areal extent of the glacierized upper catchment of the Gangotri is some 258.56 km^2, made up of the Gangotri system itself lying recumbent over 109.03 km^2, the Chaturangi spread over 72.91 km^2, the Raktvarn stretched over 45.34 km^2 and the Kirti covering an area of 31.28 km^2. This glacial complex contains around 40 cubic km (km^3) of ice. Four other valley glaciers, Maitri, Meru, Bhrigupanth and Manda with a total glacierized extent of 29.41 km^2, do not contribute to the Gangotri glacier, but drain directly into the Bhagirathi that joins the Alaknanda to form the Ganga.[2]

During a 61-year period between 1936 and 1996, the Gangotri glacier receded by as much as 1,147 m, out of which an 850 m long recession happened during a 25-year period between 1971 and 1996. In a three-year period between 1996 and 1999, the Gangotri retreated by another 76 m. When these rates of recent retreat are contrasted with the 2,000 m retreat recorded over the last 200 years, a significant acceleration in recession becomes obvious. Available data show that the rate of retreat in 1971 was 19 m per year, which accelerated to 34 m in 2007. These recent higher rates of retreat made some experts and environmentalists speculate that due to global warming the Gangotri glacier may completely disappear by 2035.[3] If that happens, they argue that the Ganga will cease to flow during the summer months and will drain only the monsoonal rains, thus becoming seasonal. I would like to mention that while the Gangotri is receding, some glaciers further west in the Himalaya are growing in size and volume! Let us investigate the issue further.[4,5,6]

Global warming is not uniform
Global warming does not mean a uniform amount of warming at each and every place on the globe. Although a vast majority of the places on this earth will become hotter

due to global warming, however strange it may seem, certain parts will, in fact, become cooler. Global warming will not make the earth uniformly dry up either, nor will it make rainfalls disappear. Although the bulk of the continental landmass will become much drier, quite paradoxically again, some places will become wetter and receive far much more rainfall. In the following section, I will present discussions to convince you my readers of my assertions that one: some places will become cooler and two: some places will receive much more precipitation, due to global warming. Let me start my discussion to explain cooling, which can occur, say for instance, at a place in higher latitude, currently kept warm by the Gulf Stream.

The Gulf Stream

The Gulf Stream is a vast oceanic current that carries warm waters from the tropics to the temperate regions of northern Europe and North America. This ocean current originates in the Gulf of Mexico, flows past the east coast of the USA and Newfoundland in Canada, and then crosses the Atlantic Ocean. It then branches into two, with the northern stream moving to northern Europe. The Gulf Stream is an 80 to 150 km wide and a 1,000 m deep river of the sea that transports 1.4 Peta Watt (1 Peta Watt is 1,000 million Mega Watt or 10^{15} Watt) of heat, which is equivalent to almost 100 times the current energy demand of the entire world. Around Cape Hatteras, on the coast of North Carolina in the US, the Gulf Stream transports water at the rate of 80 million cubic meter per second. The Gulf Stream is much bigger than any river system of the world, in fact, the combined release of all waters from all rivers flowing into the Atlantic is only 0.6 million cubic m (mcm) per second.[7]

As the Gulf Stream proceeds north, the warm waters undergo cooling due to evaporation. The evaporative loss makes the waters heavier due to increased salinity. By the time the Gulf Stream reaches the North Atlantic Ocean, its saltier heavier denser waters sink in the relatively less salty and less dense waters. The Gulf Stream then reverses its direction of travel, to embark on a southward journey.

The Gulf Stream has significant localized effects, on the climate of the east coast of Florida and Massachusetts in the US, and on the west coast of Britain, which is a good few degree warmer than the east coast. The warming effect of the Gulf Stream is most dramatic in the western islands of Scotland, so much so that the small township of Plockton (latitude 57.33°N) that is located east of the Isle of Skye, has a mild climate that allows subtropical cabbage-palm-trees to grow. The local climate in Plockton, in the absence of the Gulf Stream, would be freezing cold as latitudinally it lies further north of Moscow (latitude 55.45°N) by almost two degrees.[8]

Due to global warming, there is every possibility that the Gulf Stream may change course, or it may lose its strength. In fact, between 1957 and 2004, heat transport by the Gulf Stream declined by a full 30% and its deep return flow weakened by 30% as well. Any change in the characteristics of the Gulf Stream, would cause a significant localized cooling in Scandinavia and in Britain. Even during a time of global warming, if this happened, the western islands of Scotland will actually experience a substantial cooling.[9] Based on these apprehensions, Hollywood produced an apocalyptic action movie in 2004 titled, The Day After Tomorrow, which became the sixth highest-grosser of that year.[10]

This very logic that global warming is not uniform, is also applicable to the Himalayan environment, wherein, certain pockets, the glaciers, instead of disappearing due to global warming, may start to grow due to a combination of reasons. Unlike the Scottish islands, the Himalaya, however, is not influenced by the Gulf Stream, but by an equally powerful agent, the monsoon, which is discussed below.

Monsoon and its effect on the Himalayan environment

The Himalayan mountain system is a vast 2,400 km long arc, sprawling from the west to the east. Width of this range varies from 400 km in Kashmir in the west, to 150 km in Arunachal Pradesh in the east. The Himalaya consists of three parallel ranges, the northern most being the Great or High Himalaya, with an average height of 6,100 m above the mean sea level (MSL). This is where more than fifty mountains that exceed 7,200 m in height exist. The Great Himalaya acts as a massive barrier that arrests both the South West or the summer monsoon, which starts around June and continues till September, and the North East or the winter monsoon, and prevents their escape to northern Asia.[11]

In hot summer months, intense incoming solar radiation (insolation) heats up the Great Indian Desert of Thar in Rajasthan and the adjoining semiarid regions of the Indian landmass very significantly, creating low pressure over the entire north and central India. Waters of the Indian Ocean also experience similar heating that causes a large-scale evaporation, leading to the production of moisture laden winds. These winds flow in to fill up the vacuum created by the low pressure and proceed north until they reach the Himalaya, which, as mentioned earlier, act as a huge wall, forcing the winds to rise higher. At high altitudes, these moist winds cool down and precipitation of rain and snow occurs. The north-eastern part of India around Cherrapunji receives copious rainfall.[12, 13]

In a slight diversion from the main course of this article, I would like to mention that the name Cherrapunji, which was the anglicized version of Sohra in the native lingo, has just been reverted to the original by the State Government of Meghalaya. Sohra receives the highest rainfall in the world of about 1,200 cm per year and also holds two unique records. The first record is for the maximum rainfall in the world of 2,299 cm in a single year between August 1860 and July 1861 and the second, for the maximum amount of rainfall of 930 cm in a single month in July 1861.

Now let us go back to the movement of the monsoon clouds, which then turn west and move along the Himalaya and over the Lower Himalayan range that occurs at an elevation between 3,700 m and 4,500 m above the MSL, in the direction of Kashmir, causing widespread rains. The intensity of the rainfall, however, decreases towards the west. The Himalaya also receives a significant amount of precipitation from the North East or the retreating monsoon of the winter months.[14]

The South West Monsoon, like the Gulf Stream, is a vast natural system of transport of energy and water and carries a comparable 1.2 Peta Watt (1,200 million Mega Watt) of heat energy. The monsoon system, both the South West and the North East combined, transports about 12,000 billion cubic m (bcm) of water vapor over the Indian landmass annually, a third of which precipitates as rain and snow. I will present a small calculation, using some round figures, to demonstrate the enormity of the volume of precipitation India receives due to the monsoon. Let me start with the annual average rainfall of India, which is about 117 cm (1.17 m) over a landmass of 3.3 million km^2. The amount of rainwater the landmass thus receives is about 3,860 billion m^3 (bcm) (1.17 m X 3.3 million km^2) or say 4,000 billion m^3 (4,000 cubic km).[15]

Over the millennia, these monsoonal precipitations have created the vast glacial environment in the Himalaya, which towards the end of the twentieth century played host to some 18,065 glaciers spread over a total area of 34,659 km^2 containing a total volume of 3,734 km^3 of ice. The vast majority of these glaciers, 9,449 to be precise, existed in the central Himalaya. The western Himalaya hosted 5,648 glaciers and the rest 2,968 occurred in the eastern Himalaya. I want my readers to realize that the Himalaya has the largest concentration of glaciers outside the polar ice caps and provides about 500 billion cubic m (500 km³) of water annually. Some 67% of these glaciers, however, exhibited recession.[16, 17, 18]

A compendium of Task Force Report just published by the National Disaster Management Authority (NDMA) of the Government of India in October 2020 states that some 10% of the total area of the Himalaya is covered by glaciers. Another 30% to 40% of the Himalayan terrain "supports the snow cover". The compendium also states that some 9,575 glaciers spread over an area of 37,500 km² exist in the Indian Himalayan region. The three great river basins of the Sindhu, the Ganga and the Brahmaputra have a combined glaciated area of 71,182 km² hosting 32,392 glaciers. The Ganga basin hosts 6,237 glaciers spread over an area of 18,393 km². The main glaciers of the Himalaya are the 74 km long Siachen, the 30 km long Gangotri, 26 km long Zemu, 19 km long Milam and Bara Shigri, stretched over a length of 30.5 km.[19, 20]

Global warming and erratic monsoon

In the previous two chapters, I have repeatedly stated that global warming will make the monsoon system more vigorous yet erratic, which in turn will affect the overall environment of the Himalaya to a significant extent. In the year 2008, the South West Monsoon reached south Andaman Sea a full five days before schedule, on the 10th of May. The monsoon then broke at the southernmost tip of the Indian landmass at Kerala on the 31st of May as scheduled and then raced to the north to arrive at New Delhi on the 15th of June, a full two weeks early, to smash a 108-year-old record.[21]

In 2009, the South West Monsoon broke on Kerala on the 23rd of May, a full one week ahead of schedule. The two consecutive early onsets of the South West Monsoon in 2008 and 2009, might have created the impression that early arrival may become the norm, but then it arrived late in certain years too. Early or late, one fact that is obvious is that monsoon has been erratic and global warming will make the erratic behavior even worse. The duration of the monsoon season will also vary; it may become shorter or even longer.

Due to the vigorous monsoon, rainfall over the entire eastern and northern parts of India and Bangladesh has become far heavier. In 2007, serious floods played havoc with the lives and properties of hundreds of millions of people, in all the states of eastern India. In 2008, eastern India received torrential rainfall too and that inundated vast areas in the states of Odisha and West-Bengal, rendering millions homeless. On the 24th of August 2008, following heavy rains in the Himalayan foothills in eastern Nepal, the Koshi river breached its bank and opened a channel in the adjoining north Bihar, it had abandoned over 200 years ago. The initial 3 km wide breach, grew at the rate of 200 m per day and the ensuing inundation instantly affected over two million people.[22]

Heavier rains in Rajasthan

A vigorous monsoon will carry more water vapor, travel much faster and will lead to higher precipitations on the landmass of India. The monsoon clouds, moreover, will penetrate deeper into the Himalaya, scale higher altitudes and cause significantly higher amounts of precipitation, high up on the mountains. The monsoon system might have already started penetrating deeper into the Himalaya and north-western India, evident from significantly higher rainfall in the first two decades of the twenty-first century, in the north western most state of India, Rajasthan, which is essentially a desert and constitutes the last stop of the South West Monsoon, before dissipation. In July 2003, the monsoon caused heavy downpours in Rajasthan leading to 9 deaths and the maximum recorded rainfall in a matter of a couple of days was 7 cm, which is very high and unusual for the desert state. In July 2007, rainfall was heavy too, due to a vigorous monsoon. The state of Rajasthan as a whole, in the year 2008 as of the 14th of August, received a rainfall of 433 mm as against 342 mm in the same period of the previous year. Nine districts of the state recorded 60% more rainfall than the average.

On the 22nd of August 2012, heavy rains of over 300 mm killed some 14 people in and around Jaipur, which is the capital of Rajasthan. This rainfall was an all-time high in thirty years.[23]

The very dry parts of Rajasthan, in fact, described as the last posts of the state, Jaisalmer and Barmer, experienced the rainiest August in 2020, when Jaisalmer received a monthly total of 146.6 mm of rain against the usual 72.2 mm and Barmer received 201 mm against the average of 103 mm.[24]

Earlier in 2019, Barmer in a 24-hour period starting on the 13th of November, received 58 mm of rain, which was the highest fall recorded in the month of November for Barmer in a decade. Barmer, in fact, had hardly received any rain in the month of November in the previous 10 years.[25]

Heavier rains at Tehri in Uttarakhand

Further evidence of more vigorous monsoons penetrating deeper in to the Himalaya, could be gleaned from the reports of regularly higher rainfall of the past few years at the sprawling 52 km^2 body of water of the vast reservoir, created by the Tehri Dam in the state of Uttarakhand. The reservoir is barely 50 km away from the Gangotri glacier. I must, however, mention that the Tehri Dam, built on the Bhagirathi, is situated at an altitude of only 770 m above the MSL whereas the Gangotri's lowest point is way above, located at a height of some 4,000 m. The state of Uttarakhand, during the period of 1 June to 11 August in the year 2013, received heavy rains measuring 1,074.9 mm, which was 41% more than the average of 764.4 mm. The "incessant" South West Monsoon of 2013, moreover, surprised India with its pace, for it was the fastest in 50 years and drenched the entire country by the 15th of June, a full one month ahead of the normal 15 July.[26, 27]

Cloudbursts in Uttarakhand in the central Himalaya

On the 16th of June 2013, the heavens opened on the Himalayan regions of Uttarakhand and the adjoining states of Himachal Pradesh and Uttar Pradesh in India and on Tibet and Western Nepal to pour very heavy monsoonal rains. The rampaging South West Monsoon, moreover, chose to deliver a lethal multiday cloudburst in Uttarakhand that caused devastating floods and landslides that would constitute India's worst natural disaster since the 2004 Indian Ocean Tsunami, discussed earlier in Chapter Two. Cloudburst, by the way, is an incidence of heavy rain, when the rate of fall is more than 100 mm per hour. The 2013 cloudburst in Uttarakhand, killed at least 5,700 people and caused massive devastation to infrastructure, particularly around the townships of Badrinath, Kedarnath and Gangotri. An analytical study of the natural and anthropogenic influences on the climate anomalies, conducted at Utah State University published in 2015, demonstrated that "northern India has experienced increasingly large rainfall in June since the late 1980s". This study strengthens my contention that with the intensification of global warming, the monsoon will become more vigorous, causing heavier precipitations on the Himalaya.[28, 29]

The 2012 South West Monsoon had wreaked havoc too, in the Himalayan region of north Indian states, particularly in Uttarakhand and Himachal Pradesh, by delivering a cloudburst on the midnight of the 3rd of August that caused extensive flash floods and landslides that killed at least 31 people and devastated the infrastructure. A major portion of the Gangotri National Highway was washed away, and the Gangotri Bridge collapsed too.[30]

Numerous cloudbursts[31] in the Himalayan region of India, in addition to the ones mentioned above, caused by the rampaging South West Monsoon, occurred in the second decade of the twenty-first century. Please allow me to mention some of them as follows: June 9, 2011 cloudburst near Jammu that killed 4 people; July 20, 2011 cloudburst in upper Manali in Himachal Pradesh that killed at least 2 people; September 14, 2012 cloudburst in Rudraprayag of Uttarakhand that killed 39 people; July 31, 2014 cloudburst in Tehri of Uttarakhand that killed 4 people; September 6, 2014 cloudburst in Kashmir that killed at least 200 people; May 8, 2016 cloudburst in Tharali and Karnaprayag in Uttarakhand and July 5, 2017 cloudburst in Haridwar in Uttarakhand.

Cloudbursts in Ladakh in the western Himalaya

The Union Territory of Ladakh, located in the western Himalaya, lies further north-west of the central Himalayan states of Himachal Pradesh and Uttarakhand. The capital of Ladakh, Leh, is situated on a high plateau some 3,500 m above the MSL and receives very little rainfall of 100 mm or so per year and is considered a "high altitude cold desert". On the midnight of the 6th of August 2010, the South West Monsoon struck a devastating cloudburst across a large part of the entire Ladakh that damaged 71 small towns and villages including Leh. The township of Leh received a very heavy rainfall of around 250 mm, in a matter of hours, and the ensuing flash floods and mudflows, caused massive damage to infrastructure and killed at least 255 people. Ladakh continued to receive cloudbursts, albeit somewhat smaller than the 2010 one, in August 2018, in July to August 2015 and on August 1, 2013, in addition to two previous ones on August 9, 2008 and in 2006. [32, 33, 34] All these numerous cloudbursts in the high western Himalaya, demonstrate that the vigorous South West Monsoon is penetrating deeper into the Himalaya.

Growth of glaciers in the western most Himalaya

The vigorous monsoon could be making the glaciers grow in the western most Himalaya. The Karakoram range in the western Himalaya, located over 500 km further north-west of the Gangotri, plays host to a number of glaciers. The most prominent glacier in the Karakoram is the 74 km long Siachen, which is not only the largest Himalayan glacier, but also the second largest in the world, outside of the polar regions. The head of this high-altitude valley glacier lies at 5,753 m above the MSL at its source at Indira Col in the north, and its snout lies at an elevation of 3,620 m in the south. A glaciologist, Mr. V.K. Raina, in his article published in the Journal of the Geological Society of India in 2007, stated that the Siachen glacier 'along its snout front has been in a rest mode', which in plain language means that the glacier was not retreating then. During my tenure with the Department of Science and Technology of the Government of India, I had interactions with Mr. Raina, and I am quite willing to accept his observation on the Siachen. I, moreover, would like to add that the neighboring 58 km long Baltoro glacier was reported to be advancing and so were the 40 km long Rimo I and Rimo II glaciers, which meant that these glaciers grew. Quite interestingly, some scientists attributed the growth of these glaciers, in this very remote part of the world, to a lack of human intervention. The average winter snowfall in this region was reported at 10.5 m then, which was not insignificant.[35, 36, 37, 38, 39, 40]

Julie Gardelle and her coworkers, in their 2012 article published in Nature Geoscience, [41] reported that the glaciers of Karakoram, stretched over an area of 20,000 km^2, experienced a slight mass gain in the early twenty-first century, between 1999 and 2008. Fifty percent of these glaciers were either stable or they grew perhaps because of the "localized climate". Julie Gardelle of the University of Grenoble in France also stated, "Given the wide extent of high mountain Asia, we cannot expect the climate to be uniform over the whole range, so a peculiar atmospheric behavior over Karakoram may not be surprising."[42]

The South West monsoonal snowfall plays a key role in the sustenance of the glaciers of the western Himalaya. Heavy and frequent monsoonal precipitations, in the future, will sustain the glaciers, stated a group of researchers in their article published in the Journal of Glaciology in June 2020. Another study demonstrated that "biomass burning" could be "the primary driver behind carbon-induced melting of glaciers" in the western Himalayan region.[43]

A combination of reasons for the retreat of the Gangotri

I have so far tried to convince you my readers that with the intensification of global warming the moisture content and intensity of the summer and winter monsoons will increase and they will penetrate deeper into the Himalaya causing more precipitation. Perhaps this is happening already, as evidenced from the earlier mentioned descriptions of the strong cyclones, severe floods, heavier rainfall in Rajasthan and cloudbursts in Uttarakhand and Ladakh and growth of glaciers in the Karakoram. If this were the case, why at least 67% of the Himalayan glaciers, particularly the Gangotri, are in recession then? Some other glaciers such as Ratakona, Pindari and Milam, in the vicinity of the Gangotri, say within a radius of a hundred km, are also in recession. I present a discussion below.

The Saraswati valley, north of the township of Badrinath, which is about 50 km from the Gangotri, hosts Ratakona glacier very close to the high-altitude Mana Pass. Situated at 5,632 m above the MSL, Mana Pass[44] has been the gateway to the Indo-Tibetan trade route since time immemorial. Ratakona glacier, near the pass, is about to dry up and it has disappeared entirely in the nearby Dhauli Ganga valley. Pindari and Milam glaciers that occur about a hundred km south east of the Gangotri, attract a vast number of tourists for trekking and a range of adventure sports, and are fast retreating too. Gyan Marwah[45] in his 2004 article stated that "Dr. Amber P. Tewari, a retired GSI (Geological Survey of India) official who has studied the glacier for over three decades" blamed rampant deforestation, particularly from the lateral moraines i.e. the embankments or the sidewalls of the retreating valley glaciers, for their recession.[46]

The recession, even the disappearance, of these glaciers is certainly due to a combination of reasons in addition to global warming. The other two main reasons are population pressure and massive deforestation.

The holy township of Badrinath, [47] at an altitude of 3,415 m above the MSL, is located on the banks of the Alaknanda and according to the 2011 Census of India, has a population of 2,438.

Although Badrinath is home to only so few, in the summer of 2006, the holy town received about 600,000 pilgrims up from 90,000 in 1961. The year 2011 brought 981,000 visitors and their number crossed a million in 2018, when 1,058,490 reached Badrinath, to pay homage to God Vishnu. The equally famous but much smaller nearby township of Kedarnath, with a population of 612 in 2011, saw over a million pilgrims too in 2019, when 1,000,821 of them landed to make obeisance to God Shiva or Kedarnath. Biomass burning, as stated earlier, could be "the primary driver behind carbon-induced melting of glaciers" in this Himalayan region too. [48, 49, 50]

A hundred years ago, no more than a few dozen souls lived here and barely a few hundred came on pilgrimage, and most importantly, they all travelled on foot. Badrinath was then the site of the holy temple and a few nondescript little dwellings, where a few sadhus lived and so was Kedarnath. In 2021, Badrinath is a sprawling township with many luxury hotels and guest houses offering spacious accommodation to these armies of tourists and pilgrims. The construction boom, moreover, shows no signs of abating. Fifty years ago, there was virtually no vehicular traffic and now the roads to Badrinath and the nearby holy towns of Kedarnath and Gangotri are choked full of armadas of buses, trucks, jeeps and cars. These modern dragons, spew obnoxious hot gases all the way up from their origin in the townships of Rishikesh and Haridwar, at the Himalayan foothills, some 300 km away. These vigorous human activities are causing significant amounts of local warming.

Each human body is a source of heat and millions trampling the sites of Badrinath, Kedarnath and Gangotri every year, give off more heat than a giant blast furnace. The heat is enough to scare the glaciers into a retreat.

I wonder where these millions of god-loving fellow Hindu sisters and brothers of mine were, when the British ruled India to a catastrophic destruction? Had this many stampeded on to Her Majesty Queen Victoria's viceroys, the all-powerful and the all-oppressive British Raj would have beaten a hasty retreat, a full half a century before 1947, and what to talk of the poor Gangotri! What chance does the Gangotri have to stand her ground, against such a sustained onslaught by such a multitude, for so long, but to retreat! I am amazed that she is still there! And let us not blame this heat on global warming for the simple reason that when a room gets warm because of an electrical heater switched on, the warming is local and not due to global causes. I have not mentioned yet, the inimical effects of the massive deforestation on the glaciers, in these areas and in the rest of the Himalaya.

Badrinath, Kedarnath, Gangotri and all the nearby townships now stand on forestland stripped bare. These human habitations were much smaller a century ago and were surrounded by thick forests, which are now completely gone. The scale of deforestation here is absolute, full one hundred percent. My readers, you may be surprised to know the extent of deforestation in the Himalaya as a whole. The dense forests have been, so denuded, in so many areas that vast patches of deserts have emerged to replace the woods. A study published as early as 2001, on the deforestation of the Himalaya in Himachal Pradesh, using remote sensing techniques, showed the forest cover reduced to a mere 17.15%.[51] This result is perhaps true for the entire Himalaya and what a shame that is for us all in India!

Forests invite rains and as we destroy the forests, the Himalaya refuses to attract the monsoonal precipitations. The local warming, moreover, that we generate because of the millions of tourists and pilgrims in the townships of Badrinath, Kedarnath and Gangotri, chases the monsoon clouds away. And the consequence is that at a time when the monsoon is getting more vigorous due to the intensification of global warming, certain pockets of the Himalaya like the Gangotri glacier may receive lesser precipitation forcing her to retreat. This is comparable to the paradox of Plockton that I elaborated on, earlier.

The retreating Gangotri and the need for creation of a series of glacial lakes

Glaciers scour the ground they travel on, and transport the unassorted mixture of clay, silt, sand, gravel and boulder, known as glacial till, they generate. Glaciers deposit the till along their flanks, as they proceed, often forming substantial embankments known as lateral moraines. These glacial rocks and debris, when deposited at the snout where the glacier ends, form the terminal moraine. These moraines, terminal and lateral, often impound glacial meltwater from the retreating glaciers to create glacial lakes, in the void left behind. There exist many natural glacial lakes in the Himalaya as well as in other temperate and polar regions of the world. In the last few decades, in fact, many glacial lakes have been forming at the termini of the glaciers in the Bhutan-Himalaya.

Terminal moraines that act as natural dams for glacial lakes are inherently weak. They often, because of natural reasons again, break, causing glacial lake outbursts. The ensuing floods are known as glacial lake outburst (GLO) floods and are a common hazard in the Himalaya. Such GLO floods are quite devastating and have wreaked havoc in the past in India, Nepal and China. Consolidation of glacial till of the moraines, particularly that of the terminal moraines, not only reduces the risk of glacial lake outbursts, but also helps in the formation of relatively stable glacial lakes. Formation of a series of such lakes at suitable locations in the Himalayan valleys where glaciers are in retreat, particularly at the Gangotri, would create sources for groundwater as well as surface water flow. In this context I remember Professor K.S. Valdiya[52, 53, 54], a much-respected eminent Himalayan geologist, who I had the good fortune of interacting with, during my tenure with the Department of Science and Technology. Dr. Valdiya had suggested the construction of a number of small-scale gravity dams, what I call micro-dams, across the upper reaches of the Bhagirathi, to impound the meltwater from the Gangotri glacier in a series of reservoirs. His decades old suggestion should be carried out to conserve the precious water. The small reservoirs may quite unwittingly attract more precipitation to the region too.

The concept of creation of a series of glacial lakes in the Himalaya at high altitudes, need not scare the extremely powerful antidam lobby of India, as there already exist many such vast natural bodies of water at considerable elevations, say over 4,000 m above the MSL. I would name a few here, such as Dashaur lake near the Rohtang pass at 4,200 m, Manimahesh lake in Chamba of Himachal Pradesh at 4,200 m, Tsomgo lake in Sikkim at 3,700 m and the largest lake Pangong Tso at 4,600 m. Pangong Tso located in Ladakh is up to 8 km wide and stretches over 134 km.

Pangong Tso, incidentally, became international headline during the India China border skirmishes of early 2020, particularly so after the sudden surprise attack by the Chinese soldiers on their unsuspecting counterparts. The attack took place in the night of June 15-16, 2020 in Galwan, on the shores of Pangong Tso that killed some 20 Indian soldiers.[55] This is the single biggest blunder committed by the Communist Party of China (CPI) in recent years. With this utterly unnecessary and unprovoked brutal attack, the CPI wiped clean all the goodwill the two countries had built in the past decades through trade and commerce, bilateral treaties and tourism. This attack came at a time, when the collective Indian memory of the previous Chinese attack on India, some six decades earlier in November 1962, was beginning to fade. The people of India will now take at least another sixty years to forgive China for this horrendous aggression. The Indian soldiers in Galwan, by the way, regrouped instantly to mount a counterattack that killed over 40 Chinese soldiers and stunned the CPI to silence for good.

The other large Himalayan lakes are Mansarovar spread over 320 square km, at an altitude of 4,600 m, above the MSL and the nearby 70 square km Rakshastal at 4,750 m. I would also like to add that these lakes are often the sources of many Himalayan rivers, like Mansarovar is for the Sindhu. Should a series of lakes be created on the upper reaches of the Bhagirathi, all the way to the Gangotri, they will impound enough water and replenish the groundwater table enough to prevent the Ganga from becoming seasonal. Glacier meltwater, incidentally, constitutes only a minor proportion, between 5% and 10%, of the overall runoff of the Ganga. The meltwater, however, is crucial for maintaining the Ganga's flow during the pre-monsoon summer months. Water impounded in the glacial lakes could well substitute for the glacier meltwater in making the Ganga perennial. The last few decades saw nature forming thousands of new lakes high in the Himalaya from the rising yield of meltwater from the glaciers.[56]

The legend of King Bhagirath persuading the Goddess Ganga to descend from Her heavenly Himalayan abode to save the famine-stricken multitudes on the plains, might not be an allegory, after all, it may well contain some elements of truth. The legend could well be the historical account of a massive civil engineering project King Bhagirath undertook to break the terminal moraine of a glacial lake to channel the water to irrigate the tabescent plains parched by a prolonged drought. Many such glacial lakes formed by retreating glaciers, after the end of the last ice age, 18,000 years ago, and are forming naturally even today. King Bhagirath utilized the water by breaching a terminal moraine then and let us harness the water for rejuvenating the Ganga by reinforcing the moraines now.

Need for massive afforestation of the Himalaya now

The occurrence of the Himalayan glaciers at various altitudes depends on a range of conditions that include total annual precipitation, altitude, latitude, topography, aspect and human interference. Glaciers in the eastern Himalaya occur at higher altitudes compared with glaciers in the central or western Himalaya. For example, the lowest average elevation of glaciers in Arunachal Pradesh in the east is at 4,350 m above the MSL, in Garhwal and Kumaun in the center it is at 4,000 m, while in Kashmir in the west it is at 3,700 m. Now due to an increase in the average Himalayan air temperature, anywhere between 0.6°C and 1.0°C, since the mid-1970s because of global warming, the snowline, which is the lower limit of perpetual snow, will move to a higher altitude. As the snowline migrates higher, the Himalayan treeline, the altitude above the MSL beyond which trees cease to grow, will rise higher too, thus making vastly larger areas available for the growth of forests.

With the intensification of global warming, an increase in rainfall in the Himalaya is a distinct possibility. As nature, moreover, provides a larger area for forests to grow by raising the treeline, a massive and sincere campaign for afforestation must be undertaken now, before the Himalayan forests lose their ability to regenerate. As a part of this afforestation campaign, every pilgrim as well as tourist, must plant a sapling of a native tree and must pay a certain amount of money towards the management of the forests. A great deal of care should be taken in afforesting the lateral moraines or the sidewalls, which traditionally supported abundant vegetation as they contained higher quantities of soil moisture. Successful regeneration of the Himalayan forests will reduce local warming, attract higher rainfall, lead to a higher retention of water in the aquifers and will contribute to a steadier supply of the runoff in the Ganga.

Conclusion

The Gangotri glacier may well disappear in the future, due to a lethal combination of massive deforestation, population pressure, the influx of pilgrims and tourists, and local and global warming. But if we start caring for the Ganga from now on, which would involve creation of a series of glacial lakes, undertaking a massive program of afforestation right from the foothills up to the elevated treeline in the Himalaya, taking drastic measures to reduce the local warming and reducing the pilgrim and tourist pressure, she will rejuvenate herself to a great extent and will continue to remain perennial. Are we resolved to look after her?

I conclude this chapter by citing the Goddess Ganga from the Mahabharata when She says, 'I will stay as long as you continue to address me respectfully by my proper name and I will leave should you use any abusive word to call me by'. This statement perhaps always had a deeper meaning and meant that the Ganga will flow perennially, if treated properly with respect and affection, but would cease to flow if mistreated. With the massive deforestation of her catchment, metaphorically, we have disrobed her to her utter degradation. Deforestation has triggered a reduction in monsoonal precipitation and lowered the groundwater reserves and the two have combined to reduce the steady round the year runoff in the Ganga and her tributaries. Deforestation, moreover, has accelerated the loss of topsoil and has increased the frequency and magnitude of the Himalayan landslides, which have collectively supplied a vast quantum of sediments that have choked the channels of flow. And the final humiliation we have caused her is by force-feeding her with vast quantities of untreated sewage discharge, virtually along the entire length of her course. With our mistreatment we have made the Mother Ganga ill. She is now showing her annoyance through the recession of the Gangotri glacier. It is time we wake up and start caring for her now on. If we do so, she will regain her health and will remain perennial, she will not leave us.

Apathy, inaction, resignation and despair are ruinous. Let mass action commence to keep the Ganga perennial. Let us rejuvenate the Ganga to save this land.

Chapter Four
Management of the Hirakud Dam on the Mahanadi

The first Prime Minister of India, Pandit Jawaharlal Nehru, invited a fifty-year-old Italian film director Roberto Gastone Zeffiro Rossellini to come to India to make some documentaries, on various aspects of the newly independent country.[1] Rossellini had earned a great reputation for himself as the most prominent director of the Italian neorealist cinema. He came in December 1956 and was charmed by the wealth of the colourful sights and sounds of everyday life in Bombay. Rossellini was even more charmed by a young attractive script writer, Sonali Senroy Dasgupta,[2] who was in her mid-twenties. Sonali was the mother of a five-year-old child and the wife of a most talented Bengali documentary film director, Harisadhan Dasgupta, whose scripts a young Satyajit Ray wrote. Besides seducing Sonali, Rossellini, then already married to the most famous Swedish Hollywood actress Ingrid Bergman, did make a few documentaries and one of them titled, "India – Matri Bhumi"[3] documented the construction of the Hirakud Dam. The narrative of the documentary at one point says that the Hirakud Dam was planned to liberate the poverty-stricken people of Odisha by breaking "the cycle of flood and famine" they routinely endured. The vast stretch of 4.8 km long and 195 m high concrete portion of the 25.8 km long dam, the documentary said, was to become "a monument to inscribe the names of all those who died in floods in Odisha" because of the Mahanadi, whose flow "was comparable to that of the Ganga". I write all these to remind you my readers that the Mahanadi was one hell of a mighty river and killed thousands of people. The Mahanadi was both a boon and a bane and not what you see now in 2021.

Inception of the Hirakud Dam project

Following a most devastating flood of 1937, Father of the Nation Mahatma Gandhi invited the most preeminent Indian civil engineer of the time, Sir M. Visvesvaraya, to devise some measures to control the Mahanadi floods. The centenarian Sir Visvesvaraya, in his 172 pages long autobiography titled "Memoirs of my working life"[4], published in 1951 in Bangalore, mentioned the invitation from Mahatma Gandhi. Sir Mokshagundam Visvesvaraya KCIE, by then, had designed a successful flood protection system for the City of Hyderabad, an achievement that had earned him celebrity status. As a Chief Engineer of the State of Mysore and then as the Diwan or the Prime Minister of the same princely state, he was the architect of the Krishna Raja Sagara Dam near Mysuru city. So great was his contributions towards the development of the state of Mysore that he was affectionately called the "Father of Modern Mysore State". This great son of India had also been knighted, Commander of the Order of the Indian Empire (KCIE), by the British, in 1915, for his contributions to the public good. Independent India would award him with the highest civilian honor of the Bharat Ratna in 1955.[5]

In his report of 1937, Sir Visvesvaraya recommended "investigation of the feasibility of constructing flood control reservoirs on...the Mahanadi..." and stated that "reservoirs if constructed will be of value to hold up the floods temporarily and release them gradually..." He also expressed his apprehension "that on account of their cost ... there is small prospect of the idea materializing in the near future". He, however, emphasized, "If a reservoir is constructed, it may prove useful in several other ways as well – for extending irrigation, generating electric power, etc. Once floods come under effective control, the whole area may be transformed into a prosperous region."[6] (p. 8-9 of June 1947 Report on Mahanadi Valley Development, Hirakud Dam Project of Central Waterways, Irrigation and Navigation Commission of India).[6]

Subsequently, Sir Visvesvaraya visited the "flood-ridden" parts of Odisha for the first time in April 1939 and was pleased to note that his proposal "for flood protection by constructing storage reservoirs in the upper reaches of the rivers had received some consideration, but he appreciated the difficulties regarding the construction of these because of ... poor financial condition of Orissa Province"[6] (p. 9 of June 1947 Report). Incidentally, Sir Visvesvaraya, born in 1860, was then 79 and was 9 years older than Gandhiji. In that pre-independence India, the Indian National Congress had formed a Government in Odisha, headed by Mr. Biswanath Das,[7, 8] who stayed in office between 19 July 1937 and 4 November 1939. This patriotic visionary Mr. Biswanath Das was the second Prime Minister of Odisha and had, in fact, formally approved Sir Visvesvaraya's visit to report remedies to control the floods of the Mahanadi. Another visionary, Mr. Nityananda Kanungo, was then the Minister for Public Works of the Government of Odisha and had extended a formal invitation to and had coordinated the visit of, Sir Visvesvaraya.[4]

Thereafter in 1945, the problem of flood control was forwarded to the Government of India, who in turn passed it on to Mr. A.N. Khosla, the Chairman of Central Waterways, Irrigation and Navigation Commission for further investigation. Mr. Ajudhia Nath Khosla, himself an eminent civil engineer, visited Odisha in May 1945 and recommended a revival of the proposal of Sir Visvesvaraya to construct a dam on the Mahanadi to create a reservoir, particularly so, "in the light of successful experiments in multipurpose river valley developments carried out elsewhere e.g., the Boulder Dam Project, the TVA, the Columbia Basin Development, the Central Valley Development in the USA."[6] A "Conference held on the 8th of November 1945, at Cuttack" in Odisha, "under the Chairmanship of Dr. B.R. Ambedkar", then "Member for Labour in the Government of India", decided to "thoroughly and expeditiously" investigate "the potentialities of the

Mahanadi river for unified multiple-purpose development, e.g. for flood control, irrigation, navigation, and hydro-electric power"[6]. (p. 9-11 of June 1947 Report).

Dr. Ambedkar, subsequently, would become the Chairman of the committee to draft the Constitution of India and would be famously known as "the Father of the Indian Constitution".

The Central Waterways, Irrigation and Navigation Commission (CWINC) of India was entrusted with the responsibility for all surveys and investigations for the Hirakud Dam project. The Governor of Odisha, Sir Hawthorne Lewis, on the 15th of March 1946, laid the foundation stone of the Hirakud Dam. A detailed project report by CWINC was produced in June 1947. The Report in its Summary and Recommendations stated, "The water of Mahanadi, if fully harnessed can, besides affording complete flood protection, to the delta areas, irrigate over 20 million acres of land, generate 4 million KW of power, provide a navigable waterway, with a minimum draught of 9 to 10 feet, extending 380 miles from the border of Central Provinces to the sea, make it possible to develop a deep sea port for Orissa ..., create extensive lakes to serve as sea plane base and afford facilities for fish culture, recreation etc."[6] (p. V of June 1947 Report).

Construction of the dam
Prime Minister Nehru laid the first batch of concrete on the 12th of April 1948 that marked the commencement of construction. The construction was completed in 1953 and the Hirakud Dam was formally inaugurated on the 13th of January 1957 by Prime Minister Nehru. Irrigation and power generation that had already commenced in 1956, achieved full potential in 1966. The Hirakud Dam project, incidentally, was the first major project of independent India, completed at a total cost of Rs100 crore (Rs1000 million).[9] The primary purpose of this multipurpose dam was flood control and

the secondary functions were irrigation, power generation, navigation, pisciculture and recreation.

The Hirakud Dam continues to be the single most important piece of infrastructure of the state of Odisha. The Hirakud reservoir has been faithfully irrigating around 155,635 hectares of land for the summer crop, khariff, and 108,385 hectares for the winter crop, rabi, every year and generates about 300 MW of electricity per annum. The Hirakud Dam has been largely successful in fulfilling its primary role of flood control and has succeeded in preventing or reducing the severity of floods in 24 out of 30 occasions.[10]

Life of the Hirakud reservoir, as stated in the Mahanadi Valley Development, Hirakud Dam Project, Volume - 1 – Report of June 1947, on page 30 is "for purposes of the project, to be on the conservative side, taken as a 100 years."[6] Considering that the dam was completed in 1953, the Hirakud is now some 70 years old. Shall we worry a little for this elderly dam? Could the Hirakud Dam collapse? The answer is yes. Having raised the possibility of a collapse, I seek a patient hearing from you my readers of my arguments presented below.

Major dam collapses of the world

The International Humanitarian Law, incidentally, regards dams as "installations containing dangerous forces",[10.a] due to the enormous disaster a failure can deliver on people and their environment. Dams have collapsed all over the world, causing enormous losses of lives and property. In the first decade of the twenty-first century, between the years 2000 and 2009, more than 200 dams collapsed worldwide. Please allow me to start with a brief description of a few catastrophic dam collapses, starting with a calamitous one in China.

Collapse of the Banqiao Dam and the Shimantan Reservoir Dam in China

In 1950, immediately after the unpleasant experience of a catastrophic inundation, the Government of China undertook a program to control the Huai river i.e. the Huang He or the Yellow river system by constructing a series of dams for flood prevention. The secondary purpose of the dams was irrigation and power generation. Under this program two major dams, the Banqiao Dam on the Ru river and Shimantan Reservoir Dam on the Hong river, in addition to a large number of smaller dams, were constructed between April 1951 and 1952. The storage capacity of the 116 m high Banqiao Dam was 492 million cubic m, out of which 375 million cubic m were kept in reservation to impound flood waters. The Shimantan Reservoir Dam had a storage capacity of 94 million cubic m, out of which 70 million cubic m were reserved for arresting floodwater. [11, 12, 13]

The initial construction of the Banqiao Dam had some design flaws that led to the appearance of cracks in the dam as well as in the sluice gates. Following the advice of Soviet engineers, both the dams were reinforced and expanded and were then termed 'iron dams', which meant that the dams could never be broken, pretty much like the Titanic was termed 'unsinkable'. The Banqiao Dam now apparently stood to protect 'once a thousand-year flood', which meant preventing a flood resulting from a downpour of 53 cm of rain, over a period of three days. The Shimantan Reservoir Dam was ready too, to protect 'once a five-hundred-year flood', which meant preventing a flood resulting from heavy rainfall of 48 cm, over a period of three days. [11, 12, 13]

After the construction of these two major dams, many smaller dams were built, initially confined to the mountains. In 1958, however, Chinese Vice Premier Tan Zhenlin, against the professional expert advice of the hydrologist Chen Xing, decreed that the smaller dams be constructed on the plains in order to give priority to irrigation. This arbitrary shift in priority by the orders of the ignorant politician, despite the protests of the knowledgeable technocrat, led to the construction of a huge reservoir on the plains. The hydrologist Chen Xing was banished to a remote part of China, as a punishment and experienced further humiliation in 1961, when he was labelled 'a right-wing opportunist' and was purged. [11, 12, 13]

At the beginning of August 1975, an unusual weather pattern caused a set of storms that poured about one meter of rain within a space of three days. The downpours started on the 5th of August, when the first storm dumped 45 cm of rain, which was 40% higher than the previously recorded fall. The second heavy rainfall of 16 hours came on the 6th of August and was followed by the third downpour that lasted 13 hours on the 7th of August. The Banqiao and Shimantan reservoirs that were designed to handle a maximum rainfall of 50 cm, over a period of three days, were filled to capacity by the 8th of August 1975. A little after midnight by 12.30 am, floodwater rose 40 cm above the crest of the Shimantan Dam, and it collapsed. Within 5 hours, 120 million cubic m of water went rushing down the Hong river. After half an hour, around 1 am, floodwater rose above the crest of the Banqiao Dam and it collapsed. A 6 m high wall of flood wave with a 12 km wide front, rushed down the Ru river emptying over 600 million cubic m of water. The floodwater raced down at a speed of about 50 km per hour, comparable to the speed of fast-moving cars on a highway. [11, 12, 13]

Collapse of the Banqiao and Shimantan dams, led to a catastrophic collapse of 62 dams downstream. The floodwaters ravaged more than a million hectares of farmland spread over 29 districts. According to the Hydrology Department of Henan Province of China, 26,000 people died from flooding and 145,000 perished during subsequent epidemics and famine. The actual number of fatalities was probably much higher than reported. This disaster made some 6 million buildings collapse and a total of around 11 million people were affected.[11, 12, 13]

The hydrologist, Chen Xing, who had opposed the dam building plans on the plains, was rehabilitated instantly. He was rushed to Beijing to urge the communist high command, to order the bombing of many of the smaller dams for the floodwaters to drain.

Collapse of the St. Francis Dam in California

The St. Francis Dam was a concrete gravity arch dam, constructed between 1924 and 1926, to create a reservoir to supply water to the City of Los Angeles. The 59 m high dam across San Francisquito Canyon, 64 km north-west of Los Angeles, created a reservoir of a storage capacity of 47 million cubic m. Soon after the construction of the dam, throughout 1926 and 1927, cracks kept appearing in the dam and its abutments. Some of the cracks, moreover, started leaking muddy water. On the 7th of March 1928, as the reservoir was filled to capacity for the very first time, more cracks appeared. Only five days later, on the 12th of March 1928, three minutes before midnight, the dam collapsed and 45 million cubic m of water that formed a 38 m high wall, rushed down the canyon destroying everything on its path. The flood wave raced south to the Pacific Ocean at Montalvo, 87 km away. The flood was 3 km wide and travelled at a speed of 8 km per hour as it reached the ocean at 5.30 am. The floods killed more than 600 people and it is remembered as the second worst natural disaster of California, after the San Francisco earthquake of 1906.[14]

The dam had broken into several large pieces. The dam's failure is attributed to the unstable basement, upon which it stood and the poor design of the dam, which was excessively tall without adequate support.

Collapse of the South Fork Dam in Pennsylvania

The 22 m high and 284 m long South Fork Dam was constructed, between 1838 and 1853, by the Commonwealth of Pennsylvania to create a huge artificial body of water that came to be known as the Lake Conemaugh. Following unprecedented incessant rainfall, on May 31, 1889, this earthen dam collapsed catastrophically releasing 20 million cubic m of water that rushed 23 km downstream, causing massive floods in Johnstown and killed 2,209 people. This constituted the largest loss of lives in the United States then.[15, 16]

Tsunami at the Vajont Dam in Italy

This dam, one of the tallest in the world with a height of 262 m, was built on the Vajont river in Erto e Casso municipality that is located 100 km north of Venice. Conceived in the 1920s, the dam was constructed between 1957 and 1960 and created a large reservoir in a geologically unstable landslide prone area. During the initial filling, on October 9, 1963, a landslide fell into the reservoir causing a 250 m high megatsunami that spilled some 50 million cubic m of water onto the adjacent towns and villages lying below. The tsunami did not destroy the dam, which remained intact and retained nearly two thirds of the volume of the storage water. This huge natural disaster caused 1,910 fatalities and the dam now stands abandoned.[17]

Collapse of Sempor Dam in Indonesia

This embankment dam on the Sempor river in Central Java Province of Indonesia was built in 1967 for multiple purposes, the main purposes being flood control, irrigation, drinking water supply, power generation and recreation. The 1 MW power plant was located at the base of the dam. An embankment dam, by the way, is typically built by the compaction of a mound of composite materials of soil, sand, silt, clay and rocks and is inherently very vulnerable to any incidence of overflow of water above its crest. On the 29th of November 1967, water from flash floods flowing into the artificial reservoir overtopped the Sempor Dam causing its failure. The resultant massive wave of water killed 160 people in three towns below and caused extensive damages to infrastructure. The dam was subsequently rebuilt, and the construction finished in 1978; the power plant was commissioned in 1980.[18, 19]

Dam failure and the Kurenivka Mudslide in Ukraine in the Soviet Union

Following heavy rains, an earthen dam constructed in a ravine to contain the loam pulp dump of brick factories, near the Babi Yar mass murder site, collapsed on 13 March 1961 near Kiev, the capital city of Ukraine in the erstwhile Soviet Union. The dam failure released a vast quantum of pulp sludge, mud, human remains and water that raced down the steep slope of the hillside on to the streets of Kiev.[20] The mudslide overwhelmed the low-lying Kurenivka residential area and the total volume of pulp settled on one of the streets was of the order of 600 thousand m^3 with a depth of some 4 m. The initial official reports stated only 145 fatalities but a 2012 comprehensive Ukrainian study by Smoliy, Goryak and Danilenko[21] estimated the death toll to be between 1,500 and 2,000 that the communist authorities never admitted. No notification of the disaster was ever published by the communists, who did their best to cover up the horrendous tragedy. Subsequent investigations, in the wake of the calamity, led to the conviction of some construction engineers and managers, who were accused of poor design and maintenance of the earthen dam that had contained loam pulp pumped from the brick factories for ten years.

State I must, my appreciation for the valor of the valiant unsung heroes of the 120 Detached Engineering Battalion and the Anti-gas Regiment of the Local Anti-Aircraft Defence soldiers of the Soviet Army, in the Kyiv Military District, for conducting the rescue and recovery operations. These operations were led by a Soviet Army Military engineering Colonel Ivan Ustinovich Kharchenko[22], who had long been decorated a Hero of the Soviet Union and had received the Gold Star and the Order of Lenin during World War II for personally defusing more than 50,000 explosives, including bombs, mines and shells.

Mention I must, that Babi Yar was a ravine on the hillside that was used as the site for many horrendous massacres committed by the Nazi German forces during World War II, the first being the extermination of all Jews of Kiev on 29-30 September of 1941, when 33,771 of them were massacred. Subsequently, Soviet prisoners of war, communists, Ukrainian nationalists and Roma or Romani Gypsies who, incidentally, trace their origin to the north-western part of the Indian subcontinent of the fifth century CE, were massacred. Babi Yar ravine held between 100,000 and 150,000 human bodies, massacred during the German occupation during World War II. The massacres came to an end only after the Soviet Red Army liberated Kiev on 22 December 1943.[23]

In 1962, the Ukrainian Communist Party announced the levelling of the Babi Yar ravine to establish a park on the site of the massacres.[23]

Bombing destruction of the Möhne Reservoir Dam in Germany

Between 1908 and 1913, two dams were constructed, one each on the two rivers, Heve and Möhne, to substantially enhance the existing storage capacity, by as much as three times, to supply water for human consumption as well as for industry, in the rapidly growing Ruhr industrial area. The reservoir so created, some 45 km east of the City of Dortmund in the state of North Rhine-Westphalia, had a holding capacity of 135 million cubic m of water. The reservoir provided drinking water, pure water for steel making, water for the canal transport system, water to generate electricity at a hydroelectric power station and controlled flood. The power station, at the base of the Möhne Reservoir Dam, generated 5.1 MW of electricity.

When commissioned, this reservoir was the largest in Europe and had displaced some 140 homesteads, home to 700 people.

This multipurpose reservoir dam complex, particularly its dams, were "identified as important strategic targets" by the British Air Ministry, before the commencement of World War II. During the war, Squadron No 617 of the Royal Air Force of Britain, dropped purpose built bouncing bombs on the Möhne Reservoir Dam and on the Edersee Dam, located in the nearby state of Hesse on 16-17 May 1943 to destroy them. The bombing caused a huge breach, of some 77 m by 22 m, in the Möhne Reservoir Dam and the Edersee Dam was damaged too. Destruction of the dams released vast quantities of water that caused catastrophic flooding in the Ruhr and Eder valleys. The inundation destroyed the power plant at the Möhne Reservoir Dam and the power plant at the Edersee Dam that generated 16 MW of electricity. The huge flood wave inflicted over 800 fatalities on the small township of Neheim-Hüsten in the Ruhr valley, whose total death toll stood at 1,579 that included some 600 German civilians and 1,026 Soviet civilian labourers including 526 women.[24, 25, 26, 27, 28, 29, 30]

Notable dam collapses in India
India has witnessed five notable dam collapses and they are:

1. Gohna lake dam in Garhwal, collapsed on 25 August 1894, due to the failure of the naturally created landslide dam that was inherently weak killing 1 person.
2. Tigra Dam in Gwalior, collapsed on 19 August 1917, due to leakages of water through the sandstone foundation killing at least 1,000 people.
3. Panshet Dam built on the Ambi river, near Pune in Maharashtra, in the late 1950s, for drinking water supply and irrigation, failed on 12 July 1961, killing at least 1,000 people. Former Secretary of Maharashtra State Irrigation Department, Mr. Madhukar Deshmukh, who was involved in the construction, in an interview

some fifty years after the tragedy, mentioned that an outlet of the 200 ft high fully earthen dam to a reservoir downstream was created at its base. Deshmukh explained, "Ideally, the arch of the conduit should have been made from RCC (Reinforced Cement Concrete). However, in those days, steel was in short supply and we were forced to use concrete blocks instead." "The force of the water was so great that it managed to dislodge the concrete blocks, which resulted in the earthen portion of the dam giving way. Had RCC been used, the accident could certainly have been averted."[31]

I think that the civil engineers who constructed the dam understood their concrete and RCC well, but did not understand water, and utterly underestimated the enormous pressure it can exert.

4. Machchu-2 Dam of Morbi in Gujarat, built on Machhu river, failed on 11 August 1979, killing at least 5,000 people. Following an intense rainfall, some 16,307 m³ per second of water started flowing into a dam designed to handle an inflow of 5,000 m³ per second, causing two huge breaches. The 762 m long breach on the left embankment and the 365 m long one on the right, caused a catastrophic dam collapse. Within 20 minutes of the failure, waters between 3.7 and 9.1 m in height, flooded the township of Morbi situated 5 km downstream, causing massive destruction.

5. Iware Dam in Ratnagiri district of Maharashtra, collapsed on 2 July 2019, due to heavy rains, causing water to flow over the dam, killing 23 people in the habitations downstream.[28]

Deliberate destruction of large dams constitutes crimes against humanity

The deliberate destruction of a 135 million cubic m capacity Möhne Reservoir Dam, utterly devastated the Ruhr valley and imagine the devastation that would occur following a purposeful destruction of a much larger dam like the Hirakud, whose reservoir capacity at 5.896 billion cubic m, i.e. 5.896 km^3, is almost 45 times bigger. A deliberate destruction of Hirakud, say for example during a war with either China or Pakistan, would utterly devastate the entire Mahanadi valley and the vast Mahanadi delta. The fatalities will be in millions. India has a large number of dammed reservoirs holding over a billion cubic m of water each and they all need protection from deliberate destruction.

Please allow me to mention the 16 largest reservoirs in India with a capacity of greater than or equal to 1,000,000 acre feet i.e. 1.2 billion cubic m or 1.2 km^3 and they are as follows: Rihand Dam of Uttar Pradesh (4.3 km^3), Idduki Dam of Kerala (1.996 km^3), Jayakwadi Dam of Maharashtra (2.909 km^3), Ujjani Dam of Maharashtra (3.14 km^3), Koyna Dam of Maharashtra (2.7974 km^3), Indira Sagar Dam of Madhya Pradesh (12.2 km^3), Sriram Sagar Dam of Telangana (3.172 km^3), Nagarjuna Sagar Dam of Andhra Pradesh and Telangana (11.561 km^3), Srisailam Dam of Andhra Pradesh and Telangana (8.722 km^3), Somasila Dam of Andhra Pradesh (2.20862 km^3), Bhakra Dam of Himachal Pradesh (9.62 km^3), Hirakud Dam of Odisha (5.896 km^3), Mettur Dam of Tamil Nadu (2.64 km^3), Sardar Sarovar Dam of Gujarat (9.5 km^3), Ukai Dam of Gujarat (7.41 km^3) and Tehri Dam of Uttarakhand (4 km^3).[32]

Proposal to protect major dams by Ballistic Missile Defence (BMD) Program

I propose that all these dams be protected by the Ballistic Missile Defence (BMD) Program of the country. Going by the reports emerging in January 2020, India has developed the capabilities to install ballistic missiles to intercept incoming missiles fired by any hostile enemy country.[33] The Government of India must install the BMD systems, around each of the above-mentioned dams on a priority basis.

Drafting of a covenant for Protection of World Dams and Reservoirs

I propose that the Government of India must negotiate and sign covenants with both Pakistan and China, explicitly stating not to attack each other's dams and reservoirs, neither during peacetime nor during any wars.

Dams and reservoirs are a heritage of humanity and need protection. Dams and their associated reservoirs, particularly the ones with a storage capacity of more than one hundred million cubic m need to be protected to avoid catastrophic failures that could endanger millions of human lives.

I, therefore, propose that a draft should be prepared for the Protection of the World Dams and Reservoirs, perhaps by the Ministry of Water Resources of the Government of India, along the lines of the United Nations (UN) Educational, Scientific and Cultural Organization (UNESCO) Convention Concerning the Protection of the World Cultural and Natural Heritage that was adopted by the United Nations General Conference at its seventeenth session in Paris, on 16 November 1972.[34][35, 36]

Such a draft, on the Protection of the World Dams and Reservoirs, should be tabled at the United Nations for discussions, to create a Covenant for the Protection of the World Dams and Reservoirs. After the enactment of the covenant, the World Dams and Reservoirs will enjoy legal protection, by an international convention administered by the United Nations.

Deliberate destruction of dams during a war be considered war crimes

Deliberate destruction of any dam with an associated reservoir over one hundred million cubic m capacity, either during an armed conflict or during peace time, by either an enemy nation or by a terror outfit, to harm human habitations, should be considered as war crimes and as crimes against humanity.

Rome Statute of the International Criminal Court in Article 8 titled War Crimes in sub-section 2.b.ii. states, "Intentionally directing attacks against civilian objects, that is, objects which are not military objectives" and in sub-section 2.b.iv. states, "Intentionally launching an attack in the knowledge that such attack will cause incidental loss of life or injury to civilians or damage to civilian objects or widespread, long-term and severe damage to the natural environment which would be clearly excessive in relation to the concrete and direct overall military advantage anticipated",[37] constitute war crimes. These articles could be applied to deliberate destruction of dams and reservoirs, over one hundred million cubic m capacity.

Salient features of the Hirakud Dam

The Hirakud Dam is one of the longest dams in the world and is a composite structure of earth, concrete and masonry. The main concrete dam that spans the two abutment hills, called *dungri* in the local lingo, is 195 m high and 4.8 km long and is flanked by 21 km long earthen dykes on either side. The overall length of the composite dam is 25.8 km that has created a reservoir, of 743 square km, at full capacity. This reservoir is the largest artificial lake in Asia, with a 640 km long shoreline. The original storage capacity of the reservoir was 5,818 million cubic m (5.8 km³), which in 1988 was revised to 5,375 million cubic m, and now in 2020 is probably around 4,800 million cubic m or even less. This 25% or so reduction in the storage capacity is due to the accumulation of sediments in the reservoir. The FRL/MWL or the Full Reservoir Level (FRL) and the Maximum Water Level (MWL) of the reservoir balance is maintained at 192.024 m or 630 ft. The Dead Storage Level (DSL) of the reservoir lies at 179.830 m or 590 ft and thus the dead portion of the storage capacity, i.e. water that cannot flow out of the reservoir so is not available, hence technically dead, is 1,800 million cubic m. The average annual inflow of water to the reservoir, fed by the two rivers the Mahanadi and the Ib, is 37 million cubic m.[38, 39, 40, 9, 6]

What can trigger a collapse of the Hirakud Dam
Unlike the St. Francis Dam of the US that collapsed in 1928, the Hirakud Dam stands on a relatively stable geological foundation. People, moreover, claim that Hirakud is located in a seismically stable peninsular India. Yes, unlike California and Japan, which are seismically very active and unstable, peninsular India is relatively stable, but is by no means absolutely free from seismic disturbances or earthquakes. Prof. Dr. S.M. Ramasamy, a former Director of the venerable Geological Survey of India (GSI) and a former Vice Chancellor of The Gandhigram Rural Institute (Deemed to be University) in his article, "Remote sensing and active tectonics of South India", has outlined a vast number of reasonably active fault systems that crisscross the peninsular India.[41, 42] These faults, which are like cracks in the earth's crust, incidentally, are the places that experience crustal movements that cause earthquakes. The Mahanadi, moreover, flows in a vast 400 km long trench like depression, some 50 to 80 km wide, bound by two deep fault systems on either side. In geology, this particular linear depression is called the Mahanadi Graben that opened up some 120 million years ago and continues to be an area prone to crustal movements, hence can experience earthquakes.[43] Graben, by the way, means trench in German and this Mahanadi Graben hosts the Hirakud Dam.

And let it be known that an earthquake can strike any part of this world.

Reservoir induced earthquake at the Koyna Dam in Maharashtra in India
On the 11th of December 1967, a strong earthquake struck Koyna, situated some 241 km away from Mumbai and located very much in the peninsular India. The India Meteorological Department (IMD) and the Central Water and Power Research Station of the Government of India, reported a magnitude of 7.5 in the Richter scale for the Koyna earthquake that killed around two hundred people, injured over a few thousand

people and rendered a good few thousand homeless. Koyna hosts a rubble-concrete dam, one of the largest of the state of Maharashtra, on the Koyna river.[44] This multipurpose Koyna Dam was constructed to provide water for irrigation, to control flood and to generate hydroelectricity. This dam, in fact generates, 1,960 MW of electricity, thus making this the largest hydroelectric power plant of India. The epicenter of the 1967 earthquake was within 5 km of the Koyna Dam, which developed large cracks.

Dr. Hari Narain and Dr. Harsh K. Gupta in their article titled "Koyna Earthquake" published in 1968 in Nature[47] stated that the depth of focus of the earthquake was 30 km and "the earthquake was felt over distances up to 700 km from the epicenter". The Koyna Dam, built in a moderately seismically active area, was probably hit by a natural earthquake resulting from movements along a fault. Equally possible it is that waters impounded in the reservoir of the dam, triggered the earthquake.

This hypothesis of reservoir induced seismicity has been proposed, among others, by an eminent seismologist of worldwide fame, Dr. Harsh K. Gupta, who I had the good fortune of working with, in the Ministry of Science of Technology of the Government of India. Padma Shri Dr. H.K. Gupta, a Leader of India's Antarctic Expedition, a former Vice Chancellor of Cochin University of Science and Technology, subsequently became the Director of National Geophysical Research Institute (NGRI) and retired as the Secretary of the Ministry of Ocean Development of the Government of India. Dr. H.K. Gupta was the founder President of the Asian Seismological Commission and currently is the President of the Geological Society of India.[45, 46] The erudite views of Dr. H.K. Gupta cannot be ignored.

Dr. Harsh Gupta et al in their 1969 article titled "A study of the Koyna earthquake of December 10, 1967", published in the Bulletin of the Seismological Society of America stated that "Seismicity in Koyna region has been found to increase with the increase of water level in the reservoir and vice-versa with a certain time lag." Dr. Harsh Gupta et al also claimed that "The two major earthquakes of this region have similar foreshock-aftershock pattern".[47,] [48, 49] These are strong claims indeed to prove their reservoir induced seismicity theory.

The large cracks developed in the Koyna Dam, following the 1967 earthquake, were completely sealed by high pressure grouting and many "internal holes were drilled to reduce the hydrostatic pressures in the body of the dam". The non-overflow part of the dam was consolidated in 1973 and the spillway portion of the dam was further strengthened in 2006, with the hope that the dam can now withstand stronger quakes than those caused by the 1967 earthquake.

On the 13th of March 2005, Koyna again was the epicenter, this time of a moderate earthquake of 5.1 on the Richter scale that was felt in faraway Mumbai. The Koyna region is seismically quite active and regularly experiences earthquakes that measure up to magnitude 5.[44] The magnitude of the 1967 earthquake, by the way, is now revised to 6.6 down from 7.5. A fault line, incidentally, runs underneath this region at a depth of some 8 km. In the second decade of the twenty-first century, an ambitious project, led by Dr. Harsh K. Gupta, was designed to drill a 7 km deep borehole in Koyna region to understand "physical, geological and chemical processes and properties of the earthquake zone in real time".[50]

Possibility of a seismic disturbance at the Hirakud Dam
In view of the above discussions on reservoir induced seismicity, we must take into consideration the possibility of the 4,800 million cubic m of water and the 1,000 million cubic m of sediments impounded by the Hirakud Dam, triggering an earthquake. I would also like to mention that the Hirakud

Dam falls in Seismic Zone III of India, which is a moderate intensity zone and may experience moderate earthquakes. The capital city of Odisha, Bhubaneswar, also lies in this Seismic Zone III, just as Ahmedabad in Gujarat that experienced a major earthquake in 2001 and Jabalpur in Madhya Pradesh that experienced a major earthquake in 1997.[51, 52, 53]

An earthquake could develop cracks in the Hirakud Dam and may even cause an immediate collapse. Any seismic disturbances, even minor seismic noises, the Hirakud Dam experiences must be monitored in a continuous basis by an array of modern digital accelerographs and seismographs. At least two strong-motion accelerographs should be installed on the body of the dam and at least two more in the immediate vicinity. Each accelerograph must record all the three components of motion and must have a natural frequency of around 20 Hz and a recording speed of about 1 cm/s (cm per second). The accelerographs will record potentially destructive shaking of the ground and the resulting vibrations of the dam. At least three seismographs must be installed in the immediate vicinity of the dam and three more on the body of the dam. The sensitive seismographs will monitor seismic activities on a continuous basis.[54, 55]

Reduction of storage capacity due to siltation

An article titled "Death of Hirakud Dam"[56] published in The Times of India in May 2018, written by a knowledgeable activist, Ranjan K. Panda, mentioned of an analysis carried out by the Central Water Commission in 1995 and subsequent studies by the dam authorities that found that "the total storage capacity had gone down by 27.35% due to siltation". Mr. Panda also mentioned of a remote sensing study that "confirmed that live storage and dead storage had declined by 17.16% and 53.72%, respectively." Mr. Panda, quite rightly so, mentioned his apprehension that these storage capacities might have declined even further, perhaps quite significantly, in the last 25 years since the studies of 1995.

If we accept a rounded estimate of 25% of the original capacity of the reservoir, presently lost to sediments deposited in the last 70 years, say of the order of one billion cubic m or one cubic km (1 km^3), we have to accept the possibility of a massive mudslide taking place within the reservoir. The bottom topography of the artificial lake and the location of the slide will determine the magnitude of the mudslide. A strong mudslide could generate a powerful tsunami, which could then smash against the Hirakud Dam causing a collapse.

A very heavy downpour in the upper reaches of the Mahanadi and the Ib rivers, at a time when least expected, could rapidly fill the reservoir. If water per chance, flows above the crest of the dam, the dam may well collapse.

The top priority, flood control, be respected

Ever since the conception of the Hirakud Dam, its primary function was flood control. Let us all be very clear on this top priority of Hirakud, it is flood control; irrigation even power generation are only secondary functions. Absolutely essential it is, therefore, that before the onset of the heavy monsoon rains, the reservoir must be kept sufficiently empty, to have a higher capacity to accommodate the runoff from the upper reaches of the Mahanadi and the Ib. Unfortunately, the pre-monsoon period, when the reservoir should be kept empty, is the peak of summer when the demand for electricity is also at its peak. So, the political masters, in order to appease their electorates often interfere in the management of the Hirakud Dam, forcing the engineers to keep the reservoir sufficiently full rather than empty, so as to have enough water to continue to generate hydroelectric power. A very heavy unexpected downpour caused either by a cloud burst or due to a storm, like the extremely severe cyclonic storm Phailin of 2013 that I have discussed in Chapter Two, could suddenly fill up the reservoir and overwhelm the dam to collapse. You may recollect that in 2013, as Phailin poised to make landfall, the sluice gates of the Hirakud Dam were flung open to lower the water level, which otherwise would have risen above the crest of the dam. As a matter of fact, after commissioning of the dam in 1957, the Maximum Water Level (MWL) was maintained at 625 ft[6] and not at 630 ft that is observed now. The MWL should be lowered to 625 ft again to keep the Hirakud Dam safe.

Please allow me to quote from the very first exhaustive report of June 1947 on the Hirakud Dam Project prepared by the Central Waterways, Irrigation and Navigation Commission (p. 35) on the subject that categorically mentions 625 ft as follows. "The reservoir level for purposes of flood control, power, irrigation and navigation will be restricted to 625 and for abnormal floods like those of 1872 and 1834 this level will be permitted to rise, up to 630.5; but as explained in Chapter IX, the reservoir level will stay above R.L.625.0 for a maximum period of 5 to 6 days only"[6]. The Report on this subject on p. 49 further states, "The additional reserve of 5 ft will afford almost complete protection even for floods of the magnitude of that of 1834."[6]

Nine out of ten undue interferences may not cause any serious problems. Yet, on those 6 out of 30 occasions in the past, when the sluice gates were forced open as a last resort to protect the dam, releasing substantial volumes of water to the already overflowing Mahanadi drainage basin exacerbating the floods, the reservoir was kept sufficiently full probably at the behest of the political bosses. The process of management of the Hirakud Dam must be respected and must not be interfered with, by politicians and bureaucrats. In the best interest of the dam, the reservoir and the people of Odisha, let the technocrats manage the Hirakud Dam.

Policy for disaster management
With the intensification of global warming and climate change, unseasonal rains will become more common and the intensity of the storms and downpours will increase. As years roll by

and as the population of the towns and cities of the already overpopulated Mahanadi basin rise, loss of human lives will be enormous, in millions, in case of a catastrophic collapse of the Hirakud Dam. As the dam gets older, moreover, chances of its collapse increase. Depending on the time of the year, the lunar cycle and the fullness of the Mahanadi, the floodwaters from a collapsed Hirakud could rush down at a speed anywhere between 10 and 50 km per hour. At present, a controlled release of water from the sluices of the Hirakud Dam, takes some 36 hours to reach the densely populated City of Cuttack, located at the apex of the Mahanadi delta, some 300 km downstream as the river flows. An uncontrolled catastrophic release of water from a collapsed Hirakud Dam, in a worst-case scenario, could overwhelm Cuttack much faster and will reach the Bay of Bengal most definitely inside 48 hours. In addition to Cuttack, the townships on the banks of the Mahanadi like Sambalpur, Sonepur, Banki and all other habitations on the Mahanadi delta right up to the port city of Paradip on sea, will be utterly devastated. The devastations will be unprecedented, and the Mahanadi delta could be wiped clean. Unfortunately, as the dam gets older, the possibilities of a collapse increase.

Until recently, no public policy document for disaster management in case of a catastrophic collapse of the Hirakud Dam existed. In October 2018, an Emergency Action Plan for the Hirakud Dam, prepared by the Central Project Management Unit (CPMU) for the Department of Water Resources of the Government of Odisha, was published.[57] This is a welcome development indeed. A more detailed study must be undertaken, to determine the likely path of the travelling wall of water from the Hirakud Dam and the length of time it will take, to reach all the various towns and cities along the Mahanadi. A contingency plan that includes an advanced warning system, should be in place to warn the townships, urging mass evacuations. Each and every habitation, starting from tiny villages to townships to large cities, along the river, should have information available as to the shortest and the safest routes for mass evacuation to safety. A public education program, for the entire population along the Mahanadi and her distributaries, on the dangers of a dam collapse, must also be administered.

Important aspects of management of the Hirakud Dam
The very first step in the proper management of the Hirakud Dam, requires the acquisition of an accurate body of knowledge on all aspects of the dam and the reservoir, including its capacity. As already mentioned, the reservoir capacity of 5,818 million cubic m at the time of the commissioning, is no longer correct, because of the accumulation of vast quantities of silts and sediments, flowing into the reservoir. An estimate of 25% reduction in the capacity, mentioned earlier, could well be correct, but must be investigated thoroughly.

Calculation of the capacity requires the construction of a three-dimensional picture of the reservoir that starts with an accurate profile of the bottom. A simple-minded assumption that the bottom of the reservoir is flat is incorrect; in fact, it could be anything but flat. The floor of the reservoir could be crisscrossed with numerous channels and may possess complicated topography, hosting many interesting sedimentary and hydrological features. Only a detailed investigation, with the help of side-scan sonar technology, can provide an accurate profile of the bottom. A side-scan sonar survey is not particularly difficult (not easy either!), requires a boat to anchor the sonar and a few pieces of equipment to record the bottom profile and must be conducted as soon as possible. The bottom profile, moreover, will keep changing virtually every year after the monsoonal influx. Survey of the bottom profile, therefore, may become necessary to be carried out, every few summers.

Based on the results of the side-scan sonar survey, a systematic program of drilling to obtain sediment cores must be conducted. The sediment cores must then be subjected to sedimentological, mineralogical, geochemical and Cs^{137} radiochemical investigations, to provide a wealth of information, including the basic information on composition, compaction and the height of the sediment piles. The information then would be used to devise an appropriate strategy for the removal of sediments. The accumulated sediments could have formed large well-compacted underwater mounds and plateaus, which would require excavation by a combination of technologies including cutter-section dredging and opencast mining.

Removal of sediments from the reservoir
The mention of opencast mining should not come as a surprise. One billion cubic m of sediments would weigh around 2 billion tons, which would require a huge open cast mining operation for excavation and removal. My calculation of the tonnage is based on the mineralogy of these riverine sediments, whose main component is quartz, possessing a specific gravity of 2.65 and the other component being mostly clay, whose specific gravity is less than that of quartz. These sediments, moreover, could possess significant porosity. I could, therefore, safely assume a rounded specific gravity of 2 for the sediments accumulated in the Hirakud reservoir.

The excavated sediments could be used to reinforce the 21 km long earthen dykes, if necessary, and to landscape the islands within the reservoir and the hundreds of km long northern and western shorelines. Bed leveler dredging, which is comparable to the operations of a bulldozer on land, could be done to flatten the floor of the reservoir to eliminate the dangers of a mudslide. The radiochemical analysis for Cs^{137}, incidentally, would show anomalies or simply higher concentrations of Cs^{137} in the sediment columns. These anomalies constitute chronological markers and correspond to nuclear fallouts, either from nuclear tests or from nuclear accidents.[58, 59] Since the Hirakud Dam was commissioned in 1957, its sediments would faithfully carry the signatures of the nuclear fallouts from the late 1950s right up to the fallout from Fukushima disaster in 2011. These faithful markers can be utilized, to calculate the rate of sedimentation, during various periods of time, in the history of the reservoir.

The Government of Odisha, in 2008, initiated a program for a limited dredging of the Hirakud reservoir through their agency, Orissa Construction Corporation (OCC), to remove some 0.7 million cubic m of sediments. Although this dredging was very small in scope and was designed essentially to facilitate the flow of water into a canal for irrigation, it was a step in the right direction. A program of regular monitoring of suspended and bed load sediments, entering the reservoir is important, for such studies will help design and construct structures to arrest the silt or at least to reduce the amount, entering the reservoir. Monitoring of the seismic activities, as described earlier, could reveal seismic stress in the region, which will help in taking necessary precautions to ensure the safety of the dam.

Conclusion

At 70, Hirakud is an aging dam, comparable to an aging human body. Just as an aging human body requires proper maintenance, so does the Hirakud Dam.

I know well that many of you my readers are wondering what happened to Sonali? Some of you have already Googled and got the answer. For all those who are still waiting eagerly to learn from me, or as people say from the horse's mouth or perhaps more appropriately from the Taurean's mouth, for astrologically I am a Taurus, must be informed that Sonali eloped with Rossellini, accompanied by her 6-year-old son, in 1957, to become his wife number three and continued to live in Italy ever after.

People in coastal Odisha can live happily ever after, if the Hirakud Dam is managed properly to save this land.

Chapter Five
Caring for the Rivers in India

The greatest poet Vyaasadev who wrote the epic Mahabharata, towards the end of his life, while still engaged in literary pursuits by the banks of the venerable Saraswati, observed that the magnificent civilization that stood beside and is nurtured by the life-giving river, will disappear due to the moral decline of the citizenry. His observation, nay prophecy, came true. What he was referring to was the greed of the citizenry and their blatant disregard for and rampant abuse of, natural resources. The massive deforestation along the entire length of the Saraswati and gross abuse of her waters, killed the river.

Growth of Indian civilization along the rivers
Indian civilization grew along the life-giving rivers of the subcontinent and the prominent rivers are the Sindhu, the Ganga, the Brahmaputra, the Yamuna, the Saraswati, the Godavari, the Krishna, the Kaveri, the Narmada, the Tapti, the Mahanadi, the Sone, the Gandak, the Ghaghara, the Kali, the Koshi, the Hooghly, the Padma, the Meghna and the Periyar. The Vedas were composed on the banks of the Sapta Sindhu, in the region of the Sapta Sindhavah, bound by the Saraswati in the east and by the Sindhu in the west, and irrigated by the Satudru (Sutlej), the Vipasa (Beas), the Asikni (Chenab), the Parusni (Ravi) and the Vitasta (Jhelum).

Shri Ram's Ayodhya stood beside the Sarayu, Valmiki wrote the epic Ramayana on the banks of the Tamrabhadra or the Tamasa, the Mahabharata unfolded beside the Yamuna, the Buddha meditated on the banks of the Phalgu, Mahavira achieved omniscience on the banks of the Rijubalika, Adi Shankara composed the famous Achyutastakam beside the

Periyar, Pitunda Metropolia flourished on the shore of the Rushikulya, gateway to the world Tamralipta flourished on the shore of the Prachi, Pataliputra prospered on the banks of the Ganga, the Chalukya dynasty reigned from the banks of the Tungabhadra, kings of the Pandyan empire ruled from the banks of the Vaigai, the Chola dynasty ruled from the Kaveri valley, the Satavahana dynasty prospered on the banks of the Godavari and the Krishna, Emperor Kharavela reigned from the shores of the Daya, "the father of linguistics" and grammarian Panini wrote the treatise Astaadhyaayii on Vyaakarana near the Sindhu, the Chanda Ashoka became the Dharma Ashoka and embraced Buddhism on the banks of the Daya, "the father of medicine" Sushruta practised medicine and surgery on the shores of the Ganga, Charaka practised and wrote the treatise on medicine Charaka Samhita on the banks of the Ganga, Vatsyayana wrote the aphorisms on love Kama Sutra beside the Ganga, Adi Shankara established Sri Kanchi Kamakoti Peetham beside the Palar or the Dakshina Pinakini, the "Prince of Poets" Kalidasa described the exceptional beauty of the Narmada in the epic Raghuvamsa, Takshashila flourished on the Sindhu, Nalanda prospered near the Panchane, Odantapuri bloomed on the banks of the Panchanan, Pushpagiri blossomed beside the Kelua, Nagarjuna shone on the banks of the Krishna, Valabhi sparkled on the shore of the Ghela, Sharada Peeth glowed at the confluence of the Madhumati or the Kishanganga and the Sandili, Vikramashila throve on the banks of the Ganga near her confluence with the Koshi, Somapura excelled on the banks of the Bhadra, Aryabhata wrote the treatise on astronomy and geography Aryabhatiyam on the banks of the Ganga, Gunadhya wrote Brihatkatha very likely on the banks of the Godavari, Banabhatta wrote Harshacharita and Kadambari on the banks of the Hiranyabahu or the Son, Bhavabhuti wrote Malatimadhava at Kalpi on the banks of the Yamuna, Adikavi Pampa author of the Kannada epics Vikramarjuna Vijay and the Adi Purana grew up on the banks of the Varada, the kings of the Vijaynagar empire ruled from the banks of the Tungabhadra, the Ahom kings who defied and defeated the Mughals flourished on the banks of the Brahmaputra, Mughals reigned from the banks of the Yamuna, Sant Dnyaneshwar authored Dnyaneshwari and Amrutanubhav on the banks of the Indrayani, Guru Nanak preached on the banks of the Ravi, Goswami Tulsidas authored the epic Ramcharitmanas on the banks of the Ganga, Kabir Das composed his innumerable poems beside the Ganga, my forebear Saint Achyutananda Das wrote the Books of Prophecies on the banks of the Chitrotpala, Rabindranath established Visva-Bharati near his "choto (little)" the Kopai, Ramakrishna taught beside the Hooghly, in recent times Mahatma Gandhi established his ashram by the Sabarmati and later on his disciple Acharya Vinoba Bhave led the Bhoodan Movement from his ashram beside the Wardha, Netaji Subhas Chandra Bose grew up on the shores of the Mahanadi, the phenomenally popular Sarat Chandra Chattopadhyay wrote his novels on the banks of the Rupnarayan, "Rupashi Banglar Kabi" Jibanananda Das wrote Banalata Sen on the banks of the Hooghly and Bharat Ratna "Xudha Kontho" Dr. Bhupen Hazarika wrote and sang on the banks of the Brahmaputra and the Ganga.

Alexander, known in Persian folklore as the Butcher of Persia, after annihilating the majestic capital city of Persepolis[1] marched further east but failed to cross the Sindhu. The valiant Hindu warriors, assembled on the banks of the Sindhu, drove him back. This marauder, incidentally, sustained a mortal thoracic injury by a poisoned arrow[2] shot by a defending soldier, and died while retreating.

The Odishan rivers of the Mahanadi and her distributaries – the Kathajodi, the Birupa, the Kuakhai, the Devi, the Daya, the Bhargavi – the Subarnarekha, the Budhabalanga, the Salandi, the Baitarani, the Brahmani, the Kharasrota, the Rushikulya, and now extinct the Chandrabhaga, the Prachi and the Chitrotpala gave the state her fertile tracts that made her a prosperous agrarian land. In olden times, these rivers provided Odisha with her marine and riverine ports that harbored huge galleons, departing for the far-off lands of Java, Sumatra, Bali, Komboja (Cambodia), Malaya, Siam and Brahmadesha (Burma), laden with precious stones, silk, expensive textile, silver filigree, gold ornaments and all manners of merchandise. This maritime trade made Odisha fabulously prosperous. The poverty stricken Odias of the twenty-first century do not realize that Odisha cradled the immensely prosperous port of Tamralipta and a world class majestic city, Pitunda Metropolia, that were recorded by the famous Greek geographer Claudius Ptolemy, in a world gazetteer that he wrote in the second century CE. Pitunda Metropolia, by the way, was located around the present-day town of Ganjam.

The land of the five rivers (Jhelum, Ravi, Chenab, Beas and Sutlej), the Punjab, in modern times has become the breadbasket of the country, thanks to the Bhakra Nangal Dam. The Hirakud dam on the Mahanadi, dams on the Tungabhadra, the Damodar, and on many other rivers across the length and the breadth of the country, mentioned in Chapter Four, have provided waters for irrigation, drinking, industry and sanitation.

Traditional Indian respect for water
And all these rivers prospered, due to the respect with which water was treated. Even today, I notice vestiges of that reverence for water among the rural Indians, when I see them bathing in the Ganga and for that matter, in any waterway, even in canals across the country. They reverentially offer a palmful of water in their folded hands, raised skywards in appreciation of the benevolence of Nature, who holds and protects us. The Vedic subtlety and the reverence for the earth and the environment are encapsulated beautifully in this age-old Sanskrit verse:

'Samudra basane devi
Parvata stana mandale

Vishnu patni namastubhyam
Paadasparsam kshyamasva me', which upon translation
reads,

Thy robes are ocean,
Mountains thy bosom,
My mother Oh Earth,
Thou the consort of Vishnu,
My deepest bow to you,
Forgive me,
For treading on thee. (Translation ND).

Vedic India saw the earth as the mother and treated the land that sustained us, with the utmost respect and humility. As a result, from the time immemorial, in this great nation of ours, we enjoyed an "abundance of food, fine water and pure air"[3], just as stated in the fourth century BCE book titled Indika, written by the Greek writer Megasthenes, in his account of the Mauryan India. Please allow me, my sisters and brothers of India, to quote a few more lines from Indika to make you feel proud and the lines are: "The inhabitants, in like manner, having abundant means of subsistence, exceed in consequence the ordinary stature, and are distinguished by their proud bearing. They are also found to be well skilled in the arts, as might be expected of men who inhale a pure air and drink the very finest water."[4] Megasthenes, by the way, was a Greek historian, writer, diplomat and Indian ethnographer, who served as the Greek ambassador of Seleucus, in the court of Chandragupta Maurya, in around 303 BCE.[5]

Now, please allow me to ask you a simple question and my question is, is there any clean water left in India? You, of course, will pull out your mineral water bottles, but let us discuss water quality in the next chapter. And could I offer you a piece of advice and that is, stop patronizing those unspeakable DFC joints (Damned Fried Chicken) and think of drinking "the very finest water" and "inhaling pure air" so that you "exceed the ordinary stature and are distinguished by your proud bearing" and become "well skilled in the arts", just like your forebear.

Modern urbanized Indians, consider themselves too smart to show any respect towards the earth, water and the environment. Today, India faces a situation where in the name of growth and modernization, blatant abuses of the rivers and waters are being encouraged and condoned. Reckless deforestation in the name of development is accelerating the death of the rivers. The rivers are the lifeblood of the country, let us save them or else we all perish. (Appendix One and Appendix Two).

Inter linking of the rivers

The Government of India supported by a favorable judgement by the Supreme Court, on the 27th of February 2012[6,7], wished to embark upon the hugely ambitious project of linking some rivers of the country. The then President of India, championed the idea too and experts started discussing the issue. Yes, in theory, benefits of interlinking the rivers could be vast, floods and droughts could be banished from the country and fresh water, the most precious natural resource, could be prevented from getting wasted by rushing into the seas.[8]

The Government of India, identified 30 River Link Projects (RLP) in the country and chose to link the Ken and the Betwa rivers in the state of Madhya Pradesh as the first RLP, to provide water for drinking and irrigation to the chronically parched Bundelkhand region. These two tributaries of the much bigger Yamuna, run parallel in two adjacent river basins, some 200 km apart. Rs18,000 crore (USD2.8 billion) Ken-Betwa River Link Project (KBRLP), envisages construction of a 77 m high dam on the Ken, to create a reservoir of 2,953 million cubic m (about 3 bcm) capacity, to store water to be channeled to the Betwa, by a 218 km long canal. This major dam on the Ken or the Karnawati, as she was called in ancient times, will create a reservoir spread over 90 km² to submerge the core of a prime forest that presently hosts a tiger sanctuary, Panna Tiger Reserve. In a 100 years' time, this most expensive artificial reservoir will get completely silted up and transformed into a patch of desert, which will then expand to destroy the forest. A much better alternative exists to this huge reservoir.

This Bundelkhand region is ideal for the construction of a good few thousand micro-dams, which will put an end to the chronic water shortage. Bundelkhand also contains many old traditional purpose-built tanks, to harvest water. These water harvesting structures, presently being neglected to death, upon rejuvenation, could easily mitigate the water crisis. A study conducted by the International Water Management Institute and the Tata Water Policy Program, says that "repairing around 146 of these tanks in Tikamgarh district, could irrigate around 29,000 hectares of land"…which "is more than half the irrigation potential (47,000 hectares) planned for Tikamgarh, Chhatarpur, Hamirpur and Jhansi districts, through the Ken-Betwa project"[9].[10]

History of river linking proposals in India

I would like to mention that the idea of linking of rivers of India is nothing new. The last independent Hindu king of Odisha, Mukundadev, also known as Mukunda Harichandan, during his 8-year reign, between 1559 CE and 1568 CE, conceived of linking the Ganga with the Mahanadi. This idea struck him in 1560 CE, when he chased Sultan Giasuddin Jallal Shah of the Suri dynasty of Bengal, who had invaded the northern part of Odisha, all the way to the Ganga at Varanasi and defeated him. There on the banks of the holy Ganga, Mukundadev got the exquisite set of stone stairs of the Triveni Ghat constructed that the Odias consider a place of pilgrimage, as holy as the Prayag. Mukundadev initiated the excavation of a canal linking the Ganga at Triveni to the Mahanadi at Cuttack. Mukundadev, unfortunately, died fighting the Muslim invaders and the state of Odisha fell into the hands of the Muslim Sultan of Bengal in 1568 CE.[11] The grandiose plan of Mukundadev of linking the two rivers was, needless to say, abandoned.

General Sir Arthur Thomas Cotton proposed a national water grid

Please allow me to praise General Sir Arthur Thomas Cotton, a British general and irrigation engineer par excellence, who started his career in 1819, at the age of 16, as a Commissioned Second Lieutenant in the Madras Engineer Group. Soon afterwards, he fought in the First Burmese War and in 1821, joined service in India, where he was attached to the Chief Engineer to Madras. Thereafter, he received an appointment as an Assistant Engineer of the Tank Department and dedicated his life to the construction of dams, irrigation and navigation canals in the entire British India. Sir Cotton built the Dowleswaram Barrage on the Godavari at Rajamahendravaram, the 1,223.5 m long Prakasam Barrage across the Krishna and the Kurnool Cuddappah Canal in Andhra Pradesh. And these are marvelous projects of engineering that have bestowed great benefits on tens of millions of people.[12]

Arthur Cotton, in 1828, started on a project of excavating the sediments that choked the old Kallanai Dam built across the Kaveri, near Tiruchirappalli, by the Chola King Karikalan in the first century BCE. After the excavation for desiltation, the 2,000-year-old dam is still fully operational now. And our Odia engineers never cared to desilt the Hirakud reservoir!

The excavation of sediments at the Kallanai Dam, provided an opportunity to Arthur Cotton and his group of engineers, to study the dam and its construction on sandbanks. With this model of the age-old dam, he designed and built the Upper Dam on the Kaveri in Mukkombu and the Lower Anaicut Dam in Anaikarai. The success of these two projects brought him the permission and funds, to build the much bigger barrages on the Godavari and Krishna mentioned above.[12]

In 1858, Cotton proposed to connect major rivers of the country and interlinking them with canals, to form a national water grid for navigation, irrigation and drinking water supply. He retired in 1860 and left India. His grand scheme, consequently, never took off and lost out to the powerful railway lobby. Arthur Cotton also proposed measures for drought relief in Odisha.

You are revered in Andhra Pradesh and you are a much admired and respected British gentleman in India. You were hated by your British superiors in the administration, essentially because of your love for the people of India. Your British superiors, moreover, initiated impeachment proceedings against you, calling for your dismissal, but somehow better sense prevailed, and you continued the good work for a people you loved. You, in fact, were so distressed by the sight of hungry famine-stricken people in Godavari district that you initiated your "ambitious plans to harness the waters of the Godavari river, for the betterment of the community".[12.]

My reverential bow to you, General Sir Arthur Thomas Cotton.

Revival of the concept of a national water grid

Padma Bhushan Dr. Kanuri Lakshman Rao, during his tenure as the Minister for Irrigation and Power of the Government of India, revived the concept of a national water grid in 1972. Dr. K.L. Rao was a brilliant well qualified engineer and under his able leadership, the Nagarjuna Sagar Dam with a storage capacity of 11.472 billion cubic m, was designed and constructed, between 1955 and 1967, across the Krishna in Andhra Pradesh.[13] The chief component of his national water grid plan was the 2,640 km long Ganga - Kaveri link, for irrigation and power generation. This link required pumped lifting of water on a vast scale over a head of 550 m, at an expected consumption of some 7,000 Mega Watt (MW) of electricity. This proposal was rejected, quite rightly so, by the Central Water Commission for being economically prohibitive.

The Garland Canal concept of 1977 was proposed by Captain Dastur and involved the construction of two canals, the first being a 4,200 km long, stretching from the Ravi in the west to the Brahmaputra in the east, along the Himalayan foothills. The 9,300 km long second canal was to garland the entire central and southern India. Both these canals were to be connected with a number of reservoirs and were to be interconnected by pipelines at two localities, Delhi and Patna. Two committees of experts, drawn from the Central Water Commission (CWC), the State Governments, the Indian Institutes of Technology (IITs), the Geological Survey of India (GSI) and the India Meteorological Department (IMD) found the proposal, quite rightly, technically infeasible. The Garland Canal proposal was consequently rejected.[14]

The Ministry of Water Resources of the Government of India, prepared a National Perspective Plan, in 1980, to develop water resources, by transferring water from surplus basins to water deficit basins, by interlinking of rivers. The plan involved development of the Himalayan and the Peninsular rivers. Thereafter, in 1982, the National Water Development Agency (NWDA) was established to undertake necessary surveys and feasibility studies. In due course, the NWDA identified 30 links, 14 for the Himalayan rivers in the north and 16 for the rivers of the peninsula in the south. This grand plan envisaged irrigation for some 37 million hectares of land, generation of 34 million Mega Watt (MW) of electricity, increased navigation, flood control and drought relief.[14]

In 1999, the National Commission on Integrated Water Resource Development, however, opposed massive inter-basin transfer of water and recommended optimal utilization of intra-basin surpluses.[14]

I am willing to support the idea of linking rivers, within the same basin (intra-basin) in deltaic coastal regions of the country and in the Sindhu – Ganga – Brahmaputra plains to facilitate irrigation, navigation and water supply. I, however, completely disagree with the idea of linking rivers of different basins (inter-basin), particularly when they are very far apart. The idea of linking the Ganga with the Kaveri is simply preposterous.

Managing the health of the rivers of India

Afforestation by the construction of a large number of micro-dams, as discussed in detail in Chapter One, will rejuvenate the smaller first and second order streams, but will not revive the big rivers that are almost choked to death, by massive deposits of sediments. Just as in matters of human health, at times medicine alone is not enough and surgery becomes necessary, similarly management of the health of the river systems, at times, requires drastic measures. Many of the rivers of India have suffered irreversible damages and must undergo surgical operations. And by surgery, I essentially mean, excavation of sediments from the riverbeds and dredging of the channels at the estuaries.

Excavation of sediments from the riverbeds of the Mahanadi and other major rivers of Odisha for their revival

Honorable Dr. B.R. Ambedkar, Labour Member to the Government of India, in his Presidential Address delivered at Cuttack Conference organized to discuss the development of the rivers of Odisha, held on the 8th of November 1945, had emphasized that the plan of embankments to manage the rivers is wrong and Odisha must adopt the methods the USA employed, for the development of the rivers like the Missouri-Mississippi (p.249).[15]

And the vast water resources of the largest river of the USA, the Missouri-Mississippi is carefully managed by extensive river-engineering, which includes systematic dredging every year, carried out by the US Army Corps of Engineers.[16]

Now in 2021, while the "Old man River", the Missouri-Mississippi, continues to flow majestically, the largest river of Odisha, the once mighty Mahanadi, whose monsoonal flow right up to the middle of the twentieth century used to be comparable to that of the Ganga, virtually lies dead for most of the year, all choked up, because of substantial deposits of sediments along its entire course. The 858 km long Mahanadi, etymologically the Great River, originates in the state of Chhattisgarh that adjoins Odisha on the west. This Great River was navigable for much of its course, starting at "The town of temples" Arang, in Raipur district of Chhattisgarh right up to its mouth, near the port city of Paradip, on the Sea of Kalinga or the Bay of Bengal. Navigation on this 700 km long course continued from time immemorial until the construction of the Hirakud Dam in 1950s.[16.a] Even after the construction of the dam, Mahanadi was navigable from the town of Sambalpur, which is located just downstream of the Hirakud Dam, right up to Cuttack, for a length of some 300 km, until the late 1980s. Hundreds of boats, laden with bamboo for making paper, used to ply a distance of some 100 km, between Daspalla and a paper mill near Cuttack at Choudwar, on the Mahanadi till the late 1980s. The faulty design of the New Mahanadi Barrage at Jobra, whose construction started in 1978, obstructed the free-flowing transportation of sediments, which then piled up to completely choke the Great River, around Cuttack.

The Mahanadi riverbed at Cuttack today is probably at a higher elevation than that of the city and only the Ring-road embankment, protects the Millennium City of Cuttack from the monsoonal floods. This massive deposition of sediments, moreover, has very drastically reduced the in-river water holding capacity of the Mahanadi.

The Government of Odisha are well aware of the problem of sedimentation that the Mahanadi confronts now. The Chief

Minister of Odisha, in 2017, wrote to the Minister for Water-resources of the Union Government of India, to make funds available for the dredging of the mouth of the Mahanadi.[17] Some islets that formed on the Mahanadi, near the Jobra Anicut of Cuttack, were partially removed by dredging that started in 2015. In this connection, I would also like to mention that the Government of Assam have decided to desilt the mighty Brahmaputra, by dredging, to mitigate the severity of the annual floods.[18, 19, 20]

I propose that the Government of Odisha take a decision, to excavate and dredge the entire length of some 400 km of the Mahanadi, right from the Hirakud Dam in Sambalpur to the river mouth, at the Bay of Bengal near Paradip. The approximate volume of sand to be excavated for the 400 km long, 1 km wide, 3 m deep stretch of the Mahanadi will be around 1.2 billion cubic m (bcm).

Some three years ago, on the 7th of March 2018, I conveyed my proposal for a comprehensive dredging of the entire length of the Mahanadi and other major rivers of Odisha, for their revival, in a letter to the Principal Secretary to the Government of Odisha, Department of Water Resources, with copies to the Secretary to the Government of India, Ministry of Water Resources of the Government of India and to the Honorable Minister for Water Resources of the Government of India. (Appendix Two).

I had mentioned the cost of this Mahanadi excavation project at around USD1.2 billion, calculated at the rate of the excavation cost of USD1 for 1 cubic meter of sediment. Now in 2021, taking the inflation into account, I would base my project cost at the rate of USD1 for 1 ton of the sediment, making the total cost of the Mahanadi excavation project USD2.4 billion. As explained in Chapter Four, 1 cubic m of sediment will weigh 2 tons, so 1.2 bcm will weigh 2.4 billion tons. The total volume of sand to be excavated from all the major riverbeds in Odisha, including the Mahanadi, will be of the order of a rounded figure of 5 bcm, which is about 10 billion tons. The total cost of excavation, therefore, will be of the order of USD10 billion.

I would also like to add that the most commonly used term, for removal of the river sediments is dredging, which becomes a misnomer in the context of most of our Indian rivers, because these days they dry up, pretty much from the month of November and remain dry, till the arrival of monsoonal rains in June. These bone-dry riverbeds are reasonably compact and must be excavated and not dredged. The estuaries and the mouths of these rivers, however, require dredging. The more appropriate term, therefore, is excavation, which, incidentally, is a cheaper process of removal of sediments too.

Some of the excavated sand and silt at Cuttack could be used to very substantially strengthen the Ring-road embankment and create waterfront property, by reclaiming a portion of the presently silted up course of the Mahanadi adjacent to the city. The Government of Odisha started dredging operations in this stretch of the Mahanadi, in 2020, to reclaim a large acreage of land for constructing a major medical complex. Well done. The Government of Odisha should now devise a plan for the excavation of the entire course of the Mahanadi and other major rivers of Odisha, like I proposed.

Huge global demand for sand

The Government of Odisha could float a tender to invite bids for the export of the excavated river sand. I say this because the volume of the worldwide trade in sand, annually, is of the order of 50 billion tons, which means that the global demand for sand is huge. [21, 22, 23] River and marine sands, moreover, are angular as opposed to the aeolian sands of the deserts, which are well rounded and not good for making the concrete mix. River and marine sands, on the other hand, are excellent because of their angularity. The world, by the way, needs 4 billion tons of concrete annually and 75% of which is sand. The world, therefore, requires 3 billion tons of sand just for making concrete alone. In 2017, China produced 2,500 million tons of cement and India produced 280 million tons. These huge volumes of cement output, require at least 3 times more sand, for preparing concrete. China dredges sand of the order of 236 million tons per annum. Sand is being used to build islands in China, in the UAE and in Singapore. Extraction of sand is a USD70 billion industry annually. About 100 billion tons of sand, worth USD2.3 billion, is stolen annually in the world. I hope that I have convinced you my readers that Odisha can easily sell 10 billion tons of sand in the international market and can make a handsome profit too, for the price of sand in the US averaged USD9 per ton, between 2007 and 2019.[24] Singapore is getting organized to spend around SGD72 billion or more, in the next 100 years, to fortify the country against the rising seas.[25] A significant portion of this huge amount will be spent on buying sand. The Government of Odisha could easily make an arrangement with the Government of Singapore, to sell the excavated sands.

Excavate the moribund Kharasrota

The Kharasrota, a distributary of the Brahmani branches off at Jenapur and flows east to the Bay of Bengal. Since the Kharasrota, which etymologically means fast flowing, sources its water from a major river like the Brahmani, which is the second largest river of the state of Odisha, its sediment load consists mostly of pure sand, a lesser proportion of silt and not much clay. The clay component, moreover, washes away because of the fast flow, without getting a chance to settle down on the riverbed. As a result, the sandbanks, the floodplains and the riverbed of the Kharasrota are composed of essentially sand, which in the absence of a large component of clay is very porous and permeable. The porosity could be as high as 50% or more. These days, this river is effectively ephemeral, and the riverbed is completely dry for eight months in a year, like all other rivers of Odisha.

In 2021, the Government of Odisha have embarked upon a mega drinking water supply project that will draw large volumes of water from the Kharasrota riverbed, to be supplied to a large number of villages in the adjacent district of Bhadrak. The project has become very contentious and divisive.

In the absence of a regular, round the year discharge of fresh water in the Kharasrota, sea water could easily penetrate these large pore spaces following a large scale drawal of water. The massive saline incursion can happen right up to the site of the project some 35 km away from the sea. This will cause saline toxicity in the agricultural fields and will make presently potable drinking water, from the many dug wells, undrinkable. All aquifers right up to the project site will experience severe saline incursion and will not produce potable drinking water anymore. The tube well water, will neither be fit for any industrial activity, nor for irrigation.

These days, when the riverine discharge dwindles, saline incursion becomes noticeable in the porous sedimentary terrain laid by the Kharasrota right up in Bharigada village, located some 30 km upstream from the sea. The river, incidentally, is some 3 km wide at this village. The Baitarani regularly gets saline water during high tide, right up to its confluence with the Kharasrota. This seawater, at present, does not enter the Kharasrota, because of the however little freshwater discharge. Once the freshwater discharge comes to an end, because of the mega project, particularly in the dry summer months, seawater will enter the Kharasrota from the Baitarani and will travel upstream, perhaps right up to the site of the mega project.

The mangrove forest at Bhitara Kanika sanctuary requires brackish water, which is a mixture of fresh river water and saline seawater, for survival. In the absence of a sizable volume of freshwater flow in the Kharasrota, this mangrove forest will be destroyed. This mangrove forest of Bhitara Kanika, moreover, apparently contains some 75% of the entire range of mangrove species of the world. People in these areas feel that the mega project will stop the flow of water downstream, right from the month of November, until the arrival of monsoon in June.

The only way the mega project will be viable, if some 10,000 micro-dams are constructed in the upper catchment areas of the Brahmani and the Baitarani, to store vast quantities of rain water in the pore spaces of the higher grounds and in the aquifers to make the flow of fresh water in the Kharasrota, a round the year phenomenon.

The entire Kharasrota riverbed must be excavated to a depth of 3 m, right from the source at Jenapur, to the site of the mega project, to enhance the water holding capacity of the river very substantially, which will ensure a round the year flow in the river, for the mega project to become viable.

Conclusion

Including the Mahanadi, all major rivers of Odisha, the Subarnarekha, the Baitarani, the Budhabalanga, the Salandi, the Kharasrota, the Brahmani, the Birupa, the Kathjodi, the Kuakhai, the Devi, the Daya, the Rusikulya are completely choked up and require excavation and dredging for their revival. A stretch of the Salandi, at the township of Bhadrak, incidentally, was dredged a few years back. If we do not revive these major rivers of Odisha, they will die and please do not forget that once the rivers die civilizations die. I have appended a news-item published on this subject, on the Times of India, in May 2017, for your information. (Appendix One). Because of these dying rivers, Odisha now faces an existential crisis.

Odisha is not alone, virtually all rivers of India, in each and every state of India, need revival now, before it is too late. Let us, therefore, revive these moribund rivers to save this land.

Chapter Six
Creating Awareness on Water Quality in the City of Cuttack

The thousand-year-old City of Cuttack, ever since its inception in the eleventh century as the Abhinab Varanasi Katak on the banks of the Mahanadi, has remained the cultural heart of the state of Odisha. This old capital of the state was the center of administration and trading and became the hub of the freedom movement in the twentieth century. The name Cuttack is the anglicized distortion of the original Odia word Katak, which etymologically means fortress. I sincerely hope that the distorted spelling is abolished soon, so that Cuttack becomes Katak again. Cuttack plays host to the most venerable academic institution of the state of Odisha, Ravenshaw, which was established in 1868 as a college and has become a university now. Cuttack, moreover, proudly hosts Orissa Medical School founded in 1875 that was eventually renamed Srirama Chandra Bhanja Medical College in 1951, the Annapurna Theatre that opened in 1936, the High Court of Odisha that was established in 1948 and the Barabati Stadium that was built in 1958. Quite justifiably, the inhabitants of this Millennium City, which is the seat of learning, healthcare, judiciary, entertainment and sports, take great pride in the customs and traditions of Cuttack. And no wonder, whatever this island City of Cuttack does, Odisha follows.

Sources of water for the island City of Cuttack

The elongated island of Cuttack that stretches eastward from Naraj in the west, is barely 25 km long and only 5 km broad at its widest. Perhaps the Athgarh Sandstone of upper Gondwana age that is prominently exposed at Naraj, on the south bank of the Mahanadi, forms the core bedrock of this island that grew with the accretion of sandbars around. Unfortunately, no systematic geophysical seismic survey of the entire city has ever been conducted, which rules out an authoritative discussion on the basement geology of this island city. Superficially, the island appears to be composed of poorly consolidated sandy sediments, deposited by the Mahanadi and her distributary the Kathajodi that branches off at Naraj and forms the southern boundary of the city. These poorly consolidated sediments at depths, below the ground surface, constitute excellent porous aquifers that have served as repositories of clean fresh water, stored over thousands of years. This fresh water was drawn by the populace, all through their existence in the last millennium, for their sustenance.

Toxification of drinking water
Around 1960s, this island of Cuttack experienced urbanization that gained considerable momentum, making this city home to a population of 610,189 in 2011, according to the provisional reports of Census India. The population now in 2021, in all likelihood, has expanded to a million. Urbanization led to the inevitable generation of solid waste as well as wastewater, volumes of which, now in the third decade of the twenty-first century, have assumed dangerous proportions. Barring a noteworthy sincere effort by the then Mayor of the City of Cuttack, Mr. Trilochan Kanungo, who had commissioned a systematic scientific study of the issue of solid waste disposal in the mid-1990s, a master plan for waste disposal for the city was never devised. An erudite patriot, Mr. Kanungo, holds a Master's degree in Mathematics from Ravenshaw in addition to a Bachelor's degree in Laws from Madhusudan Law College of Cuttack. Mr. Kanungo, moreover, was a member of Odisha Legislative Assembly (MLA) and a Member of the Parliament (MP) of India. I pay my tribute to this gentleman of great integrity, while expressing deep anguish that Cuttack failed to see the grand vision of this visionary.

Consequently, solid waste that included household garbage, night soil, municipal garbage, industrial waste, medical waste, and the solid component of sewage, dredged manually from the innumerable putrid stagnant drains of Cuttack, was never disposed properly. Solid waste was, in fact, dumped indiscriminately in the low-lying areas, by the rivers, on either side of the city. The innumerable stagnant drains of Cuttack just alluded to, in the absence of a master plan, have nowhere to flow. A wastewater treatment plant constructed long ago, got overwhelmed by the sheer volume of sewage and broke down. The plant was subsequently abandoned. Sewage water from the drains leading to this treatment plant, inundated a vast stretch of area, which now stands transformed as a putrid bog, with the sole purpose of assaulting the senses of smell and sight.

In due course, these garbage dumps on the low-lying areas were reclaimed by sand filling and upon this reclaimed land, grew housing estates like the various sectors of the Cuttack Development Authority (CDA). Inhabitants of these areas, often residing in beautifully constructed luxurious buildings, or shall I say palaces, generally unaware of the solid waste buried beneath their plots, assumed that they lived in their own little pieces of paradise, until rudely awakened by a dark coloration of water that they drew from the borewells sunk on their premises. Such dark colored water, left in a pot exposed to air for a while, turns red. This I believe is due to the presence of ferrous iron, bound to organic compounds present in the water, drawn from the ground below, which upon oxidation, due to contact with the atmospheric oxygen present in air, turns into ferric iron and the water gains a reddish hue. Such waters in CDA, prove that the solid wastes buried beneath the housing plots have, in fact, contaminated groundwater below. Mechanism of this contamination is simple and involves percolating rainwater, infiltrating the solid waste buried underground and carrying the extracts from the waste, to the unconfined aquifers, hosted in poorly consolidated sediments below. Groundwater residing in the aquifers, ends up thoroughly contaminated by a range of obnoxious organic compounds as well as deadly pathogens. Sewage wastewater, lodged in innumerable putrid stagnant drains laid across the length and breadth of the city, percolate into aquifers regularly, on a daily basis, to thoroughly toxify groundwater. Contamination of groundwater by the drains, in fact, is going on at least for the last 60 years, since the early 1960s.

I have also received reports of yellowish colored water, issuing from pipelines of drinking water, supplied by the Cuttack Municipal Corporation. Drinking water supply, in some poorly maintained localities of the city, is certainly being contaminated by sewage wastewater, through leakages in the pipelines. Such toxification of municipal water supply engendered many deadly outbreaks of jaundice, every year without fail, from 2014 to 2019.[1]

Cuttack only three decades ago, right up to the end of the 1980s, boasted over a thousand ponds of various sizes, scattered all over the city. These rainfed artificial reservoirs not only constituted a source of water for ablutions and domestic use, but also served as traps to harvest rainwater that recharged groundwater. Unfortunately, however, these ponds were never maintained properly, in fact, most of them were terribly neglected, so much so that they came to be used as pits for disposal of household solid waste. Domestic sewage also flowed freely into these ponds. The ponds, upon receiving an abundant supply of nitrates, phosphates and other nutrients and minerals from the wastewater and solid waste, gradually became eutrophic. The eutrophic ponds nurtured a profuse growth of a range of aquatic plants, like water hyacinth that eventually perished and decayed, making the ponds a veritable cesspool of organic matter and a range of nasty chemicals. The severe water pollution of the ponds was never addressed, nor were they ever renovated, not even desilted.

These putrid cesspools, covered with a thick mattress of water hyacinth, however, continued to recharge aquifers unabated, with thoroughly polluted water that eventually toxified groundwater.

Obnoxious water hyacinth menace

Water hyacinth grows so thick that it chokes the diffusion of atmospheric gases into the water below and deprives the aquatic fauna of life sustaining oxygen, thereby restricting the growth of the fish population. Water hyacinth, by the way, is native to the Amazon basin of Latin America and was introduced to Kolkata by Lady Hastings, the wife of the First British Governor-General, towards the end of the eighteenth century, as an aquatic ornamental plant.[2]

Since the arrival in the 1790s, this prolific species has invaded virtually all bodies of water and waterways of eastern India. In the 1920s and 1930s Bengal, water hyacinth had seized water bodies totaling some 10,000 square km and caused an annual damage of the order of Rs6 crores (Rs60 million). Water hyacinth, moreover, created havoc by engendering the deadly diseases of malaria, cholera and diarrhea and earned the epithets of 'Blue devil', 'Terror of Bengal' and 'Curse of Bengal'[3].

Water hyacinth, so exasperated the fiery Bengali Rebel Poet or "Bidrohi Kobi" Padma Bhushan Mr. Kazi Nazrul Islam that in the late 1920s, he wrote a poem inciting a rebellion to eradicate the obnoxious weed. An English translation of the said poem by Dr. Iftekhar Iqbal is presented below.

"Destroy this water hyacinth
They are not plants, but children of foreign devils
Destroy them in full
Put them on fire and burn them to ashes
They are the enemy of life and a strangler
They are the teeth of a monster, the wings of a cannibal

Destroy this water hyacinth
They are the agents of malaria, famine and the hell
They are the harbinger of bad luck and devastating plague
One by one, they swallow rivers and canals,
Rivulets, streams, ponds, fields and drains
Destroy this water hyacinth
They are the curse of Bengal, poisonous sin
Let's clear them from the roots
They have turned the green Bengal into graveyard
They are the devil's ambassador
Destroy this water hyacinth
Hoods of black snakes' peep through their leaves
They are the endless breeds of goblins who live forever
Brothers, if they don't die, we all die
Eliminate them, please don't listen otherwise
Destroy this water hyacinth."[3]

Please allow me to incite you my readers, to eradicate water hyacinth from the aquatic bodies and waterways of India.

Dr. Iftekhar Iqbal, by the way, holds a Ph.D. in history from Cambridge University and is a much-accomplished academician of the University of Dhaka, currently teaching at the Universiti Brunei Darussalam of Brunei. I thank you Dr. Iqbal for your permission to quote your translation of Kazi Nazrul Islam's poem in its entirety. I hope that your translation creates awareness in India, on the dangers of the toxic water hyacinth.

Water hyacinth, however, has a rich protein content that makes it a livestock feed in Assam and West Bengal. This weed, moreover, makes good bedding material for mushroom farming, forms compost for fish food planktons, becomes a source of cellulose, makes good green manure to raise soil fertility and is used in rough paper production. The roots of this aquatic weed absorb, precipitate and concentrate toxic metals like lead, cobalt, zinc, manganese, nickel, copper, cadmium, iron, mercury, selenium and silver from waste waters. Water hyacinth, therefore, could be cultivated in and harvested from, wastewater, for its treatment. Water hyacinth can also replace cow dung to generate biogas.[4] I, therefore, propose that we exhaust the existing supply of water hyacinth in productive ways, to the point of its eradication for good.

Sand filled toxic ponds

Now, reverting to the story of the ponds in Cuttack, I would like to mention that in the last three decades, some 900 of these were sand filled, without ever receiving any treatment for the organic matter and pathogen rich silt, lying at the bottom. Houses were built on these reclaimed patches of land, which continue to toxify the aquifers, pretty much like the housing plots in CDA, discussed earlier.

The extent of toxification of groundwater, from a combination of sources in the city, as of today, is difficult to sum up authoritatively. Going by anecdotal evidence, contaminations have occurred in many locations in various sectors of CDA and in some other parts of the city. The extent of contamination, could only be established by a systematic scientific investigation.

Remedial measures

Wall mounted water filters of various makes have become quite popular these days. Such water filters, however, may not be good enough, to purify the earlier discussed contaminated waters, drawn from borewells as well as from the damaged municipal pipelines. Old fashioned boiling of water, particularly so, at the elevated temperature of 121°C and at a higher pressure, encountered in normal pressure cookers, is excellent. Boiling water in a pressure cooker, will very efficiently kill pathogens, break down a range of nasty organic compounds and precipitate dissolved solids. The so boiled water, after cooling, could be poured into a filtration unit to produce safe and clean drinking water.

Ensurance of cleanliness of drinking water, by boiling and filtration is only an immediate solution for the short term. A long-term approach to ensure a supply of clean drinking water, for the populace, would require careful maintenance of the pipelines, which can easily eliminate the problem of contamination, by sewage wastewater at damaged leaky sites. A far more important approach to ensure purity of fresh water in aquifers, however, would start with the designing of a protocol for the collection of solid waste in the city and creation of a master plan, for their disposal in purpose-built lined-sanitary-landfills. Medical waste must be burnt by incineration or pyrolysis, in purpose-built facilities. A master plan must be devised for the transportation of sewage wastewater in pipelines, laid above the ground, to a number of wastewater treatment plants, constructed at strategic locations of the island city. Such a method of transportation would significantly reduce percolation of wastewater into the aquifers below, which in turn will stop toxification of groundwater.

The 100 odd ponds that still continue to exist in Cuttack, must be excavated, desilted and renovated, so that their water quality improves very substantially. These reservoirs of fresh water can then continue to recharge the aquifers below, without ever contaminating them.

Creation of awareness is paramount
People of Cuttack must become aware of the life-threatening issue of toxification of drinking water supply in their city. The use of the term life-threatening is not an exaggeration, as some of you might think; the phrase is a reminder of the stark reality. In this context, please allow me to cite the case of "Cancer Train", an epithet being used to describe an overnight daily Bathinda – Bikaner Passenger train that commences its journey from the agricultural heartland of Punjab, Bathinda district to Bikaner in Rajasthan. Approximately 60% of the passengers of this 12-coach train, packed to capacity, are

cancer patients, drawn from all over Punjab, on their way to Acharya Tulsi Regional Cancer Treatment & Research Institute in Prince Bijay Singh Memorial Hospital, in Bikaner. And all these cases of cancer are attributed to consumption of toxic water, drawn from aquifers and canals, thoroughly toxified by pesticides. Pesticides, incidentally, have been used extensively in the last six decades, in agricultural fields of Punjab, to boost the production of food-grains, since the days of the Green Revolution of the 1960s.[5]

Please allow me to mention that Japan noted the harmful effects of synthetic chemical pesticides in agriculture, way back in the 1960s and chose to devise biodegradable pesticides for application, to eliminate the problem of groundwater pollution. We must introduce biodegradable pesticides in India.

Groundwater pollution in Cuttack has reached dangerous levels and that requires the creation of awareness among the populace, through talks, speeches, meetings in community functions and in academic institutions, discussions in electronic media and by written articles in the print media. People of Cuttack must become vigilant of the issues of solid waste disposal, wastewater disposal, renovation of putrid ponds and they must demand remedial action. Once the people of Cuttack become aware, people of the rest of Odisha will also wake up to the problems of water pollution they face. People of Cuttack must ensure the elimination of age-old practice of indiscriminate disposal of garbage.

I appeal to you my sisters and brothers of Cuttack to pay heed to the advice that I offer, not for my sake, but for the sake of your children, grandchildren, great grandchildren, for the future generations and the future of Cuttack. If you do not become aware of the massive ongoing toxification of drinking water now, and if you do not initiate any mass action to demand remedial action by the authorities, I assure you that in another two decades you will experience a paradoxical situation of rising wealth and seriously declining health. Do wake up and stop the contamination of drinking water, do preserve the water quality and do take remedial measures to purify the groundwater that sustains you.

Importance of fresh water

Please do not forget, even for a second, how very precious water is! Water is the prime limiting factor for the sustenance, growth and development of human civilization. From a human perspective, this planet has no dearth of land, but has a serious shortage of fresh water that makes large areas of the world uninhabitable. This precious natural resource and its quality must be managed carefully, simply for the very survival of our human species.

Contamination of fresh water

Fresh water, be it on the surface or underground, is being contaminated, save for a few exceptions like Japan, everywhere in the world. Odisha, obviously, is no exception. In a state like Odisha, where rainfall is seasonal and restricted only to a few months in the year, surface water is not available everywhere. The townships and the villages that are fortunate to be located on the banks of the rivers, show a callous disdain for their life-giving waters. Release of untreated raw sewage and industrial effluents into these waters is routine and no one shows any concern at all. These river waters, consequently, show very high concentrations of coliform bacteria, which are essentially derived from human and animal feces. Total Coliform (TC) bacterial count has, therefore, become a standard indicator of water quality. The Total Coliform count of the two largest rivers of Odisha, Mahanadi and Brahmani, is of the order of 60,000 pieces per 100 ml of water.[6] I request you my readers to contrast these counts with the World Health Organization's (WHO) recommended water quality for human consumption that states that coliform bacteria "must not be detectable in any 100-ml sample".[7] Needless to say, the quality of these waters is extremely poor, but people still consume it because they have no choices. They of course, suffer consequently, from all manners of illnesses. Many lives are lost every year due to diseases, which are completely preventable.

People in many parts of Odisha, draw their supply of water from the ground below. Groundwater from the right geological formations is generally clean and water quality is invariably good. Groundwater, however, must be managed properly, for it is not an inexhaustible source of fresh water and a balance between drawal and recharge must be maintained.

Cities sinking due to excess drawal of groundwater

Excessive drawal of groundwater, combined with the enormous weight of concrete structures, built on areas of poorly consolidated sediments is causing widespread land subsidence in many cities of the world. The capital of Indonesia, Jakarta, home to over 10 million is sinking at an alarming rate of between 3 and 25 cm per year, essentially because of excessive drawal of groundwater. Barely 40% of the people of Jakarta receive piped water, supplied by the authorities, while the rest 60% of this vast sprawling coastal city, draw their water from borewells sunk deep, to draw from the aquifers, making the city sink like a 'deflating balloon'.[8] The subsidence could have been stopped, by putting a strict end to the drawal of groundwater and by resorting to a supply of surface water from artificial reservoirs. The capital of Japan, Tokyo, faced the problem of land subsidence, in the 1960s, due to the postwar rapid urbanization that saw the construction of many concrete structures, including high-rise buildings. The subsidence, of the order of 10 cm per year, in the coastal mega city of Tokyo was completely stopped by putting a strict ban on drawal of groundwater. The aquifers were then artificially recharged. I give a lot of credit to the law-abiding disciplined people of Japan, who always cooperate whole heartedly with any measures announced by the government, for the public good.

The Japanese adopted corrective measures, just in time, to rid the problem of land subsidence. The measures have been so effective that Tokyo, presently the largest city of the world and home to some 28 million, has no problems of subsidence now.

The problem of land subsidence in Jakarta is so advanced that adoption of corrective measures will not solve this crisis now, could only buy some 20 to 30 years of time, at best, before the city sinks into oblivion. The Government of Indonesia, in fact, has decided to build a brand-new capital city in the province of East Kalimantan, on the island of Borneo, at a huge cost of USD32.79 billion, and to abandon Jakarta to its sinking fate.[9]

The capital of Thailand, Bangkok, is known as the Venice of the East, because of the presence of innumerable canals. These waterways, were dug, when this city was established in the second half of the eighteenth century and flowed above the sea level. In this third decade of the twenty-first century, many of these canals, perhaps a majority of them, flow below the sea level. This vast coastal city, home to over 10 million, is sinking at the rate of 1 to 2 cm per year. The capital of the Philippines, Manila, is the most densely populated city in the world and has a population of 12 million. This coastal city is sinking at the rate of 10 cm per year, essentially because of unregulated excessive drawal of groundwater. The largest city of Viet Nam, Ho Chi Minh City, home to some 9 million, has sunk by 50 cm in the last 25 years, again due to excessive drawal of groundwater.[10]

In this discussion so far, I only gave examples of coastal cities of the world, but let me assure you that land subsidence is not confined to the coast. Some vast inland cities like the Mexico City, sprawled on a lakebed is sinking at the rate of 25 cm per year. A full 70% of the water, consumed by the 21 million inhabitants of this enormous city, is drawn from the aquifer below. This huge drawal of groundwater, makes the water table fall by a meter a year and makes the city sink rapidly.[11]

I have a strong feeling that some of the coastal cities of India, in addition to riverine cities like Cuttack, built on poorly consolidated soft sediments, are undergoing subsidence under the heavy weights of concrete constructions. Some high-rise buildings of Kolkata have tilted appreciably, while many have developed cracks, all certainly because of land, subsidence. A study conducted by the Geological Survey of India, found that between 2016 and 2019, the Salt Lake City area of Kolkata experienced annual subsidence of 2 cm.[12] The land subsidence in Kolkata is essentially, because of the excessive drawal of groundwater. Systematic studies will reveal, land subsidence in many coastal and riverine cities of India, again because of the excessive drawal of groundwater. A proper study must be conducted, to assess the rate of land subsidence in Cuttack.

Excessive drawal of groundwater in coastal habitations causing saline incursion

In coastal areas of Odisha, excessive drawal of groundwater creates yet another problem. In the absence of enough fresh water to recharge the aquifers, and the close proximity to the sea, makes seawater seep in, to fill in the vacuum, created by excessive drawal. This phenomenon, known as saline incursion, renders groundwater brackish and unfit for human consumption.

Excessive unregulated drawal of groundwater is taking place virtually in all cities and towns of Odisha. In Cuttack, such drawal is making the water table decline very rapidly, so much so that many borewells routinely go dry every year. The coastal town of Puri is experiencing a rapid decline in the water table, due to excessive drawal of groundwater too. Two dug wells, Ganga and Yamuna, on the premises of the Jagannath temple of Puri that supply water for the daily rituals of the temple that includes cooking of snacks, sweets, lunch and dinner for thousands of pilgrims, these days dry up every summer, because of the falling water table. The only solution is to raise the water table in Puri, which can be done by freeing up the two well identified earmarked recharge areas of the city, at Talabania and Baliapanda, of the unauthorized unlawful constructions that severely hinder percolation of rainwater. During my teenage years, some fifty years ago in Puri, I remember seeing the formation of vast shallow lakes at the two recharge areas, after every heavy rainfall. These lakes do not form anymore, because there is no space for them. The Honorable High Court of Odisha, in fact, decreed to clear the unauthorized constructions, following a Public Interest Litigation (PIL) filed by an idealistic schoolmate of mine, presently engaged as a Senior Advocate of the Odisha High Court, Mr. Ashok Kumar Mohapatra. Ashok also officiates as the Acting President of the Committee of the Learned Scholars (Mukti Mandap Pandit Sabha) of the Jagannath temple. I hope that the Puri Administration, takes the necessary steps and removes the unlawful constructions from the earmarked recharge areas. I commend you Ashok, my brave friend, for filing this PIL and winning the case, to obtain a favorable decision for the public good of Puri and for the good of the Jagannath temple.

From time to time, I hear an unwise suggestion casually flung, both in the print and electronic media, to deepen the two dug wells further, so as to reach some imaginary deeper freshwater aquifers, to ensure that the wells remain perennial and prevent the annual summer desiccation. I stand by my assertion of the term "imaginary", because this aquifer in Puri is merely a thin shallow one and any further digging of the wells, will only breach the freshwater aquifer and reach the brackish water layers below, forming due to saline incursion.

Virtually all coastal habitations in Odisha, are facing the problem of saline incursion, so much so that in summer months, most of the dug wells in these places, instead of producing fresh water are delivering brackish water.

Public awareness is vital

Legislation and governments can play a role in keeping fresh water clean, but a bigger role must be played by the people, who in the very first place should be taught the importance of water quality. People must be educated, on the dangers of excessive drawal of groundwater and they must understand the need for a drawal recharge balance. People must also learn that decline in water quality will substantially damage, public health and wellbeing and ultimately the economic growth. People must be trained, to develop a better sense of hygiene in every aspect of life and to stop disposing of waste into the waterways. Legislation must be enacted: (a) to regulate drawal of groundwater, (b) to make rainwater harvesting mandatory, so that it can be used for groundwater recharge, and (c) to place an upper limit on the height of the high-rise buildings in the cities that are experiencing subsidence.

High quality of water in Japan

Hiroshima, my adopted city, because of its geology, geography and climate is endowed with an abundance of fresh water. Outstanding management practices for water use and wastewater disposal, in addition to the meticulous Japanese cleanliness and hygiene, which are truly exemplary, have ensured excellence of the water quality of Hiroshima. Many small, medium and large industries are, consequently, based in Hiroshima and are engaged in a range of activities from food processing to mineral water bottling to breweries that are dependent on high-quality fresh water. Hiroshima also hosts major industrial behemoths like SHARP, MAZDA and Mitsubishi, who are significant users of high-quality water. Japan is generally seen as a country of high-technology and as a major manufacturer of automobiles, machinery, robots, scientific instruments, medical devices, steel and shipbuilding etc. This image of Japan is correct, but we must also realize that Japan is a clean and tidy nation, with an abundant supply of very high-quality fresh water.[13, 14, 15]

Let us improve our water quality in India to save this land.

REFERENCES

Chapter One
Eastern India must not become a desert
1. Quit India Movement. https://en.wikipedia.org/wiki/Quit_India_ Movement, Retrieved on 28 November 2019.
2. Lebra, Joyce C. 1977. Japanese trained armies in South-East Asia, New York, Columbia University Press, ISBN 0-231-03995-6.
3. Indian Independence League. https://en.wikipedia.org/wiki/Indian_ Independence_League. Retrieved on 28 November 2019.
4. Iwaichi Fujiwara. https://en.wikipedia.org/wiki/Iwaichi_Fujiwara. Retrieved on 28 November 2019.
5. Indian_National_Army. https://en.wikipedia.org/wiki/Indian_ National_Army. Retrieved on 28 November 2019.
6. Tomoyuki_Yamashita. https://en.wikipedia.org/wiki/Tomoyuki_ Yamashita. Retrieved on 28 November 2019.
7. Twenty-Fifth_Army_(Japan). https://en.wikipedia.org/wiki/Twenty-Fifth_Army_(Japan). Retrieved on 28 November 2019.
8. Rash Behari Bose. https://en.wikipedia.org/wiki/Rash_Behari_Bose. Retrieved on 28 November 2019.
9. Japanese conquest of Burma. https://en.wikipedia.org/wiki/Japanese_ conquest_of_Burma. Retrieved on 28 November 2019.
10. Archibald Wavell. https://en.wikipedia.org/wiki/Archibald_ Wavell,_1st_Earl_Wavell. Retrieved on 28 November 2019.
11. American-British-Dutch-Australian Command. https://en.wikipedia. org/wiki/American-British-Dutch-Australian_Command. Retrieved on 28 November 2019.
12. Shojiro Ida. https://en.wikipedia.org/wiki/Sh%C5%8Djir%C5%8D_ Iida. Retrieved on 28 November 2019.
13. Harold Alexander. https://en.wikipedia.org/wiki/Harold_Alexander,_1st_ Earl_Alexander_of_Tunis, Retrieved on 28 November 2019.
14. Malayan Campaign. https://en.wikipedia.org/wiki/Malayan_ campaign. Retrieved on 28 November 2019.
15. Anglo-Burmese War. https://en.wikipedia.org/wiki/Anglo-Burmese_ Wars. Retrieved on 28 November 2019.
16. Bengal Famine of 1943. https://en.wikipedia.org/wiki/Bengal_ famine_of_1943. Retrieved on 28 November 2019.
17. Vritra. https://en.wikipedia.org/wiki/Vritra. Retrieved on 28 November 2019.

18. Bengal Famine of 1943. Wikipedia, https://en.wikipedia.org/wiki/Bengal_famine_of_1943. Retrieved on 28 November 2019.

19. Mishra, Pankaj. August 6, 2007, Exit Wounds, The legacy of Indian partition. The New Yorker https://www.newyorker.com/magazine/2007/08/13/exit-wounds. Retrieved on 28 November 2019.

20. Leo Amery. Wikipedia, https://en.wikipedia.org/wiki/Leo_Amery. Retrieved on 28 November 2019.

21. Orissa Famine of 1866. https://en.wikipedia.org/wiki/Orissa_famine_of_1866. Retrieved on 29 November 2019.

22. Sahu,N.K. Mishra, P.K. and Sahu, J.K. 1981. History of Orissa, Nalanda, Cuttack.

23. Durant, Will. The Case For India. 1930, Simon and Schuster, New York, https://www.vifindia.org/sites/default/files/139221701-The-Case-for-India-1930.pdf. Retrieved on 30 November 2019.

24. Patnaik, Utsa and Patnaik, Prabhat. 2016. A Theory of Imperialism, Columbia University Press, https://cup.columbia.edu/book/a-theory-of-imperialism/9780231179799. Retrieved on 30 November 2019.

25. A Theory of Imperialism. http://resistir.info/livros/patnaik_theory_of_imperialism.pdf. Retrieved on 30 November 2019.

26. Tharoor, Shashi. 2017. Inglorious Empire. What the British did to India, Aleph (India), Inglorious Empire, https://en.wikipedia.org/wiki/Inglorious_Empire, Retrieved on 30 November 2019.

27. 'A Beastly People…', The Hindu – Ramachandra Guha. 7 October 2011. http://ramachandraguha.in/archives/%E2%80%98a-beastly-people%E2%80%A6%E2%80%99.html. Retrieved on 30 November 2019.

27a. Guha, Ramachandra. 2008. India After Gandhi, PAN Books. https://www.academia.edu/36099051/india_after_gandhi_by_guha.pdf. Retrieved 30 November 2019.

28. 1951 Census of India. https://en.wikipedia.org/wiki/1951_Census_of_India. Retrieved on 30 November 2019.

29. Rice production in India. https://en.wikipedia.org/wiki/Rice_production_in_India. Retrieved on 30 November 2019.

30. Agriculture in India. https://en.wikipedia.org/wiki/Agriculture_in_India. Retrieved on 30 November 2019.

31. Krishnaswami Ramiah. https://en.wikipedia.org/wiki/Krishnaswami_Ramiah. Retrieved 30 November 2019.

32. Green Revolution. https://en.wikipedia.org/wiki/Green_Revolution. Retrieved on 30 November 2019.

33. Benjamin Peary Pal. 2007. Search for New Genes. Academic Foundation. pp. 19–. ISBN 978-81-7188-632-6, M.S. Swaminathan, Benjamin Peary Pal: A Tribute. https://books.google.co.jp/books?id=01fnNWME9woC&pg=PA19&redir_esc=y#v=onepage&q&f=false, Retrieved on 30 November 2019.

34. Norman Borlaug. https://en.wikipedia.org/wiki/Norman_Borlaug. Retrieved on 30 November 2019.
35. Food for peace. https://en.wikipedia.org/wiki/Food_for_Peace. Retrieved on 30 November 2019.
36. Chidambaram Subramaniam. https://en.wikipedia.org/wiki/Chidambaram_Subramaniam. Retrieved on 30 November 2019.
37. M.S.Swaminathan. https://en.wikipedia.org/wiki/M._S._Swaminathan. Retrieved on 30 November 2019.
38. Paddock, William and Paddock, Paul (1967), Famine 1975!: America's decision: Who will survive? Little, Brown, 1967 – 276.
39. Famine 1975!: America's decision: Who will survive? https://en.wikipedia.org/wiki/Famine_1975!_America%27s_Decision:_Who_Will_Survive%3 F. Retrieved on 30 November 2019.
40. India posts record food grain production in '08 crop year. https://economictimes.indiatimes.com/news/economy/indicators/india-posts-record-food-grain-production-in-08-crop-year/articleshow/2972825.cms?from=mdr. Retrieved on 30 November 2019.
41. Record rice output to propel India's food grain production to 281.37 million tonnes in 2018-19. https://economictimes.indiatimes.com/news/economy/agriculture/record-rice-output-to-propel-indias-foodgrain-production-to-281-37-million-tonnes-in-2018-19/articleshow/68200557.cms?from=mdr. Retrieved on 30 November 2019.
42. Yoshida, Tadanori. December 10, 2018. China's record rice yield — a blessing for global grain consumers. https://asia.nikkei.com/Economy/China-s-record-rice-yield-a-blessing-for-global-grain-consumers. Retrieved on 30 November 2019.
43. Rice Production in the World (Country-Wise Production). http://www.yourarticlelibrary.com/essay/rice-production-in-the-world-country-wise-production/25492. Retrieved on 30 November 2019.
44. Yuan Longping. https://en.wikipedia.org/wiki/Yuan_Longping. Retrieved on 30 November 2019.
45. Profile: Yuan Longping, father of hybrid rice, Xinhua 2019-09-26. Editor: huaxia. http://www.xinhuanet.com/english/2019-09/26/c_138424119.htm. Retrieved on 30 November 2019.
46. Livestock population in India by Species. nddb.coop. https://www.nddb.coop/information/stats/pop. Retrieved on 30 November 2019.
47. Role of Livestock in Indian Economy — Vikaspedia. http://vikaspedia.in/agriculture/livestock/role-of-livestock-in-indian-economy. Retrieved on 30 November 2019.
48. World Livestock. 2011. Livestock in food security - FAO. http://www.fao.org/3/i2373e/i2373e.pdf. Retrieved on 30 November 2019.
49. Small ruminant production in the developing countries - FAO. http://www.fao.org/3/ah221e/AH221E13.htm, Retrieved on 30 November 2019.
50. Jitendra. 17 October 2019. Goats, sheep drive India's livestock numbers. Down to Earth. https://www.downtoearth.org.in/news/

economy/goats-sheep-drive-india-s-livestock-numbers-67302. Retrieved on 26 January 2021.

51. Black Saturday Bushfires, https://en.wikipedia.org/wiki/Black_Saturday_bushfires. Retrieved on 30 November 2019.

52. Read, Paul. November 18, 2019. Arson, mischief and recklessness: 87 per cent of fires are man-made. https://www.smh.com.au/national/arson-mischief-and-recklessness-87-per-cent-of-fires-are-man-made-20191117-p53bcl.html. Retrieved on 30 November 2019.

53. The Amazon in Brazil is on fire - how bad is it? BBC News. https://www.bbc.com/news/world-latin-america-49433767. Retrieved on 30 November 2019.

54. Ullendorff Edward The Queen of Sheba 1 - The University of Manchester. https://www.escholar.manchester.ac.uk/api/datastream?publicationPid=uk-ac-man-scw:1m269. Retrieved on 30 November 2019.

55. Forestry in Ethiopia. https://en.wikipedia.org/wiki/Forestry_in_Ethiopia. Retrieved on 30 November 2019.

56. Das, Alekh Prasad. Jibanara Daka; an autobiography.1994. Sri Lalita Prakasani, Bhubaneswar.

57. Das, Nachiketa. Kaya Yoga: Road to happiness, health and longevity. 2018. Notion Press, Chennai. ISBN 978-1-64249-702-1.

58. River Development Project of Water system Senogawa. https://www.pref.hiroshima.lg.jp/uploaded/attachment/11088.pdf. Retrieved on 30 November 2019.

59. Topography. Odisha Government Portal. https://www.odisha.gov.in/content/topography. Retrieved on 30 November 2019.

60. Dam Safety Activity Report. August 2018. Department of Water Resources, Government of Odisha. http://www.dowrodisha.gov.in/DamSafety/Dam%20Safety%20activity%20report.pdf. Retrieved on 30 November 2019.

61. Human, Joe, Pattanaik, Manoj. 2000. Community Forest Management: A Casebook from India. London: Oxfam.

62. Harrabin, Roger. 2015. 'Water man of India' Rajendra Singh bags top prize. BBC environment analyst. 21 March 2015. https://www.bbc.com/news/science-environment-32002306. Retrieved on 30 November 2019.

63. Narendra Modi Wikipedia. https://en.wikipedia.org/wiki/Narendra_Modi#cite_note-Shah_BS-153. Retrieved on 30 November 2019.

64. Panchayati Raj & Drinking water, Government of Odisha. Topography. Odisha Government Portal. https://odishapanchayat.gov.in/English/demographic.asp. Retrieved on 30 November 2019.

65. Singha, Minati. 'Orange alert' across Odisha as temperature crosses 46 degree Celsius.TNN.May 15, 2017. Retrieved on 30 November 2019.

66. Odisha signs agreement to invest Rs. 1,115 crore for groundwater recharge IANS, Bhubaneswar, August 10, 2018. https://www.business-standard.com/article/news-ians/odisha-signs-agreement-to-invest-rs-1-115-c. Retrieved on 30 November 2019.

67. 14,588 check dams built in Odisha in 10 years: Minister. 12 March 2020. Sambad English. https://sambadenglish.com/14588-check-dams-built-in-odisha-in-10-years-minister. Retrieved on 11 February 2021.

Chapter Two
Sea level rise and inundation of coastal India

1. Sea Level Change. https://www.ipcc.ch/site/assets/uploads/2018/02/WG1AR5_Chapter13_FINAL.pdf. Retrieved on 1 December 2019.
2. Lu, Denise and Flavelle, Christopher. Oct. 29, 2019. Rising seas will erase more cities by 2050, new research shows. https://www.nytimes.com/interactive/2019/10/29/climate/coastal-cities-underwater.html. Retrieved on 2 December 2019.
3. Kulp, Scott A. & Strauss Benjamin H. 2019. New elevation data triple estimates of global vulnerability to sea-level rise and coastal flooding. Nature Communications volume 10, Article number: 4844 (2019). https://www.nature.com/articles/s41467-019-12808-z. Retrieved on 2 December 2019.
4. Ice age. https://en.wikipedia.org/wiki/Ice_age. Retrieved on 2 December 2019.
5. Sea level rise. https://en.wikipedia.org/wiki/Sea_level_rise. Retrieved on 2 December 2019.
6. Mission to planet earth TOPEX/POSEIDON NASA/CNES Press Kit. August, 1992. https://www.jpl.nasa.gov/news/press_kits/topex_poseidon.pdf. Retrieved on 10 December 2019.
7. TOPEX/POSEIDON. https://en.wikipedia.org/wiki/TOPEX/Poseidon. Retrieved on 10 December 2019.
8. Greenland Lost 12.5 Billion Tons of Ice in a Single Day. https://www.smithsonianmag.com/smart-news/greenland-lost-record-breaking-125-billion-tons-ice-single-day-180972808/. Retrieved on 10 December 2019.
9. Leahy, Stephen. January 21, 2019. Greenland's ice is melting four times faster than thought—what it means. New science suggests Greenland may be approaching a dangerous tipping point, with implications for global sea-level rise. National Geographic. https://www.nationalgeographic.com/environment/2019/01/greeland-ice-melting-four-times-faster-than-thought-raising-sea-level/. Retrieved on 10 December 2019.
10. Recent Antarctic ice mass loss from radar interferometry and regional climate modelling, Nature Geoscience 1(2):106-110 · January 2008. https://www.nature.com/articles/ngeo102. Retrieved on 11 December 2019.
11. Third Assessment Report — IPCC, ipcc.ch/assessment-report/ar3/. Retrieved on 11 December 2019.
12. Rajendra K. Pachauri. https://en.wikipedia.org/wiki/Rajendra_K._Pachauri. Retrieved on 11 December 2019.
13. Aryabhata. https://en.wikipedia.org/wiki/Aryabhata. Retrieved on 11 December 2019.

14. Woolard, George Prior. 1949. Gravity anomalies and the nature of the Earth's crust. https://agupubs.onlinelibrary.wiley.com/doi/abs/10.1029/TR030i002p00189. Retrieved on 11 December 2019.

15. Is sea level the same all across the ocean? The sea level varies around the globe. https://oceanservice.noaa.gov/facts/globalsl.html. Retrieved on 11 December 2019.

16. Why will sea level rise not be the same everywhere?, https://www.earthobservatory.sg/faq-on-earth-sciences/why-will-sea-level-rise-not-be-same-everywhere. Retrieved on 11 December 2019.

17. Sea level rise. https://www.globalchange.gov/browse/indicators/global-sea-level-rise. Retrieved on 11 December 2019.

18. Flooded Future: Global vulnerability to sea level rise worse than previously understood. October 29th, 2019. Climate Central. https://www.climatecentral.org/news/report-flooded-future-global-vulnerability-to-sea-level-rise-worse-than-previously-understood. Retrieved on 11 December 2019.

19. Marine archaeology in the Gulf of Cambay. https://en.wikipedia.org/wiki/Marine_archaeology_in_the_Gulf_of_Cambay. Retrieved on 11 December 2019.

20. Chengappa, Raj. February 11, 2002. Ancient city discovered off Gujarat coast, could be oldest in the world. India Today. https://www.indiatoday.in/magazine/cover-story/story/20020211-ancient-city-discovered-off-gujarat-coast-could-be-oldest-in-the-world-795877-2002-02-11. Retrieved on 11 December 2019.

21. Badrinaryan, Badrinaryan. Gulf of Cambay: Cradle of Ancient Civilization. https://www.archaeologyonline.net/artifacts/cambay. Retrieved on 11 December 2019.

22. Rohde, Robert A. File: Holocene Sea Level.png. https://commons.wikimedia.org/wiki/File:Holocene_Sea_Level.png. Retrieved on 11 December 2019.

23. Rohde, Robert A. File: Post-Glacial Sea Level.png. https://commons.wikimedia.org/wiki/File:Post-Glacial_Sea_Level.png. Retrieved on 11 December 2019.

24. Sea level rise. https://en.wikipedia.org/wiki/Sea_level_rise. Retrieved on 11 December 2019.

25. Last Glacial Period – Wikipedia. https://en.wikipedia.org/wiki/Last_Glacial_Period. Retrieved on 26 October 2020.

26. Porter. S.C. 2001. Snowline depression in the tropics during the Last Glaciation. Quaternary Science Reviews 20 (2001) 1067}1091. https://www.ldeo.columbia.edu/~peter/Resources/Seminar/readings/Porter,%202001(Snowline%20lowering).pdf. Retrieved on 26 October 2020.

27. Kalsi. S.R. 2006. Orissa super cyclone – A Synopsis. MAUSAM, 57, 1 (January 2006), 1-20 551.515.2 (541.5) (1) https://metnet.imd.gov.in/mausamdocs/15711_F.pdf. Retrieved on 26 October 2020.

28. Revisiting the super cyclone that hit Odisha in 1999. https://www.hindustantimes.com/india/revisiting-the-super-cyclone-that-hit-

odisha-in-1999/story-S0lDY1STwdrVdMravThCZK.html. Retrieved on 26 October 2020.

29. Basin Details (Mahanadi & Eastern Rivers Organization). http://www.cwc.gov.in/mero/about-basin. Retrieved on 26 October 2020.

30. 1999 Odisha Cyclone - Wikipedia. https://en.wikipedia.org/wiki/1999_Odisha_cyclone. Retrieved on 26 October 2020.

31. Cyclone Sidr - Wikipedia. https://en.wikipedia.org/wiki/Cyclone_Sidr. Retrieved on 26 October 2020.

32. Cyclone Nargis – Wikipedia. https://en.wikipedia.org/wiki/Cyclone_Nargis. Retrieved on 26 October 2020.

33. Cyclone Fani – Wikipedia. https://en.wikipedia.org/wiki/Cyclone_Fani. Retrieved on 18 November 2020.

34. Cyclone Bulbul – Wikipedia. https://en.wikipedia.org/wiki/Cyclone_Bulbul. Retrieved on 18 November 2020.

35. Cyclone Phailin – Wikipedia. https://en.wikipedia.org/wiki/Cyclone_Phailin. Retrieved on 18 November 2020.

36. INDIA Cyclone Phailin in Odisha, October 2013. Rapid Damage and Needs Assessment Report. Government of Odisha. https://ncrmp.gov.in/wp-content/uploads/2014/03/Odisha-Phailin-report-Final.pdf. Retrieved on 26 November 2020.

37. United Nation praises Odisha's handling of Cyclone Phailin, calls it a landmark in disaster management. All India Press Trust of India. October 15, 2013 NDTV. https://www.ndtv.com/india-news/united-nation-praises-odishas-handling-of-cyclone-phailin-calls-it-a-landmark-in-disaster-management-537847. Retrieved on 26 November 2020.

38. Ashis Senapati. Ashis. 17 August 2015. Down to Earth. UN felicitates Odisha for its disaster management model during Phailin. State first in Southeast Asia to get a thumbs up by the international body. https://www.downtoearth.org.in/news/un-felicitates-odisha-for-its-disaster-management-model-during-phailin-43087. Retrieved on 26 November 2020.

39. Forecast on Cyclone Phailin was "more or less" accurate: IMD. The Economic Times. October 13, 2013. https://economictimes.indiatimes.com/news/politics-and-nation/forecast-on-cyclone-phailin-was-more-or-less-accurate-imd/articleshow/24089041.cms. Retrieved on 30 November 2020.

40. Cyclone Phailin: India Meteorological Department wins battle over forecasts. October 14, 2013. All IndiaAgence France-Presse. NDTV. https://www.ndtv.com/india-news/cyclone-phailin-india-meteorological-department-wins-battle-over-forecasts-537584. Retrieved on 30 November 2020.

41. (PDF) Report on Phailin Cyclone 2014 - ResearchGate. https://www.researchgate.net/publication/296614126_Report_on_Phailin_Cyclone_2014. Retrieved on 30 November 2020.

42. Hirakud Dam – Wikipedia. https://en.wikipedia.org/wiki/Hirakud_Dam. Retrieved on 30 November 2020.

43. Hirakud Dam Project. http://dowrodisha.gov.in/Projects/MajMed/DetailsCompletedOngoing/Ongoing/CEUMB/Hirakud%20System%20(Completed)/SFHirakud.pdf. Retrieved on 30 November 2020.

44. Hirakud.pdf – Central Water Commission. http://www.cwc.gov.in/sites/default/files/hirakud.pdf. Retrieved on 30 November 2020.

45. Temporal analysis of area-capacity curve for hirakud reservoir. http://ethesis.nitrkl.ac.in/5803/1/E-18.pdf. Retrieved on 30 November 2020.

46. Hirakud HE Project - Odisha Hydro Power Corporation Ltd. http://www.ohpcltd.com/Hirakud/project. Retrieved on 30 November 2020.

47. Capacity boost for Hirakud dam- The New Indian Express. February 14, 2019. https://www.newindianexpress.com/states/odisha/2019/feb/14/capacity-boost-for-hirakud-dam-1938712.html. Retrieved on 30 November 2020.

48. Emergency Action Plan Hirakud Dam – Prepared by Central Project Management Unit (CPMU). Prepared for Department of Water Resources, The Government of Odisha. October 2018. http://www.dowrodisha.gov.in/Emergency%20Action%20Plan/Emergency%20Action%20Plan/Hirakud.pdf. Retrieved on 30 November 2020.

49. Laxman Singh Rathore - Wikipedia. https://en.wikipedia.org/wiki/Laxman_Singh_Rathore. Retrieved on 30 November 2020.

50. Odisha hit by over nine lakh lightning strikes this year. Jacob Koshy. November 09, 2019. The Hindu. https://www.thehindu.com/news/national/other-states/odisha-hit-by-over-nine-lakh-lightning-strikes-this-year/article2993293.ece. Retrieved on 25 November 2020.

51. Doppler radar to be commissioned in Odisha's Gopalpur next month. February 28, 2016. The Economic Times. https://m.economictimes.com/news/science/doppler-radar-to-be-commissioned-in-odishas-gopalpur-next-month/articleshow/51176911.cms. Retrieved on 25 November 2020.

52. Uma Charan Mohanty – Wikipedia. https://en.wikipedia.org/wiki/Uma_Charan_Mohanty. Retrieved on 25 November 2020.

53. With an alert system in place, lightning deaths in Odisha down by over 30%. Debabrata Mohanty
The Hindustan Times. July 15, 2019. https://www.hindustantimes.com/india-news/with-an-alert-system-in-place-lightning-deaths-in-odisha-down-by-over-30/story tFTEw5Bz1jcNtkeyLFAAML.html. Retrieved on 25 November 2020.

54. Coral reef – Wikipedia. https://en.wikipedia.org/wiki/Coral_reef. Retrieved on 17 November 2020.

55. Early Holocene sea level rise – Wikipedia. https://en.wikipedia.org/wiki/Early_Holocene_sea_level_rise. Retrieved on 17 November 2020.

56. Younger Dryas – Wikipedia. https://en.wikipedia.org/wiki/Younger_Dryas. Retrieved on 18 November 2020.

57. Younger Dryas impact hypothesis – Wikipedia. https://en.wikipedia.org/wiki/Younger_Dryas_impact_hypothesis, Retrieved on 18 November 2020.

58. Antonio Zamora. Younger Dryas Global Deluge. You Tube. May 17, 2019. https://www.youtube.com/watch?v=EFhPW103zko. Retrieved on 18 November 2020.

59. Mausala Parva – Wikipedia. https://en.wikipedia.org/Mausala_Parva. Retrieved on 16 November 2020.

60. Diana L. Eck (26 March 2013). India: A Sacred Geography. Three Rivers Press. p. 382. ISBN 978-0-385-53192-4.

61. Dvaraka. https://en.wikipedia.org/wiki/Dv%C4%81rak%C4%81. Retrieved on 19 December 2019.

62. A painting depicting Krishna's Dwarka, made during Akbar's reign, from the Smithsonian Institution. https://en.wikipedia.org/wiki/Dwarka#/media/File:Dwarka.jpg. Retrieved on 19 December 2019.

63. Tsunami – Wikipedia. https://en.wikipedia.org/wiki/Tsunami. Retrieved on 4 November 2020.

64. List of tsunamis – Wikipedia. https://en.wikipedia.org/wiki/List_of_tsunamis. Retrieved on 4 November 2020.

65. East Molokai Volcano – Wikipedia. https://en.wikipedia.org/wiki/East_Molokai_Volcano. Retrieved on 7 November 2020.

66. Stirling, Andrew (1822) An Account, Geographical, Statistical and Historical of Orissa Proper, or Cuttack; The Asiatic Researches, Vol. 15. Reprinted in Chapter Six titled Orissa: Chronology and History in Hunter W.W., Stirling Andrew, Beames John and Sahu N.K. (2009) A History of Orissa, Edited by N.K. Sahu, 480 pages, New Age Publications, Cuttack-753002, ISBN: 81-88337-24-2

67. Tsunami Facts and Information; Australian Government, Bureau of Meteorology. http://www.bom.gov.au/tsunami/info/index.shtml. Retrieved on 17 January 2020.

68. How deep is the ocean? - NOAA's National Ocean Service. https://oceanservice.noaa.gov/facts/oceandepth.html. Retrieved on 17 January 2020.

69. Bay of Bengal - Wikipedia. https://en.wikipedia.org/wiki/Bay_of_Bengal. Retrieved on 17 January 2020.

70. Barren Island (Andaman Islands) - Wikipedia. https://en.wikipedia.org/wiki/Barren_Island_(Andaman_Islands). Retrieved on 17 January 2020.

71. Hydrogen production – Wikipedia. https://en.wikipedia.org/wiki/Hydrogen_production. Retrieved on 2 November 2020.

72. Green Hydrogen Market Size & Analysis Report, 2020-2027. https://www.grandviewresearch.com/industry-analysis/green-hydrogen-market. Retrieved on 2 November 2020.

73. 2004 Indian Ocean earthquake and tsunami - Wikipedia. https://en.wikipedia.org/wiki/2004_Indian_Ocean_earthquake_and_tsunami. Retrieved on 17 January 2020.

74. Methane clathrate – Wikipedia. https://en.wikipedia.org/wiki/Methane_clathrate. Retrieved on 3 November 2020.

75. Clathrate hydrate – Wikipedia. https://en.wikipedia.org/wiki/Clathrate_hydrate. Retrieved on 3 November 2020.

76. 'Methane hydrate': A new energy source discovered off Andhra coast. The National Herald. 27 February 2019. https://www.nationalheraldindia.com/national/methane-hydrate-a-new-energy-source-discovered-off-andhra-coast. Retrieved on 3 November 2020.

77. Large Deposits of Potentially Producible Gas Hydrate Found in Indian Ocean. USGS. 25 July 2016. https://www.usgs.gov/news/large-deposits-potentially-producible-gas-hydrate-found-indian-ocean. Retrieved on 3 November 2020.

78. Countries affected by the 2004 Indian Ocean earthquake and tsunami – Wikipedia. https://en.wikipedia.org/wiki/Countries_affected_by_the_2004_Indian_Ocean_earthquake_and_tsunami. Retrieved on 2 November 2020.

79. 2011 Tohoku earthquake and tsunami – Wikipedia. https://en.wikipedia.org/wiki/2011_T%C5%8Dhoku_earthquake_and_tsunami. Retrieved on 4 November 2020.

80. Kei Sasaki, Kaoru Nakamura, Kenji Takeno, Hidenori Shinkawa, Nachiketa Das, Ken Sasaki. 2015. Removal of Radioactivity from Sediment Mud and Soil and Use for Cultivation of Safe Vegetables in Fukushima, and Removal of Toxic Metals Using Photosynthetic Bacteria. Journal of Agricultural Chemistry and Environment, 2015, 4, 63-75.

81. Kei Sasaki, Kenji Takeno, Hidenori Shinkawa, Ken sasaki, Nachiketa Das. 2015. Removal of Radioactivity and Recovery of Radioactive Cs from Sediment Mud and Soil in Fukushima, Japan Using Immobilized Photosynthetic Bacteria. Advanced Materials Research Vol. 1091 (2015) pp 125-130. Trans Tech Publications, Switzerland doi:10.4028/www.scientific.net/AMR.1091.125

82. Das, Nachiketa, Morikawa, Hiroyo, Sasaki, Ken. 2015. Discovery of Radon in Hot Spring Waters of Odisha in Eastern India, Asian Journal of Water, Environment and Pollution, Vol. 12, No. 4, pp. 71-77.

83. Genbaku Kensui: Dedication of Water Ceremony for the Victims of the A-Bomb. 2013. Written by Ken Sasaki, Translated by Ken Sasaki with Nachiketa Das. Published by Meisui-Bio Research Institute Research and Development Centre, Hiroshima Kokusai Gakuin University, 6-20-1, Nakano, Akiku, Hiroshima, 739-0321, Japan.

84. The Great Wall of Japan: 101 East, Al Zazeera. July 31, 2020. You Tube.

85. Maddy, July 31, 2009, Champaka Raman Pillai – The forgotten freedom fighter. https://maddy06.blogspot.com/2009/07/champaka-raman-pillai-forgotten-freedom.html. Retrieved on 17 December 2019.

86. Indugopan G.R. 27 September 2016, Chempaka Raman Pillai: The freedom fighter who coined 'Jai Hind'. https://english.manoramaonline.com/lifestyle/news/chempaka-raman-pillai-indian-revolutionary-freedom-fighter.html. Retrieved on 17 December 2019.

87. Wright Tom. November 11, 2011. Why Delhi? The Move From Calcutta. The Wall Street Journal. https://blogs.wsj.com/indiarealtime/2011/11/11/why-delhi-the-move-from-calcutta/. Retrieved on 17 December 2019.

88. Netherlands. https://en.wikipedia.org/wiki/Netherlands. Retrieved on 17 December 2019.

89. Delta Works. https://en.wikipedia.org/wiki/Delta_Works. Retrieved on 17 December 2019.

90. Integrated Coastal Zone Management Project, Odisha. http://www.iczmpodisha.org/index.htm. Retrieved on 17 December 2019.

91. Mars Orbiter Mission. https://en.wikipedia.org/wiki/Mars_Orbiter_Mission. Retrieved on 17 December 2019.

92. Amos Jonathan. Why India's Mars mission is so cheap - and thrilling. 24 September 2014. https://www.bbc.com/news/science-environment-29341850. Retrieved on 17 December 2019.

93. Indian Space Research Organisation - Wikipedia. https://en.wikipedia.org/wiki/Indian_Space_Research_Organisation. Retrieved on 17 December 2019.

94. Chandrayaan-1. https://en.wikipedia.org/wiki/Chandrayaan-1. Retrieved on 17 December 2019.

95. Chandrayaan-2. https://en.wikipedia.org/wiki/Chandrayaan-2. Retrieved on 17 December 2019.

96. Keling. https://en.wikipedia.org/wiki/Keling. Retrieved on 17 December 2019.

97. Patel Kandarpa. Maritime Relation of Kalinga with Sri Lanka. OHRJ, Vol. XLVII, No. 2. https://magazines.odisha.gov.in/Journal/Journal2/pdf/ohrj-017.pdf. Retrieved on 17 December 2019.

98. Kallanai Dam. https://en.wikipedia.org/wiki/Kallanai_Dam#cite_note-:0-2. Retrieved on 17 December 2019.

99. Karikala. https://en.wikipedia.org/wiki/Karikala. Retrieved on 17 December 2019.

100. Sagarmala. http://sagarmala.gov.in/about-sagarmala/background. Retrieved on 17 December 2019.

101. Sagar Mala. https://en.wikipedia.org/wiki/Sagar_Mala_project. Retrieved on 17 December 2019.

Chapter Three
Can global warming make the Ganga run dry?

1. Ganges - Wikipedia. https://en.wikipedia.org/wiki/Ganges. Retrieved on 6 December 2020.

2. Gangotri Glacier - Wikipedia. https://en.wikipedia.org/wiki/Gangotri_Glacier. Retrieved on 6 December 2020.

3. Fred Pearce. Flooded out. 5 June 1999, Magazine issue 2189, New Scientist. https://www.newscientist.com/article/mg16221893-000-flooded-out/ Retrieved on 6 December 2020.

4. Ajay K. Naithani, H. C. Nainwal, K. K. Sati and C. Prasad: Geomorphological evidences of retreat of the Gangotri glacier and its characteristics. Current Science, 2001, Vol. 80, No. 1, 87-94. http://www.ias.ac.in/currsci/jan102001/87.pdf. Retrieved on 6 December 2020.

5. Retreat of the Gangotri Glacier - NASA Earth Observatory. Article at Earth Observatory driven by NASA, 22 Jun 2004. https://earthobservatory.nasa.gov/images/4594/retreat-of-the-gangotri-glacier. Retrieved on 6 December 2020.

6. Lal, P. Vaka, D. S. Rao, Y. S. 15 November 2018. "Mapping surface flow velocities of siachen and gangotri glaciers using terrasar-x and sentinel-1a data by intensity tracking". ISPRS Annals of the Photogrammetry, Remote Sensing and Spatial Information Sciences. IV-5: 325–329. doi:10.5194/isprs-annals-IV-5-325-2018. https://www.isprs-ann-photogramm-remote-sens-spatial-inf-sci.net/IV-5/325/2018/. Retrieved on 6 December 2020.

7. Gulf Stream - Wikipedia. https://en.wikipedia.org/wiki/Gulf_Stream. Retrieved on 6 December 2020.

8. Plockton - Wikipedia. https://en.wikipedia.org/wiki/Plockton. Retrieved on 6 December 2020.

9. Neil C. Wells. 08 January 2016. The North Atlantic Ocean and climate change in the UK and northern Europe. https://rmets.onlinelibrary.wiley.com/doi/full/10.1002/wea.2558. Retrieved on 6 December 2020.

10. The Day After Tomorrow – Wikipedia. https://en.wikipedia.org/wiki/The_Day_After_Tomorrow. Retrieved on 6 December 2020.

11. Himalayas - Wikipedia. https://en.wikipedia.org/wiki/Himalayas. Retrieved on 6 December 2020.

12. Monsoon of South Asia - Wikipedia. https://en.wikipedia.org/wiki/Monsoon_of_South_Asia. Retrieved on 6 December 2020.

13. Cherrapunji - Wikipedia. https://en.wikipedia.org/wiki/Cherrapunji. Retrieved on 8 December 2020.

14. Lower Himalayan Range - Wikipedia. https://en.wikipedia.org/wiki/Lower_Himalayan_Range. Retrieved on 8 December 2020.

15. Water - MoSPI. http://mospi.nic.in/sites/default/files/reports_and_publication/statistical_publication/social_statistics/comp_SECTION%206_16mar16.pdf. Retrieved on 8 December 2020.

16. Chander P. Vohra. A Brief Overview of the State of Glaciers in the Indian Himalaya in the 1970s and at the End of the 20th Century. Satellite Image Atlas of Glaciers of the World Glaciers of Asia— Glaciers of India— Satellite Image Atlas of Glaciers of The World. Edited By Richard S. Williams, Jr., and Jane G. Ferrigno U.S. Geological Survey Professional Paper 1 3 8 6 –F– 5. https://pubs.usgs.gov/pp/p1386f/pdf/F5_India.pdf. Retrieved on 8 December 2020.

17. Syed Iqbal Hasnain, Rajesh Kumar, Safaraz Ahmad and Shresth Taya. A Study of Selected Glaciers under the Changing Climate

Regime. Satellite Image Atlas of Glaciers of The World Glaciers of Asia— Glaciers of India— Satellite Image Atlas of Glaciers of The World. Edited By Richard S. Williams, Jr., and Jane G. Ferrigno U.S. Geological Survey Professional Paper 1 3 8 6 –F– 5. https://pubs.usgs.gov/pp/p1386f/pdf/F5_India.pdf. Retrieved on 8 December 2020.

18. Raina, V. K. and Srivastava D. 2008. Glacier atlas of India. Geological Society of India. Bangalore. 315pp. https://www.geosocindia.org/index.php/bgsi/article/view/56014.   https://www.cambridge.org/core/journals/journal-of-glaciology/article/vk-raina-and-d-srivastava-2008-glacier-atlas-of-india-bangalore-geological-society-of-india-315pp /E138296A9A8190D933932DECEAF25F12. Retrieved on 8 December 2020.

19. Compendium of Task Force Report on NDMA Guidelines Management of Glacial Lake Outburst Floods (GLOFs). October 2020. National Disaster Management Authority, Ministry of Home Affairs, Government of India. http://www.ndma.gov.in/sites/default/files/PDF/Guidelines/NDMA-Compendium_GLOF_Oct%202020.pdf. Retrieved on 8 December 2020.

20. Glaciers in Ganga Basin. http://117.252.14.242/Gangakosh/Water%20Resources/glaciers.htm. Retrieved on 8 December 2020.

21. Monsoon reaches Delhi, breaking 108-year-old record | June 15, 2008. The Times of India. https://timesofindia.indiatimes.com/city/delhi/Monsoon-reaches-Delhi-breaking-108-year-old-record/articleshow/3130790.cms

22. 2008 Bihar flood - Wikipedia. https://en.wikipedia.org/wiki/2008_Bihar_flood. Retrieved on 10 December 2020.

23. 14 dead as heavy rain lashes Rajasthan, Jaipur flooded. Aug 23 2012.Express News Service. http://archive.indianexpress.com/news/14-dead-as-heavy-rain-lashes-rajasthan-jaipur-flooded/991831/. Retrieved on 10 December 2020.

24. Jaisalmer and Barmer, the last posts of Rajasthan have rainiest August. 1 Sep 2020. Skymet Weather Team. https://www.skymetweather.com/content/weather-news-and-analysis/jaisalmer-and-barmer-the-last-posts-of-rajasthan-have-rainiest-august/. Retrieved on 10 December 2020.

25. Barmer in Rajasthan records unusual November rains after a decade. November 14, 2019. Skymet Weather Team. https://www.skymetweather.com/content/weather-news-and-analysis/barmer-in-rajasthan-records-unusual-november-rains-after-a-decade/. Retrieved on 10 December 2020.

26. Tehri Dam – Wikipedia. https://en.wikipedia.org/wiki/Tehri_Dam. Retrieved on 10 December 2020.

27. Utpal Bhaskar. THDC confident of managing rising water levels at Tehri dam. 12 Aug 2013. Mint. https://www.livemint.com/Industry/jYOD2Ndutf2FC6gGlVcdFP/THDC-confident-of-managing-rising-water-levels-at-Tehri-dam.html. Retrieved on 10 December 2020.

28. 2013 North India floods - Wikipedia. https://en.wikipedia.org/wiki/2013_North_India_floods. Retrieved on 10 December 2020.

29. Cho, Changrae; Li, Rong; S.-Y., Wang; Jin-Ho, Yoon; Robert R., Gillies. 29 April 2015. "Anthropogenic footprint of climate change in the June 2013 northern India flood". Climate Dynamics. 46 (3–4): 797. Bibcode:2016ClDy...46..797C. doi:10.1007/s00382-015-2613-2. S2CID 129575971. Retrieved on 10 December 2020.

30. 2012 Himalayan flash floods - Wikipedia.https://en.wikipedia.org/wiki/2012_Himalayan_flash_floods. Retrieved on 10 December 2020.

31. Cloudburst - Wikipedia. https://en.wikipedia.org/wiki/Cloudburst. Retrieved on 10 December 2020.

32. 2010 Ladakh floods - Wikipedia. https://en.wikipedia.org/wiki/2010_Ladakh_floods. Retrieved on 10 December 2020.

33. Preksha Sharma. 11 January 2018. Ladakh Floods: A Timeline of Disaster. The Wire. https://thewire.in/environment/ladakh-floods-timeline-disaster. Retrieved on 10 December 2020.

34. Cloudburst in Leh Triggers Flashflood, Property Damage. August 9, 2018 6:19 PM | Skymet Weather Team. https://www.skymetweather.com/content/weather-news-and-analysis/cloudburst-in-leh-triggers-flashflood-property-damage/. Retrieved on 10 December 2020.

35. Siachen Glacier - Wikipedia. https://en.wikipedia.org/wiki/Siachen_Glacier. Retrieved on 10 December 2020.

36. Raina, V.K. and Sangewar. C. 2007. Siachen Glacier of Karakoram Mountains, Ladakh – its secular retreat. J. Geol. Soc. India, 70(1), 11–16.

37. The melting of the Siachen glacier - India Environment Portal.10 Mar 2009. Rajeev Upadhyay. Current Science, Vol. 96, no. 5, pp. 646 to 648. 10 March 2009. http://www.indiaenvironmentportal.org.in/files/The%20melting%20of%20the%20Siachen%20glacier.pdf. Retrieved on 10 December 2020.

38. Taylor, J. M., Environment and Climate News, The Heartland Institute, 11 January 2006.

39. Sharmila Kher. 04 July 2015. Glacial melt? Need more studies – Down to Earth. https://www.downtoearth.org.in/news/glacial-melt-need-more-studies-2608. Retrieved on 10 December 2020.

40. Swaminathan S Anklesaria Aiyar. Jan 20, 2010. IPCC imperialism on Indian glaciers - The Economic Times. https://m.economictimes.com/swaminathan-s-a-aiyar/ipcc-imperialism-on-indian-glaciers/articleshow/5478293.cms. Retrieved on 10 December 2020.

41. Julie Gardelle, Etienne Berthier and Yves Arnaud. April 2012. Slight mass gain of Karakoram glaciers in the early twenty-first century. Nature Geoscience 5(5):322-325. https://www.researchgate.net/publication/232759925_Slight_mass_gain_of_Karakoram_glaciers_in_the_early_twenty-first_century. Retrieved on 10 December 2020.

42. Matthew Knight. April 17, 2012. Study: Glaciers in western Himalayas bucking global melting trend. https://www.cnn.com/2012/04/17/world/asia/glacier-himalayas-gain-mass/index.html. Retrieved on 8 December 2020.

43. Mayank Aggarwal. 15 July 2020. How glaciers in the western Himalayas are reacting differently to climate change and human activities. Mongabay. https://india.mongabay.com/2020/07/how-glaciers-in-the-western-himalayas-are-reacting-differently-to-climate-change-and-human-activities/. Retrieved on 8 December 2020.

44. Mana Pass - Wikipedia. https://en.wikipedia.org/wiki/Mana_Pass. Retrieved on 10 December 2020.

45. Gyan Marwah. August 2004. Ganges - A River of No Return? The South Asian.com.

46. Gangotri glacier - The South Asian. http://www.the-south-asian.com/aug2004/Gangotri_glacier.htm. Retrieved on 10 December 2020.

47. Badrinath - Wikipedia. https://en.wikipedia.org/wiki/Badrinath. Retrieved on 11 December 2020.

48. Badrinath Pilgrimage Stats - Number of Pilgrims Visiting. https://www.sacredyatra.com/badrinath-pilgrimage-stats.html. Retrieved on 10 December 2020.

49. Kedarnath - Wikipedia. https://en.wikipedia.org/wiki/Kedarnath. Retrieved on 10 December 2020. Kedarnath Pilgrimage Stats - Numbers of Pilgrims Visited. https://www.sacredyatra.com/kedarnath-pilgrim-stats.html. Retrieved on 10 December 2020.

50. Mayank Aggarwal. 15 July 2020. How glaciers in the western Himalayas are reacting differently to climate change and human activities. Mongabay. https://india.mongabay.com/2020/07/how-glaciers-in-the-western-himalayas-are-reacting-differently-to-climate-change-and-human-activities/. Retrieved on 8 December 2020.

51. P. K. Joshi, Sarnam Singh, Shefali Agarwal and P. S. Roy. 25 April 2001. Forest cover assessment in western Himalayas, Himachal Pradesh using IRS 1C/1D WiFS data. Current Science. Vol. 80, No. 8, pp. 941-947. https://www.jstor.org/stable/24105804. Retrieved on 8 December 2020.

52. Valdiya. KS. 1993. High Dams in the Himalaya. PAHAR Publication. High dams in the Himalaya.pdf http://14.139.206.50:8080/jspui/bitstream/1/131/1/HIGH%20DAMS%20IN%20THE%20HIMALAYA.pdf. Retrieved on 12 December 2020.

53. K. S. Valdiya. 25 September 1992. Must we have high dams in the geodynamically active Himalayan domain? Current Science.Vol. 63, No. 6 (25 September 1992), pp. 289-296 https://www.jstor.org/stable/24095437.

54. Valdiya. KS 1997. High dams in Central Himalaya in the context of active faults, seismicity and societal problems. Journal of Geological Society of India, Vol. 49, pp. 479–494, 1997.

55. Dinakar Peri, Suhasini Haidar and Ananth Krishnan. June 16, 2020. Indian Army says 20 soldiers killed in clash with Chinese troops in the Galwan area. https://www.thehindu.com/news/national/indian-army-says-20-soldiers-killed-in-clash-with-chinese-troops-in-the-galwan-area/article31845662.ece. Retrieved on 12 December 2020.

56. Owen King. 2 February, 2020. Melting Himalayan glaciers forming thousands of lakes, but not all water drains downstream. https://theprint.in/environment/melting-himalayan-glaciers-forming-thousands-of-lakes-but-not-all-water-drains-downstream/357325/. Retrieved on 8 December 2020.

Chapter Four
Management of the Hirakud Dam on the Mahanadi River

1. Roberto Rossellini - Wikipedia. https://en.wikipedia.org/wiki/Roberto_Rossellini. Retrieved on 14 December 2020.

2. Shedding light on Rossellini-Sonali Dasgupta affair - Times of India. Dilip Padgaonkar. 18 June, 2015. https://timesofindia.indiatimes.com/world/rest-of-world/Shedding-light-on-Rossellini-Sonali-Dasgupta-affair/articleshow/47714421.cms. Retrieved on 14 December 2020.

3. Hirakud dam construction, 1958 from India, Matri Bhumi by Roberto Rossellini, YouTube. Nov 22, 2011. https://www.youtube.com/watch?v=xOat2hTapMQ. Retrieved on 14 December 2020.

4. Sir M. Visvesvaraya. Memoirs of my working life. 1951. Bangalore. Pages 105-106 https://archive.org/details/VisvesvarayaAutobiography. Retrieved on 14 December 2020.

5. M. Visvesvaraya - Wikipedia. https://en.wikipedia.org/wiki/M._Visvesvaraya. Retrieved on 14 December 2020.

6. Mahanadi Valley Development, Hirakud Dam Project, Volume - 1 – Report. The Central Waterways, Irrigation and Navigation Commission. 12 June 1947. Chairman A. N. Khosla. hirakud.pdf - Central Water Commission. http://www.cwc.gov.in/sites/default/files/hirakud.pdf. Retrieved on 14 December 2020.

7. Biswanath Das - Wikipedia. https://en.wikipedia.org/wiki/Biswanath_Das. Retrieved on 14 December 2020.

8. Biswanath Das, Patriot with a difference, Gurukalyan Mohapatra, Orissa Review, January 2006. http://magazines.odisha.gov.in/Orissareview/jan2006/engpdf/Biswanath_Das.pdf. Retrieved on 14 December 2020.

9. Hirakud Dam - Wikipedia. https://en.wikipedia.org/wiki/Hirakud_Dam. Retrieved on 29 December 2020.

10. Ranjan K Panda. India's Hirakud dam: Disaster in the making | PreventionWeb.net. 15 September 2017. https://www.preventionweb.net/go/55173. Retrieved on 14 December 2020.

10.a. Customary IHL - Rule 42. Works and Installations Containing dangerous forces. https://ihl-databases.icrc.org/customary-ihl/eng/docs/v1_rul_rule42. Retrieved on 4 February 2021.

11. Yi Si (1998). "The World's Most Catastrophic Dam Failures: The August 1975 Collapse of the Banqiao and Shimantan Dams". In Qing, Dai (ed.).. The river dragon has come! The Three Gorges Dam and the fate of China's Yangtze River and its people. Armonk, NY: M.E. Sharpe. pp. 25–38. ISBN 9780765602053. Retrieved 15 December 2020.

12. Typhoon Nina–Banqiao dam failure | Chinese history [1975] https://www.britannica.com/event/Typhoon-Nina-Banqiao-dam-failure. Retrieved 15 December 2020.

13. 1975 Banqiao Dam failure - Wikipedia. https://en.wikipedia.org/wiki/1975_Banqiao_Dam_failure. Retrieved 15 December 2020.

14. Collapse of the St. Francis Dam - Wikipedia. https://en.wikipedia.org/wiki/St._Francis_Dam. Retrieved on 14 December 2020.

15. South Fork Dam - Wikipedia. https://en.wikipedia.org/wiki/South_Fork_Dam. Retrieved on 15 December 2020.

16. Johnstown Flood - Wikipedia. https://en.wikipedia.org/wiki/Johnstown_Flood. Retrieved on 15 December 2020.

17. Vajont Dam - Wikipedia. https://en.wikipedia.org/wiki/Vajont_Dam. Retrieved on 15 December 2020.

18. Sempor Dam - Wikipedia. https://en.wikipedia.org/wiki/Sempor_Dam. Retrieved on 17 December 2020.

19. Embankment dam - Wikipedia. https://en.wikipedia.org/wiki/Embankment_dam. Retrieved on 17 December 2020.

20. 1961 Kurenivka mudslide - Wikipedia. https://en.wikipedia.org/wiki/1961_Kurenivka_mudslide. Retrieved on 17 December 2020.

21. Smoliy, V. A.; Goryak, G. V.; Danilenko, V. M. (2012). Куренівська трагедія 13 березня 1961 р. у Києві: причини, обставини, наслідки. Документи і матеріали [Kurenivka Tragedy March 13, 1961 in Kiev: Causes, Circumstances, Consequences. Documents and materials] (in Ukrainian). Institute of Ukrainian History NAN Ukraine. p. 18. ISBN 978-966-02-6392-5.

22. Ivan Kharchenko - Wikipedia. https://en.wikipedia.org/wiki/Ivan_Kharchenko. Retrieved on 17 December 2020.

23. Babi Yar - Wikipedia. https://en.wikipedia.org/wiki/Babi_Yar. Retrieved on 17 December 2020.

24. Möhne Reservoir - Wikipedia. https://en.wikipedia.org/wiki/M%C3%B6hne_Reservoir. Retrieved on 19 December 2020.

25. List of hydroelectric power station failures – Wikipedia. https://en.wikipedia.org/wiki/List_of_hydroelectric_power_station_failures. Retrieved on 19 December 2020.

26. Operation Chastise - Wikipedia. https://en.wikipedia.org/wiki/Operation_Chastise. Retrieved on 19 December 2020.

27. 1992: famous failures: revisiting major dam catastrophes Marla J. Barnes. Famous Failures: Revisiting Major Dam Catastrophes. Hydro Review Magazine. https://damfailures.org/wp-content/uploads/2015/07/116_Famous-Failures.pdf. Retrieved on 15 December 2020.

28. Dam failure - Wikipedia. https://en.wikipedia.org/wiki/Dam_failure. Retrieved on 15 December 2020.

29. Dam Failure by John T. Christian and Gregory B. Baecher. September 9, 1999. Dam Failure - Civil, Environmental and Architectural. August 28, 2002. http://ceae.colorado.edu/~amadei/CVEN3698/PDF/Damfailure.pdf. Retrieved on 17 December 2020.

30. The Deadliest Dam Failures in History: Oishimaya Sen Nag on June 26 2018 in World Facts. https://www.worldatlas.com/articles/the-deadliest-dam-failures-in-history.html. Retrieved on 15 December 2020.

31. What went wrong at Panshet Dam. July 12, 2011. DNA. https://www.dnaindia.com/india/report-what-went-wrong-at-panshet-dam-1565039. Retrieved on 16 December 2020.

32. List of largest reservoirs in India - Wikipedia. https://en.wikipedia.org/wiki/List_of_largest_reservoirs_in_India. Retrieved on 19 December 2020.

33. Indian Ballistic Missile Defence Programme - Wikipedia https://en.wikipedia.org/wiki/Indian_Ballistic_Missile_Defence_Programme. Retrieved on 19 December 2020.

34. Convention Concerning the Protection of the World Cultural and Natural Heritage. https://legal.un.org/avl/ha/ccpwcnh/ccpwcnh.html. Retrieved on 21 December 2020.

35. Convention Concerning the Protection of the World Cultural and Natural Heritage. https://whc.unesco.org/en/conventiontext/. Retrieved on 21 December 2020.

36. World Heritage Site - Wikipedia. https://en.wikipedia.org/wiki/World_Heritage_Site. Retrieved on 21 December 2020.

37. War Crimes - the United Nations. https://www.un.org/en/genocideprevention/war-crimes.shtml. Retrieved on 21 December 2020.

38. Hirakud Dam. https://web.archive.org/web/20081102205725/http://sambalpur.nic.in/hirakud%20dam.htm. Retrieved on 23 December 2020.

39. Salient Features of Hirakud Hydro Electric Project, Burla. http://www.ohpcltd.com/Hirakud/silent. Retrieved on 23 December 2020.

40. Hirakud HE Project - Odisha Hydro Power Corporation Ltd. http://www.ohpcltd.com/Hirakud/project. Retrieved on 23 December 2020.

41. (PDF) Remote sensing and active tectonics of South India. Ramasamy S.M. 2006. https://www.researchgate.net/publication/248977579_Remote_sensing_and_active_tectonics_of_South_India. Retrieved on 23 December 2020.

42. Ramasamy S.M. 2006. Remote sensing and active tectonics of South India. International Journal of Remote Sensing 27(20):4397-4431. DOI: 10.1080/01431160500502603. Retrieved on 23 December 2020.

43. Frank Lisker and Stefan Fachmann. 2001. Phanerozoic history of the Mahanadi region, India. Journal of Geophysical Research, Vol.

106, No. B10, Pages 22,027-22,050, October 10, 2001. Phanerozoic history of the Mahanadi region, India - Wiley. https://agupubs.onlinelibrary.wiley.com/doi/pdf/10.1029/2001JB000295. Retrieved on 29 December 2020.

44. Koyna Dam - Wikipedia. https://en.wikipedia.org/wiki/Koyna_Dam. Retrieved on 23 December 2020.

45. Harsh Gupta - Wikipedia. https://en.wikipedia.org/wiki/Harsh_Gupta.Retrieved on 23 December 2020.

46. Harsh K. Gupta. 1992. Reservoir Induced Earthquakes (Developments in Geotechnical Engineering). Elsevier Science. P.382. ISBN 9780444889065.

47. Narain, H., Gupta, H. 1968. Koyna Earthquake. *Nature* 217, 1138–1139 (1968). https://doi.org/10.1038/2171138a0. Retrieved on 23 December 2020.

48. Harsh Gupta;Hari Narain; B. K. Rastogi; Indra Mohan. 1969. A study of the Koyna earthquake of December 10, 1967. Bulletin of the Seismological Society of America (1969) 59 (3): 1149–1162. https://pubs.geoscienceworld.org/bssa/article-lookup/59/3/1149. Retrieved on 23 December 2020.

49. https://en.wikipedia.org/wiki/1967_Koynanagar_earthquake 1967 Koynanagar earthquake - Wikipedia. Retrieved on 23 December 2020.

50. "Major project to study earthquake activity at Koyna". The Hindu Business Line. 21 March 2011. https://www.thehindubusinessline.com/economy/Major-project-to-study-earthquake-activity-at-Koyna/article20111617.ece. Retrieved on 24 December 2020.

51. Earthquake zones of India - Wikipedia. https://en.wikipedia.org/wiki/Earthquake_zones_of_India. Retrieved on 24 December 2020.

52. Quake shadow hangs on Orissa - Telegraph India. 2 Jan 2005. https://www.telegraphindia.com/india/quake-shadow-hangs-on-orissa/cid/683518. Retrieved on 24 December 2020.

53. Earthquake - OSDMA. https://www.osdma.org/earthquake-2/?lang=en. Retrieved on 24 December 2020.

54. Nasrat Adamo, Nadhir Al-Ansari, Varoujan K. Sissakian, Jan Laue (September 2020). Dam Safety: Use of Seismic Monitoring Instrumentation in Dams. (PDF) Dam Safety: Use of Seismic Monitoring Instrumentation in dams. https://www.researchgate.net/publication/344426649_Dam_Safety_Use_of_Seismic_Monitoring_Instrumentation_in_Dams. Retrieved on 24 December 2020.

55. Seismic Instrumentation Of Dams - TRID Database. https://trid.trb.org/view/37239. Retrieved on 24 December 2020.

56. Death of Hirakud Dam | Bhubaneswar News - Times of India. Ranjan K Panda.13 May 2018 https://timesofindia.indiatimes.com/city/bhubaneswar/death-of-hirakud dam. Retrieved on 24 December 2020.

57. Emergency Action Plan Hirakud Dam – Dept of Water Resources, Government of Odisha. http://www.dowrodisha.gov.in/

Emergency%20Action%20Plan/Emergency%20Action%20Plan/ Hirakud.pdf. Retrieved on 24 December 2020.

58. Philip N. Owens, Desmond E. Walling, Qingping He, Jo Shanahan & Ian D. L. Foster (1997) The use of caesium-137 measurements to establish a sediment budget for the Start catchment, Devon, UK, Hydrological Sciences Journal, 42:3, 405-423, DOI. 10.1080/02626669709492037 To link to this article: https://doi.org/10.1080/02626669709492037. https://www.tandfonline.com/doi/pdf/10.1080/02626669709492037. Retrieved on 29 December 2020.

59. Hewitt W. Jeter. 2000. Determining the Ages of Recent Sediments Using Measurements of Trace Radioactivity. Terra et Aqua – Number 78 – March 2000. http://iadc.stage.mobilem.net/wp-content/uploads/2017/02/ article-determining-the-ages-of-recent-sediments-using-measurements-of-trace-radioactivity-78-03.pdf. Retrieved on 29 December 2020.

Chapter Five
Caring for the rivers in India

1. Persepolis - Wikipedia. https://en.wikipedia.org/wiki/Persepolis. Retrieved on 18 January 2021.

2. Alexander the Great's Life-Threatening Thoracic Trauma. 5 Aug 2018. https://www.ncbi.nlm.nih.gov/pmc/articles/PMC6089630/. Retrieved on 18 January 2021.

3. Indica (Megasthenes) - Wikipedia. https://en.wikipedia.org/wiki/ Indica_(Megasthenes). Retrieved on 18 January 2021.

4. Megasthenes: Indika [c. 350 – c. 290 BC] – Advocatetanmoy Law Library. 10 May 2018. https://advocatetanmoy.com/2018/05/10/ megasthenes-indika/. Retrieved on 18 January 2021.

5. Megasthenes - Wikipedia. https://en.wikipedia.org/wiki/Megasthenes. Retrieved on 18 January 2021.

6. In Re: Networking Of Rivers vs on 27 February, 2012. 27 February 2012. https://indiankanoon.org/doc/41857247/. Retrieved on 18 January 2021.

7. Supreme Court go-ahead for interlinking rivers - Down To Earth. 28 February 2012. Bharat Lal Seth. https://www.downtoearth.org. in/news/supreme-court-goahead-for-interlinking-rivers-36857. Retrieved on 18 January 2021.

8. Indian Rivers Inter-link - Wikipedia. https://en.wikipedia.org/wiki/ Indian_Rivers_Inter-link. Retrieved on 18 January 2021.

9. Pipe Dreams: Why Interlinking Ken-Betwa Will Not Solve Bundelkhand's Water Crisis. 4 July 2020. Tish Sanghera. https://www. indiaspend.com/pipe-dreams-why-interlinking-ken-betwa-will-not-solve-bundelkhands-water-crisis/. Retrieved on 18 January 2021.

10. UP to get less Ken-Betwa water in non-monsoon period as Modi Govt revises river linking deal. 31 December, 2020. Moushumi Das Gupta. https://theprint.in/india/governance/up-to-get-less-ken-betwa-

water-in-non-monsoon-period-as-modi-govt-revises-river-linking-deal/576319/. Retrieved on 18 January 2021.

11. Panigrahi K.C. 1981. History of Orissa. Publisher, Kitab Mahal, Cuttack, Odisha, India.

12. Arthur Cotton - Wikipedia. https://en.wikipedia.org/wiki/Arthur_Cotton. Retrieved on 18 January 2021.

13. Kanuri Lakshmana Rao - Wikipedia. https://en.wikipedia.org/wiki/Kanuri_Lakshmana_Rao. Retrieved on 18 January 2021.

14. Citizens voice alarm over recent Supreme Court judgement on interlinking of rivers. 25 April 2012. Amita Bhaduri. https://www.indiawaterportal.org/articles/citizens-voice-alarm-over-recent-supreme-court-judgement-interlinking-rivers. Retrieved on 18 January 2021.

15. Ambedkar's Contribution to Water Resources Development. Second Edition, 2016. Central Water Commission. Ministry of Water Resources River Development and Ganga Rejuvenation. Sewa Bhawan, R.K. Puram New Delhi 110066. Download - Central Water Commission. http://cwc.gov.in/sites/default/files/ambedkars-book_1.pdf. Retrieved on 21 January 2021.

16. Alexander, J.S., Wilson, R.C., and Green, W.R., 2012, A brief history and summary of the effects of river engineering and dams on the Mississippi River system and delta: U.S. Geological Survey Circular 1375, 43 p. https://pubs.usgs.gov/circ/1375/C1375.pdf. Retrieved on 21 January 2021.

16.a Mahanadi - Wikipedia. https://en.wikipedia.org/wiki/Mahanadi. Retrieved on 4 February 2021.

17. Naveen Writes Gadkari to Deepen Mahanadi River Mouth, Sujit Kumar Bisoyi, March 22, 2017, The Times of India). https://timesofindia.indiatimes.com/city/bhubaneswar/Naveen-writes-Gadkari-to-deepen-Mahanadi-river-mouth/articleshow/57774359.cms. Retrieved on 21 January 2021.

18. Assam to start dredging of Brahmaputra to combat floods, erosion. Updated: 23 Aug 2016. https://www.livemint.com/Politics/kUg9ihLOTI8wAmnQbWpEaL/Assam-to-start-dredging-of-Brahmaputra-to-combat-floods-ero.html. Retrieved on 21 January 2021.

19. Assam to start dredging of Brahmaputra to combat flood,erosion. Aug 23, 2016. https://economictimes.indiatimes.com/news/politics-and-nation/assam-to-start-dredging-of-brahmaputra-to-combat-flooderosion/articleshow/53832810.cms. Retrieved on 21 January 2021.

20. Assam prepares to spend Rs. 40,000 crore on an economically unfeasible project Banjot Kaur. 30 November 2017. https://www.downtoearth.org.in/news/water/brahmaputra-s-dredging-vacillations-59164. Retrieved on 21 January 2021.

21. Why the world is running out of sand - BBC Future - BBC.com. 8 Nov 2019. Vince Beiser. https://www.bbc.com/future/article/20191108-

why-the-world-is-running-out-of-sand. Retrieved on 21 January 2021.

22. The World in a Grain. The Story of Sand and How It Transformed Civilization. Vince Beiser. Aug 2018. 304 pages..https://www.amazon.in/World-Grain-Story-Transformed-Civilization/dp/0399576428. Retrieved on 21 January 2021.

23. Sand Trade: World is running out of sand – Why there is now a black market for it, You Tube, Tech Insider, June 6, 2018.

24. Average U.S. price of sand and gravel 2007-2019. 19 November 2020. Raynor de Best. https://www.statista.com/statistics/219381/sand-and-gravel-prices-in-the-us/. Retrieved on 21 January 2021.

25. Sinking Cities. Phanawat Ayanaputra And Ken Lohatepanont. 2 Sep 2019. The Bangkok Post. https://www.bangkokpost.com/world/1740904/sinking-cities. Retrieved on 7 January 2021.

26. "Orange alert' across Odisha as temperature crosses 46 degree Celsius. Minati Singha| The Times of India. TNN | May 15, 2017. https://timesofindia.indiatimes.com/city/bhubaneswar/orange-alert-across-odisha-as-temperature-crosses-46-degree-celsius/articleshow/58686010.cms.. Retrieved on 21 January 2021.

Chapter Six
Creating awareness on water quality in the City of Cuttack

1. Jaundice affects 38 in a fortnight in Cuttack | Cuttack News. Lalmohan Patnaik. 3 Jul 2019. https://timesofindia.indiatimes.com/city/cuttack/jaundice-affects-38-in-a-fortnight-in-cuttack/articleshow/70047148.cms. Retrieved on 7 January 2021.

2. Water Hyacinth—Invasion with good intent? Arunita Bose. 1 June, 2019. Research Matters. https://researchmatters.in/sciqs/water-hyacinth%E2%80%94invasion-good-intent. Retrieved on 7 January 2021.

3. How the deadly water hyacinth invaded Bengal | The Daily Star. Iftekhar Iqbal. 24 Dec 2018 https://www.thedailystar.net/in-focus/news/how-the-deadly-water-hyacinth-invaded-bengal-1677862. Retrieved on 7 January 2021.

4. Biological Control of Weed Water Hyacinth - TechGape. Aquatic Weed Water Hyacinth: A Friend or Foe? Dr. Arvind Singh. 2015. https://www.techgape.com/2015/03/aquatic-weed-water-hyacinth-control.html. Retrieved on 7 January 2021.

5. The shocking tale of India's 'Cancer Train'. Poulomi Das. Jun 10, 2016. Business Insider India https://www.businessinsider.in/the-shocking-tale-of-indias-cancer-train/articlesho. Retrieved on 7 January 2021.

6. Assessment of Quality of river water in the state of Odisha-A case study of the Rivers Kuakhai, Daya and Bramhani Avijit Majumder, Bijaya Bhusan Nanda, Abhaya Kumar Naik, SatyaN Misra.May 2019.International Journal of Innovative Technology and Exploring Engineering (IJITEE) ISSN: 2278-3075, Volume-8 Issue-7C May

2019. https://www.ijitee.org/wp-content/uploads/papers/v8i7c/G10140587C19.pdf. Retrieved on 14 January 2021.

7. Guidelines for drinking-water quality - World Health Organization. https://www.who.int/water_sanitation_health/dwq/2edvol3a.pdf. Retrieved on 14 January 2021.

8. Jakarta, the fastest-sinking city in the world. By Mayuri Mei Lin & Rafki Hidayat. BBC Indonesian. 12 August 2018. https://www.bbc.com/news/world-asia-44636934. Retrieved on 7 January 2021.

9. Indonesia picks Borneo island as site of new capital - BBC News. 26 Aug 2019. https://www.bbc.com/news/world-asia-49470258. Retrieved on 7 January 2021.

10. Sinking Cities. Phanawat Ayanaputra And Ken Lohatepanont. 2 Sep 2019. The Bangkok Post. https://www.bangkokpost.com/world/1740904/sinking-cities. Retrieved on 7 January 2021.

11. Why This City of 21 Million People Is Sinking 3 Feet Every Year. Cole Mellino. Mar. 05, 2016 https://www.ecowatch.com/why-this-city-of-21-million-people-is-sinking-3-feet-every-year- Retrieved on 7 January 2021.

12. That Sinking Feeling | Kolkata News - Times of India.14 Mar 2020. https://timesofindia.indiatimes.com/city/kolkata/that-sinking-feeling/articleshow/74620245.cms. Retrieved on 7 January 2021.

13. Genbaku Kensui: Dedication of Water Ceremony for the Victims of the A-Bomb, (2013). Written by Ken Sasaki, Translated by Ken Sasaki with Nachiketa Das. Published by Meisui-Bio Research Institute Research and Development Centre, Hiroshima Kokusai Gakuin University, 6-20-1, Nakano, Akiku, Hiroshima, 739-0321, Japan.

14. Das, Nachiketa. 2008. Excellent waters in Hiroshima: A review of pioneering endeavours of water-tasting and water-quality. Journal of the Geological Society of India 71(4):468-472.

15. Das, Nachiketa, Morikawa, Hiroyo, Sasaki, Ken (2015). Discovery of Radon in Hot Spring Waters of Odisha in Eastern India, Asian Journal of Water, Environment and Pollution, Vol. 12, No. 4, pp. 71-77.

APPENDIX ONE

'Orange alert' across Odisha as temperature crosses 46 degree Celsius

Minati Singha| TNN | May 15, 2017, 20:18 IST

BHUBANESWAR: People in Odisha reeled under severe heat wave conditions on Monday as maximum temperature in the state crossed 46 degree Celsius mark at Balangir. IMD issued orange alert - a warning for severe heat wave, across the state for next two days.

"Balangir recorded 46.2 degree Celsius the highest temperature of the season so far on Monday. The heat wave situation is likely to persist till May 20 and temperature may increase another one degree in interior areas," said director of IMD's Bhubaneswar Centre, Sarat Chandra Sahu.

Normal life was thrown out of gear in the state as at least five urban centres have recorded temperature above 45 degree Celsius and 16 centres recorded above 40 degree Celsius on Monday.

"It is like an undeclared curfew in most towns in western Odisha as the heat is quite unbearable even at seven in the morning. Unless anyone has an urgent work, one should not go out as it may turn fatal," said Newton Ray, a resident of Sambalpur town where mercury reached 45.7 degree Celsius on Monday.

A crippling water shortage and unscheduled power cuts in several parts of the state has made the life miserable for common men. People in Telkoi block in Keonjhar district have called a 12-hour bandh on Monday protesting frequent power outages in the region.

Expressing concern over the rising temperature experts blamed the rise in temperature essentially to the loss of forest cover of western and central Odisha and drying up of rivers and water bodies.

"Forest cover of Odisha must be raised substantially by proper management of water by construction of some 60, 000 micro dams in the mountainous parts of the state. All major rivers of the state are dead, and they must be revived by an extensive program of dredging so that they can hold water. Once rivers die civilizations die. Odisha is facing that kind of an unprecedented crisis. The state must revive all derelict and dying ponds by proper excavation and renovation and the programme of afforestation must be intensified," said Nachiketa Das, geologist.

Environmentalists said, the government should take a multi-pronged approach. "The state government must make it mandatory to install solar panels, rainwater harvesting, and rooftop gardening on all buildings across the state particularly so in the urban areas," Das said.

Rising temperatures have reportedly killed 38 people across the state so far while the state government has confirmed five deaths due to sunstroke this season. The IMD has also predicted that rain and thunder showers may occur at isolated places in the next two days. Some north Odisha pockets have received Norwester on Monday.

APPENDIX TWO

Letter to the Principal Secretary to the Government of Odisha, Department of Water Resources, with copies to the Secretary to the Government of India, Ministry of Water Resources, Government of India; The Honourable Minister for Water Resources, Government of India.

RE: Comprehensive dredging of the entire length of the River Mahanadi and other major rivers of Odisha for their revival.

To

The Principal Secretary to the Government of Odisha
Department of Water Resources
The Secretariat, Bhubaneswar, Odisha, 751001
E: wrsec.od@nic.in wrsec.or@nic.in
C.c. The Secretary to the Government of India
Ministry of Water Resources, Government of India, New Delhi.
The Honourable Minister for Water Resources
Ministry of Water Resources, Government of India, New Delhi.
E: egov-mowr@nic.in

Date: 7 March 2018

RE: Comprehensive dredging of the entire length of the River Mahanadi and other major rivers of Odisha for their revival

Dear Sir

I propose that the Government of Odisha carry out comprehensive dredging of the entire length of the River

Mahanadi and other major rivers of Odisha for their revival. I present below my arguments in support of my proposal.

Honourable Dr. B. R. Ambedkar, Labour Member to the Government of India, in his Presidential Address delivered at Cuttack Conference organised to discuss the development of the rivers of Odisha, held on the 8th of November 1945 had emphasised that the plan of embankments to manage the rivers is wrong and Odisha must adopt the methods the USA employed for the development of the rivers like the Missouri-Mississippi (p.249, Ambedkar's Contribution to Water Resources Development).

The vast water resources of the largest river of the USA, the Missouri-Mississippi is carefully managed by extensive river-engineering, which includes systematic dredging every year, carried out by the US Army Corps of Engineers.

Now in 2018, while the "Old man River" the Missouri-Mississippi continues to flow majestically, the largest river of Odisha, the once mighty Mahanadi, whose monsoonal flow right up to the middle of the twentieth century used to be comparable to that of the Ganga lies dead, all choked up, because of substantial siltation along its entire course. The Mahanadi riverbed near the City of Cuttack today is probably at a higher elevation than the city, and the Ring-road embankment protects the Millennium City of Cuttack from the monsoonal floods. This massive siltation, moreover, has very drastically reduced the water holding capacity of the Mahanadi.

The Government of Odisha are aware of the problem of siltation that the Mahanadi confronts now. Last year the Chief Minister of Odisha, appealed to the Minister for Water-resources of the Union Government of India to make funds available for the dredging of the mouth of the River Mahanadi (Naveen Writes Gadkari to Deepen Mahanadi River Mouth, Sujit Kumar Bisoyi, March 22, 2017, The Times of India).

Some islets that formed on the River Mahanadi, near the Jobra Anicut of the City of Cuttack are being removed by dredging (Islets may endanger Jobra barrage at Cuttack. June 23, 2015. OrissaPOST). Access to the source of Sasan Canal that originates from the Hirakud Reservoir of the Mahanadi was dredged in 2008 (Dredging in Hirakud reservoir in progress. June 15, 2008, oneindia). In this connection, I would also like to mention that the Government of Assam have decided to de-silt the mighty Brahmaputra River by dredging to mitigate the severity of the annual floods (Assam to Start Dredging of Brahmaputra to combat floods. August 23, 2016, LiveMINT).

I propose that the Government of Odisha take a decision to dredge the entire length of some 400 km of the River Mahanadi, right from the Hirakud Dam in Sambalpur to the river mouth at the Bay of Bengal near Paradip. The approximate volume of sand to be dredged for the 400 km long, 1 km wide, 3 m deep stretch of the Mahanadi will be around 1.2 bcm (billion cubic meters). The cost of this Mahanadi dredging project will be around USD1.2 billion calculated at the rate of the dredging cost of USD1 for 1cubic meter.

Some of the dredged sand and silt near the City of Cuttack could be used to very substantially strengthen the Ring-road embankment and create water front property by reclaiming a portion of the presently silted up course of the Mahanadi adjacent to the City. The Government of Odisha could also float a tender inviting bids for the export of the river sand, which is angular as opposed to the well rounded aeolian desert sand, and has a huge demand all over the world.

Hirakud Reservoir that has lost some 30 per cent of its capacity to siltation, must also be dredged. The dredging of Hirakud Reservoir, however, must be preceded by a detailed bathymetric study of the reservoir. Other major rivers of Odisha like the Subarnarekha, the Budhabalanga, the Salandi, the Baitarani, the Brahmani, the Birupa, the Kathjodi, the

Kuakhai, the Rusikulya are all silted up and require dredging for their revival. If we do not revive these major rivers of Odisha, they will die, and once rivers die civilizations die. So, let us revive these moribund rivers and save this land. I have appended a news-item published on this subject, on the Times of India, in May 2017, for your information.

With best wishes and kind regards

Yours sincerely

Prof. Nachiketa Das

Professor Nachiketa Das is a scientist, an academic, an administrator, a creative writer, a practitioner of Kaya Yoga and an activist to save this land. Professor Das is dedicated to the promotion of water conservation, groundwater recharge by the construction of a very large number of micro-dams, excavation of the rivers, afforestation and preservation of water quality. Professor Das also promotes international relations and the quality of human life worldwide. Professor Das holds a B.Sc. Geology Honours degree from Utkal University of Odisha, an M.Sc. in Geology (Environmental Sciences) from the Jawaharlal Nehru University of New Delhi and started his academic career as a Lecturer in Geology of Utkal University, posted at the then Ravenshaw College, which became a university in 2006.

Professor Das availed a Commonwealth Academic Staff Scholarship tenable in the UK, awarded by the Association of Commonwealth Universities, London, for pursuing research in The University of Glasgow and the Scottish Universities Research and Reactor Centre at East Kilbride, Scotland and received the degree of Ph.D. in Geochemistry. After completion of Ph.D. Professor Das joined Harvard University as an Officer and conducted pioneering postdoctoral research on the chemical evolution of oceans. Professor Das, thereafter, joined the Ministry of Science & Technology of the Government of India as a Senior Scientific Officer Grade One and managed several national and international programmes of scientific research in the general area of earth, atmosphere and environmental sciences.

Professor Das worked as an Environmental Chemist of the La Trobe University of Melbourne in Australia, as a Geochemist and project leader of Chemostratigraphic Correlation project and Fluid History Analysis project of the Commonwealth Scientific Industrial Research Organisation – Division of Petroleum Resources – (CSIRO – DPR) of Sydney in Australia, as a Director – International of Bridge Business College in Sydney, as a Consultant to the Department of Foreign Affairs and Trade (DFAT) and the Department of Industry Science and Tourism (DIST) of the Commonwealth Government of Australia to promote Australia India Bilateral Cooperation in Science and Technology, as a Director of NRI Enviro-Geo-Tech Australia in Sydney, as a Special Associate Professor of the Department of Earth and Planetary Systems Science of Hiroshima University in Japan, and as a Visiting Professor of the Department of Bio-Recycling of Hiroshima Kokusai Gakuin University (HKGU) in Japan.

At HKG University, Professor Das conducted pioneering research in the removal of radioactivity and toxic heavy metals from soils, sediments and waters of Fukushima area, contaminated by radioactive pollution following the nuclear disaster at Daiichi nuclear power plant of Fukushima in 2011.

Dr. Das worked as the Professor of Geology of Ravenshaw University in Odisha in India and held many administrative positions of the university such as the Dean of Administration, the Chief Warden of Hostels, the Dean of the School of Earth Sciences and Regional Studies, the Head of the Department of Geology et cetera. Professor Das is also the President of a Hiroshima based company, Hiroshima Energy and Minerals Kabushiki Kaisha.

Professor Das Chaired the Indo-Norwegian Bilateral Cooperation on Geothermal Energy and shortlisted three hot springs in India for investigation, following which exploratory drilling was undertaken at Puga Valley in Ladakh for the utilisation of geothermal resources. Professor Das is also an expert member of several national committees of India, such as, Expert Committee on Geothermal Energy Resources and Management, Expert Committee on Landslide Hazard Mitigation, Expert Committee on Post Graduate Colleges of Fund for Infrastructure in Science and Technology (FIST) Program, Technical Advisory Committee (TAC) for the National Atlas and Thematic Mapping Organisation (NATMO) of Kolkata and Earth Sciences Subject Expert Committee for question setting for National Eligibility Test (NET).

Professor Das has appeared as an expert commentator and analyst on geology, mining, water resources, check dams, excavation of rivers, disaster management, floods, cyclones, tsunamis, earthquakes, natural hazard mitigation, environmental management, removal of radioactivity, sea level rise, climate change, international cooperation, education and many topical societal issues in the news and discussion programmes of All India Radio, Doordarshan TV, OTV, E-TV, Kalinga TV, Kanak TV, S-TV, Nakshyatra TV, News 7 TV of Odisha in India and on NHK TV, RCC TV, Hiroshima Home TV and TSS TV of Hiroshima in Japan. Professor Das has written over fifty scientific and popular articles and reports, published in refereed journals, magazines and on the internet.

Following the nuclear agreement signed between President Obama and Prime Minister Modi, the most prestigious Forbes magazine of the USA, in an article titled, "Nuclear Options – Obama in India" written by an eminent geochemist and columnist Dr. James Conca, on the 4th of February 2015, mentioned and cited Professor Das, as follows:

"Dr. Nachiketa Das, Professor of Geology at Ravenshaw University of Cuttack in India, feels that the Indo-U.S. Nuclear Deal signed by President Obama and Prime Minister Modi **"will provide the much needed legitimacy to the entire nuclear establishment of India on the world stage."** Which translates into a big expansion of nuclear activity with many international partners. Having worked in uranium geochemistry to clean-up of Fukushima, Professor Das even predicts that India will close the entire Nuclear Fuel Cycle." http://www.forbes.com/sites/jamesconca/2015/02/04/nuclear-options-obama-in-india/

Professor Das is an award-winning creative writer and has written four books and they are: Kichhi Katha (a collection of short stories in Odia language), Berlin Berlin (a travel story in Odia language), Kaya Yoga: Road to happiness, health and longevity and Save This Land. Professor Das collaborated with the author Professor Dr. Ken Sasaki to translate a book on water chemistry and water quality management from the original Japanese into English, titled, Genbaku Kensui: Dedication of Water Ceremony for the Victims of the A-Bomb. Professor Das is currently working on a literary fiction titled, A Seeker's Journey.

Professor Das is a Citizen of Australia, an Overseas Citizen of India, and a Permanent Resident of Japan.

Professor Das is married to Ms. Shizuka Imamoto, a high school teacher and librarian, from Hiroshima in Japan.